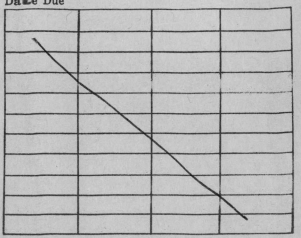

STENDHAL

By Armand Caraccio

Translated by Dolores Bagley

NEW YORK UNIVERSITY PRESS   1965

▼

Part One

The Life of Henri Beyle

I am considered an extremely witty and
very insensitive man, a roué even, and
I see that I have constantly been occupied by unhappy love affairs . . .
The Life of Henri Brulard

1 · Childhood and Adolescence in Grenoble

(1783-99)

IT IS DIFFICULT to imagine modern Grenoble, bursting at the seams and teeming with cosmopolitan life, as it was when Henri Beyle was born there in the gloomy rue des Vieux Jésuites on January 23, 1783.

However, if one climbs to the Bastille and once contemplates the immovable round of the Alps which Stendhal loved, as intensely as did Jean-Jacques Rousseau, one's gaze is inevitably drawn toward the city; and there, thanks to a network of old streets, can be distinguished the narrow limits of that "ignoble Cularo," which must have pursued the writer like "the memory of a rotten indigestion."

This contrast between the frame of mountains whose majestic span inspired him to awe and the shabby and ill-smelling city whose spirit and aspect he detested enables one to understand his everlasting love for Alpine life and his instinctive loathing for that nest of ugliness in which he was born and from which he early dreamed of escaping.

Grenoble was, nevertheless, the seat of a parliament, and its social life was free enough to have inspired in Choderlos de Laclos, who occupied a garrison there from 1769 to 1775, his *Liaisons Dangereuses*. The young Stendhal hardly suspected its flourishing commerce of flowers and sighs, which might possibly, several years later, have reconciled him to his native city. At best, he received candied nuts from the hand of a woman, so they say, on whom the character of Mme. de

3

Merteuil was based. But Beyle had a far sturdier appetite, which Grenoble could hardly satisfy.

One has only to stroll past number fourteen rue Jean-Jacques Rousseau (formerly the rue des Vieux Jésuites) in order to imagine what his childhood was like. How could his father have confined his gay young wife, Henriette Gagnon, between such somber walls? Life was hard for this extremely taciturn being—"the most Dauphinois of men"—whom Henri Beyle was soon to regard as his enemy.

The population of Grenoble is composed of the residue of neighboring mountain races, who have by no means forgotten the harshness of their ancestral existence in the relative sweetness of Grésivaudan. Their character still makes itself felt: "The Dauphinois has a way of keeping to himself; he is sharp, opinionated, argumentative. . . . While the Provençal vents himself in monstrous insults, the Dauphinois reflects and keeps counsel with his heart. . . ."

The Beyles originally came from Vercors. One finds traces of them even in the early seventeenth century. One Jean Beyle, son of Ambroise, a merchant draper of Lans around 1650, appears on the lists of procurers sworn into parliament; he filled the post of official treasurer and inherited the estate of Furonières, at Claix, of which Henri Beyle was so fond. Joseph's son, Pierre, to whom he willed the house on the rue des Vieux Jésuites, was worth approximately £20,000 in 1755. At the age of twenty he filled the position of procurer; this man was the paternal grandfather of Henri Beyle. Chérubin-Joseph, Beyle's father, was born on the 29th of March, 1747. Finding himself an orphan before his eighteenth year, he was forced to assume certain responsibilities as the eldest—responsibilities which darkened his outlook. A simple clerk at his beginnings, he was to serve for fifteen years before being received into parliament as an *avocat* in 1780. The following year he married, launched into numerous real estate speculations, and was to struggle throughout his life with financial difficulties. Due to Stendhal's autobiographical work, *The Life of Henri Brulard*, Chérubin Beyle has a very poor reputation. An argument in his behalf must be hazarded, without hesitation.

His atavism and the material difficulties he was forced to

face, with ten sisters and two brothers on his hands, explains to some extent his timidity, his introversion, his meticulousness, his pettifogging, and even his miserly nature. He learned the value of money early, and if his unlucky—though not unreasonable—speculations finally ruined him ("agriculturomania," the raising of merino sheep), bad luck had its share in this defeat. Chérubin Beyle, who was one day to become an assistant to Grenoble's mayor and a Knight of the Legion of Honor, would certainly not have managed his affairs so badly had he not floated so much of his capital: "There has been a canker in my father's fortune ever since . . . because he borrows at 8%," his son observed bitterly.

To the familial goods already indicated, Chérubin added the sturdy house on the rue de Bonne, built between 1803 and 1806, which Stendhal sold in 1817. He also acquired, in 1800, the Arthaudière estate at Cheylas, which he completely resold in 1806. He purchased lots on the rue des Vieux Jésuites and the Rue Neuve. He possessed some land at Sarcenas and some pastures at Echirolles, for he had briefly entertained a project of importing Swiss dairy cows. He had a bourgeois concern for decorum. His death in 1819 caused his son, who misinterpreted his real tenderness, the most bitter disappointment—over the evaporation of his long awaited inheritance.

Patient in his ambition, as Chérubin frequented the nobility of the cloth, the desire came to him of escaping from the bourgeoisie; he pretended to believe himself a noble, if somewhat fallen in state, and assumed a title in the official records. Thus it is that Henri Beyle's birth record states him to be "the legitimate son of the *noble* Chérubin-Joseph Beyle." In the Armorial of Dauphiné can be found the arms of his grandfather, Joseph.

Little disposed to confidences, the father and the son lived side by side without ever becoming acquainted with each other. There is no doubt, however, of Chérubin Beyle's fondness for his children. Marie-Henri was the oldest; Pauline-Eléanore was born on March 21, 1786; and Marie-Zénaïde-Caroline was born on October 10, 1788. Their mother died in 1790, as a result of confinement. So it was that Chérubin Beyle was left alone, after eight years of profound love for this woman. She was ten years younger than he; he had asked for her hand in marriage when he was thirty-five, after having acquitted himself of his duties to his brothers and sisters, and after his position seemed to him to be assured. He was by no means handsome, and to make matters worse, he was scarred by smallpox; in spite of a nature which was crafty in business and reactionary in politics (he was once imprisoned as a suspect during the Reign of Terror), Chérubin was possessed of solid qualities. He was a friend of the law, of honesty; and if he was severe with others, he was equally so with himself.

One can imagine the pain that Chérubin must have suffered, his most intimate companion stricken from him. Having an innate horror of emotion, however, he suffered and was silent. Had it not been for his fatherly duty, he would have taken holy orders. As it was, he forced himself daily to holy services. At the end of ten years, Henriette's room was still as closed as a sanctuary. His outward severity, which never prevented him from dangling the tiny Marie-Zénaïde on his knee, masked a sensitive soul that had savored the taste of *La Nouvelle Héloïse*.[1] This worship of his deceased wife's memory is revealing in its secrecy, for it indicates that within the pettifogging and sometimes dully bourgeois soul of Chérubin Beyle, there existed something passionate which is worth touching upon. But the child Stendhal never guessed this and the narrowness of his education, which shocked his sensibilities, did the rest. Whence his reaction. He has been reproached for dubbing Chérubin "the bastard." Without denying the term's irreverence, we know today that this was a slang expression common to all his comrades at the École Centrale.

Whatever may have been the differences between father and son, from whom did Stendhal inherit his propensity for stubbornness, his constant need to hide his tremulous nature, if not from his father?

For his mother, whom he lost when he was seven and whose image he transfigured with all the adornments of memory and dream, Stendhal had a veritable adoration. Certain admissions and subtle allusions in *The Life of Henri Brulard* have

---

[1] A sentimental novel by Jean-Jacques Rousseau.

prompted discussion of an Oedipus complex, but such a thing is purely speculative.

She was an attractive brunette, rosy and plump, lively and frivolous; relatively little is known about her. She was the daughter of Dr. Gagnon, an extremely literate man, and although she was undoubtedly cultured, she was not a bluestocking. Beyle afterward found in her room a copy of *The Divine Comedy*. She embroidered, had an innate talent for painting, some wit, a bit of vanity, and a touch of capricious coquetry. She was the joy and the fanciful spirit of the household. It was to her that Henri Beyle owed his taste for the arts and his almost feminine delicacy.

When he considered his double heritage, Henri Beyle felt nothing but revulsion at the thought of those mountain people who had once come from the plateau of Vercors, prompted by social ambition. Everything, on the other hand, inclined him toward the maternal branch of his family: "I thought of myself as a Gagnon, and I never thought of Beyle except with a repugnance which still persists in 1835." With a secret desire as deep as instinct, he suggested in 1832: "Through my mother, whom I resemble, I am perhaps of Italian blood." [2]

Beyle used to imagine that the Gagnons, natives of Bédarrides, had descended from one Guadagni or Guadagnoni family, who had followed the papacy to Avignon, or who had once been forced into exile by some beautiful crime. Although this was strictly a matter of hypothesis, it captivated his imagination.

Stendhal had a tender and trusting nature which happiness might have mellowed; but after his mother's death he felt himself living in a hostile world, and he retired into his shell. It was not long before he began to oppose his father's ideas, and his harsh confessions denounce the blackness of Chérubin's soul. He never forgave him for his avariciousness, nor for the real estate speculations which completely obsessed him. Nor could he pardon his father's ugliness, which he had partially inherited. But he reproached him, above all, for loving him merely "as a son who would continue the family."

2 Tr. note: Other sources indicate his Italian ancestry to have since been confirmed.

He was not aware of the paucity of the revenues Chérubin derived, despite all his purchases and sales. Proclaiming his scorn for money—and this scorn was sincere—Beyle suffered so much from the lack of sufficient paternal subsidies that the shoes he wore while he was living in Paris possessed holes: "and I needed all my spirit to slip my poor foot, painted black with ink, underneath the hole," he confessed to Pauline.[3] Forty years later this detail was to reappear in The Charterhouse of Parma.

Early misunderstandings heavy with consequences! And yet in speaking about his son, Chérubin had confided to his brother-in-law, Romain Gagnon: "I insist that he be happier than I am." This was possibly not very much to desire, but his words came from the heart.

Still, it must be noted to Chérubin Beyle's credit that Dr. Gagnon, who always maintained his regard for him, had better discerned his true nature and more justly appraised the hard conditions of his existence.

As one walks from the rue des Vieux Jésuites to the place Grenette, where Doctor Gagnon resided, the horizon expands with every step and one conceives that there can exist a disinterested exercise of the intelligence.

Dr. Gagnon was the most renowned physician in the city. Personally well cared for, he carried a cane in his hand, a cocked hat under his arm, and sported a wig with three neat rows of curls. Since the exercise of his craft only partially absorbed him, he busied himself with his grandson's intellectual education.

A true disciple of Fontenelle,[4] a friend of celebrities, a philosopher with a sense of his time, a philanthropist—he made himself a guardian of the arts and sciences. He was "eminent," in the real sense of the word, an "oracle of the bourgeoisie."

He was witty and kind, finely literate, and an assiduous reader of Voltaire and Horace—a bust of Voltaire adorned the

3 Tr. note: Other sources indicate that Stendhal's extravagance was the cause of his penury. Accounts of his allowance vary.

4 Fontenelle, Bernard le Bovier de (1657–1757). A nephew of Corneille, whose prose writing was characterized by the rational, scientific method.

mantle of his drawing room and he had made a pilgrimage to Ferney, Voltaire's home. When Rousseau passed through Grenoble, he had had the philosopher serenaded with an air from "The Village Soothsayer." Still a classicist, but without narrowness, Dr. Gagnon put himself affectionately at the disposal of his young grandson.

The opinionated child, however, did not inherit the old man's smiling skepticism, which made the doctor an enemy of all excess, a modest patriot, a tolerant spirit filled with respect for religion, and a man of refinement, as prized by the bourgeoisie and nobility for his manners and culture as he was esteemed by the populace for his goodness. Henri Gagnon convinced the child at an early age that nothing in the world was as valuable as a good book, the fruit of careful observation, which had nothing vague or empty about it:

My grandfather communicated to me his veneration for literature. Horace and Hippocrates were other men as familiar to me as Romulus, Alexander, or Numa. M. Voltaire was another, as familiar as that imbecile of a Louis XVI, whom he mocked, or that roué of a Louis XV, whom he reproached for his filthy manners.

This thoughtful, even alarming, affection for his grandson, through whom Dr. Gagnon continued to cherish his deceased daughter, is very moving. After his mother's death, with which "vanished all the joy of his childhood," Henri could not have had a better companion.

But his discretion prevented the indulgent doctor from unduly substituting himself for Chérubin, who in no way possessed the same open-mindedness. Also, there was no way to shelter the young Henri from his father's stifling discipline. He never knew one child of his own age; he never played marbles: "How I envied the nephew of our shoemaker, Madame Barthélemy."

Uncomprehending tutors bullied him, or at least gave him the impression of being bullied, which amounts to the same thing, psychologically speaking. Should Dr. Gagnon be blamed for having assured his grandson one day that he would inherit at least "15,000 francs' income so that he might eat as he thought fit" without having to work? This piece of confirmed bourgeoisie indicates that Dr. Gagnon briefly shared Henri

Beyle's hopes, although after 1816 the latter no longer entertained a great many illusions about his paternal fortune. Chérubin left, namely, 120,000 francs in debts, without counting an annual income of 2,500 francs, and he scarcely once returned to Stendhal the redeemed mortgages, except for a sum of about 5,000 francs.[5]

Two women in Stendhal's immediate environment left their mark on him. One of them was his aunt Séraphie Gagnon, whom he despised. She was utterly without beauty; he regarded her as his "evil genius," and Chérubin's ally in the "tyranny" he suffered. (This tyranny was soon reinforced by the Abbé Raillane, "the most influential bigot in the city," who aggravated Beyle's instinctive anticlericalism.) Séraphie, who was in charge of the household after her sister's death, vigorously imposed her authority. Although Stendhal implies that his father was having an affair with Séraphie, the assertion has no basis. An earnest Royalist, Séraphie was horrified by the excesses of the Revolution; reason enough for the child to enthusiastically welcome this Revolution, which so displeased those about him. Dr. Gagnon once gave shelter to two suspected priests during the Reign of Terror; their vulgarity shocked and repelled the young boy. Although he ran away one day and sneaked into the Jacobin club, contact with the masses generally disgusted him. His youthful vitality, his desire to assert himself by rebelling, caused him to participate in a childish but dangerous plot against the Tree of Fraternity, which stood opposite the Tree of Liberty in the place Grenette. Because his family's convictions were opposed to his free development, there instinctively took root within Stendhal a hatred for all conformism.

Although the young Henri had suffered in tearless sorrow the death of Henri Gagnon's butler, "poor Lambert," his only friend, when Séraphie Gagnon passed away at the age of thirty-six he threw himself upon his knees to thank God for his great deliverance from this "devil in petticoats." He had already rejoiced over the condemnation of the king because it had so distressed those about him. Thus, a total lack of understanding placed a barrier between this cantankerous

5 Tr. note: Other sources give other versions of these sums.

woman and this child of repressed sensibility, who donned a
mask of wickedness as a reaction.

His "good genius," on the other hand, was his great-aunt
Elizabeth, a sister of Dr. Gagnon, in whom survived all the
enthusiasms of the southern soul. She had a marked influence
on the avid and precocious child. An aging *grande dame*, dressed
to the teeth, she hid her traditional patriotism and her indom-
itable energy beneath an outward reserve. Her pride ill-concealed
her tenderness. Nourished by the *Library of Novels*,[6] she used
to express her admiration by saying: "That is as beautiful as *Le
Cid*." To her Stendhal owed his taste for romantic and heroic
adventures: "She had . . . shaped my heart, and it is to my
aunt Elizabeth that I owe the odious Spanish pretensions of
nobility into which I fell during the first thirty years of my life."

Such were the origins of Henri Beyle in that closing eighteenth century. The echo of revolutionary convulsions, hardly
very evident in Grenoble, had nevertheless affected him. The
barely defined character of his nature left a great deal to be
divined about the disparate heredities which composed it. To
those he owed a part of his originality and a certain bittersweet
taste—the taste of a fruit whose ripening is anything but harmonious.

Did he find in his sisters any of the affection which might
have reduced the strain of his adolescence? For Zénaïde, six
years his junior, he felt no sympathy; he mistrusted her, for she
was a "tattletale" and always sided with his aunt Séraphie. She
occupied only an insignificant place in his life. It was otherwise
with Pauline, who was as impatient as he with the familial
yoke. Far from calming his revolts, she fostered them, taking
up even the frenzy of his resentments, with just as much in-
comprehension and injustice.

But from the standpoint of personal rapport, what an at-
tentive and docile confidante she was, despite her indolence! She
was the object of his first feminine friendship, his first disciple in
the science of ideology. This confidence was sweet to him for
a long time, and the letters they exchanged, filled with frankness, permitted him to clarify his own opinions. In 1806 she

6 A publication which contained extracts from contemporary novels.

married François Daniel Périer-Lagrange and was widowed in
1816. Henri Beyle briefly envisaged living with her; but the
years, without breaking their bonds, gradually loosened them.
Without ever abandoning her, he drifted away from her.

Henri Beyle's *bête noire* was the Abbé Raillane, his tutor.
On could undoubtedly risk an argument, here again, concerning
extenuating circumstances, but not without certain limitations.
From the standpoint of Stendhalian psychology, it is not the
accuracy of such related fact which matters, but the persistence
of the *impression felt*. The Abbé Raillane may well have been
less monstrous than Stendhal depicted him, but this changed
neither the sincerity nor the violence of the feelings he lastingly
inspired in the boy. For although Stendhal's memory for facts
was sometimes inaccurate, his memory for the evolution of his
sensibility was tenacious.

This refractory, highly insensitive priest was "small, skinny,
very pinched, greenish in hue, with a false eye and a loathsome
smile." *The Life of Henri Brulard* refers to him as "a black
scoundrel." Doubtless, he lacked tact, above all. Every offense
was equal in the eyes of this implacable tutor, who taught the
Ptolemaic system because the church approved it. Denouncing
the dangers of liberty, he succeeded only in exasperating his
student to a hatred for religion, a taste for independence, a need
for logic and clarity, and a horror of virtue.

Whence arose Beyle's impetuous lack of discipline, his disgust for Grenoble and its right-thinking middle class, and that
thirst for truth which no scruple could prevent him from pursuing. Always on the defensive, the child sank into a misan-
thropy which caused people to misjudge him. They thought him
deceitful. Actually, "This is a tenderness turned sour"—"Beyle
puts a mask of comedy over a tragic soul and from now on he
will always play a role—except in front of himself." Keen, passionate, argumentative—from these qualities they wanted to
create a model of bourgeois distinction. He was to become,
instead, a precocious, if not always serene, observer of human
nature, and a most clearsighted observer of himself.

Young Henri Beyle suffered, "but he suffered from his youthful hatred," and that desire for vengeance which his uncomprehending entourage imposed on him would spur him to open

shyly to the gentlest of emotions and, oddly enough, to those of love. That feeling of hatred, so carefully fashioned to fortify a young, ambitious will, burst like a trespasser into a heart born for affection. Confusing "liberty" with "revolt," he early felt himself to be a free soul. "Family, I detest you!" he was already proclaiming. Tradition, authority, and faith were repudiated. How could he help but have had the desire to escape—to escape from his home, from his cramped milieu—to escape from *"Cularo!"*

This escape, however, was no easy thing. A foundation at the École Centrale and the École Polytechnique was necessary so that Henri Beyle might attain his ends.

The age was breaking with the tradition of the Collèges de Jésuites. The new era no longer needed latinists or humanists. In the autumn of 1796 an École Centrale, where the sciences were to be honored above all, was founded in Grenoble. Henri Beyle was thirteen years old when they enrolled him there, amid the flower of the bourgeoisie, where he was to attend classes until 1799. These were years of good fellowship; he had already received the nickname *chinois* [7] (though some believe it to have dated from his Milan years, around 1800). He made friends with François Bigillion, whose high-strung and romantic young sister, Victorine, inspired a bashful but very keen emotion in him. He marveled at her budding bosom. He was to keep for many years his friendship with Fortuné Mante, his cousin Romain Colomb, Louis Crozet, Louis-François de Barral, Félix Faure, Jean Plana, and Edouard Mounier. The strolls through Grenoble, the ritual visits to the Furonières estate at Claix, revealed to him the beauty of his native country, elevating if sometimes stifling. In the evening, he used to gaze from the bend of the Isère River out upon the Voreppe and the "lovely orange color" that etched its contour. Beyond was the unknown. Beyond was liberty, life, love—beyond was glory.

Henri Beyle soon understood that escape depended on his preparation for the École Polytechnique. The Abbé Gattel, general professor of grammar and logic, gave him an early taste

[7] "The Chinaman," a nickname given him because of his very small eyes.

for reasoning. His curiosity about foreign intellectual trends was stimulated by the literature class of Dubois Fontanelle, publisher of *L'Année Littéraire* (The Literary Year). The Italian painters were unveiled to him, with bombastic enthusiasm, by the painter Jay in his elementary art history course. He was particularly intrigued by mathematics, and he worked for three years "like Michelangelo working on the Sistine," for he intended to distinguish himself in one field, "giving no quarter to hypocrisy or vagueness," and it was upon mathematics that he placed so many of his temporal hopes. At last he had found a teacher of quick and certain judgment and vigorous intelligence, open to new ideas—Gabriel Gros.

Beyle shined in mathematics, and Dr. Gagnon felt a great deal of pride in him. As the century reached its end, his examination period arrived. He passed it with flying colors. In November, 1799, the young student left for Paris with one of his father's friends. Chérubin Beyle accompanied the young candidate to the coach. He was moved; he wept. Stendhal, absolutely joyous at escaping from the years he had felt to be tyrannical, found his father "ugly" and experienced no other emotion.

Before his departure, however, Beyle's uncle, Romain Gagnon, had dispensed to him an additional parting gift. A rather odd man, he was an unambitious lawyer whose elegant delicacy caused one to overlook his laziness and partially excused his ignorance and a certain fatuity. The young Beyle admired his uncle's worldliness and amorous conquests. It was quite a recommendation for a Grenoble woman to have "resisted M. Romain Gagnon." The latter sympathized with his nephew, and occasionally burdened himself with him when he went to the theater—oh ill-advised! For he symbolized to the adolescent from the outset a masculine ideal which was to prove inaccessible.

From the moment Beyle left Grenoble he adhered to a virile language which he probably considered healthy, holding to the persuasion of fashionable gentlemen that one succeeds in the world not through mathematics but through women. How, then, must the paralyzed lover of Virginie Cubly, a young actress he admired at the Grenoble theater, have thought of this exhortation! For this was a chaste, respectful, religious love for a little ruffled figure, with a serious and sometimes melancholy aspect. The very sight of her name on a poster was a blow to his heart. But Henri Beyle's fiery temperament was joined with the timidity Cabanis described. Virginie Cubly was always unaware of the existence of the most passionate of her idolators. One day fate put them face to face, in the Jardin de Ville: "I was almost sick . . . finally I took flight, as if the Devil were carrying me along the railing"—and without his having been seen. So went his first campaign!

For the first time he was leaving his native city. From this moment on, he was to take a giant leap toward the world. What roads he would travel in the next forty years! To the clatter of wheels which bore him away, he shook the dust of Grenoble from his heels, without any regret, without any melancholy concerning his young past.

The Grenoble life of that time had, in fact, hardly taught him everything there was to know. Although he may have visited a few very devout old ladies, who parsimoniously doled him sweets and pleasurelessly embraced him, they introduced him to absolutely none of those "lovely women who don't forget." Romain Gagnon, in revealing his affairs to him, had clearly given him an urge to kick over the traces, but for that he needed an ease which was not his lot. His deeper nature responded much more readily to the somber ardours, in the manner of Jean-Jacques Rousseau. Despite the fire of his temperament it was his fate, even in adolescence, to love more than he was loved. Fearful and mute with women, he let his desires slowly ripen in his heart; he would love, with La Fontaine, "with the somber pleasure of a melancholy heart."

How to become a Don Juan when a passionate and tender soul is joined with natural timidity—to say nothing of a precocious stoutness and thankless features! His grandfather, however, had one day given him this assurance: "You are ugly, but no one will ever reproach you for your ugliness."

2 · First Contact with Paris (1799-1800) *

Discovery of Italy (1800-1801) * Second

Sojourn in Paris (1802-1805) * Marseilles

Interlude (1805-1806)

ACTUALLY, the ingenuous Henri Beyle, who cared very little about a scientific career, went to Paris in search of romantic love and literary fame. He noted at that time, in his *Thoughts*: "I am a man whose existence is perhaps least given to chance because I am dominated by an excessive passion for fame, to which I relate everything."

Restless adolescence—a troubled age! He had wept over the cadences of Rousseau's *La Nouvelle Héloïse*, but he had also taken keen pleasure in the *Tales* of La Fontaine, and even in *Felicia*, a scatological novel by André de Nerciat. He felt himself torn between conflicting ambitions and was disappointed by a Paris which had no mountains. Like Chateaubriand twelve years before, he found there only a "vast desert of men." Even the Île de France itself always seemed "lacking in majesty" to him, although "imaginations like Genlis', unsanctified by the Alps, by melancholy, or by unhappy love affairs" might not perceive this. He did not dream of dominating Paris, like Rastignac, nor of winning riches. His greatest joy would be, first of all, to be delivered from every chain, to be free to imagine, before discovering her, that incomparable being who was destined for him.

There was no longer any question of attending the École Polytechnique; he did not bother to take the entrance examination, which was to admit several of his friends. In the absence of an engineering career, he would serve his apprenticeship in literature and in the world. As for literature, the era was delighting in La Harpe, Lemercier, Fabre d'Eglantine—but was discovering Mme. de Staël and Chateaubriand as well. As far as the world was concerned, this was the very liberal one of the Directoire, which had not yet completely forgotten the airs and graces of Louis XVI.

Henri Beyle fell ill in the face of the difficulties which assailed him; and he would have foundered in despair had it not been for the protection of his powerful cousins, the Darus, in high favor with Bonaparte—and extremely deserving, besides— who introduced him into the Military Bureau.[1] When Dr. Gagnon informed them by letter of the precarious existence of their little provincial relative, they rooted him out of his lodgings, where he was suffering with pleurisy, and they installed him in their home.

Pierre Daru, an indefatigable worker, was the "great man" of the family. He later became Quartermaster General of the Grand Army, and Napoleon's Secretary of State. Not that Daru was dreaming of military glory for his young relative, only a probationary period of three years in actice service which would eventually open the doors of the Intendance (or Administration) to him. Daru was yet to reckon, however, with the capriciousness of a protégé whose steadfastness in the face of a career was hardly his strong point. Henri Beyle already had too great a taste for literature and had persuaded himself, on viewing a production of *Le Cid*, that the only thing worth doing was writing for the stage. He thought he possessed the genius of a Molière and, on his arrival, he hastened naïvely to ask Cailhava for his *Art of Comedy* in order to study the rules of the genre. Nothing in life mattered to him but the lover's passion and the writer's fame.

But these things were more difficult to meet and conquer than he had imagined! No carriage accident deposited in his arms that beautiful damsel in distress who straightaway became his mistress. Alone in his garret in the Saint-Germain, he suffered—and the universe barely noticed his distress. An individualist by nature, he felt within himself the force and the will to be a lone knight in the world. Not that he refused eventual aid, but he knew how to scorn it as well. For fifteen years the

1 Beyle became one of 700 clerks who worked for Pierre Daru.

Darus were to do their utmost to maintain his fragile bark in
their wake, with varying success. Henri Beyle was to owe them
the only years he knew of shining success.

Pierre Daru, scholar, functionary, and statesman, was extremely fond of literature, but a conformist to the Empire style.
A lion for work, according to Napoleon, his authoritative temperament never reconciled itself to the changeableness of his
young cousin. He persisted, nevertheless, in promoting the
youth's career, although Beyle's spelling—he had an affectation
of writing the French *cela* with two "l's"—exasperated him.
Pierre Daru, who had never watched without bewilderment as
Beyle entered his drawing room "with the air of a monk" and
a timidity that prohibited him from leaving for his handker-
chief, was later amazed to learn that Beyle had published several books. Despite a certain incompatibility of temperament,
however, Beyle always regarded Daru as his benefactor. Up
until her premature death in 1817, the Countess Daru, as well,
continued to maintain her friendship for him and her protection. Beyle later reproached himself for his ingratitude toward
them.

In this new circle he discovered a second master in seduction,
Martial, the brother of Pierre. An artillery lieutenant, Assistant
Commissary, and then Commissary of War, Under Inspector of
Reviews before he joined the Army of Italy in 1800, Intendant
to Brunswick in 1806, and then Intendant to the Crown Goods
in the Department of the Tiber and Lake Transimene, Martial
was to give Beyle a warm welcome in Milan, Brunswick, and
Rome. He taught the writer what little he would ever know
"about the art of conducting oneself with the ladies." The
handsome Martial collected mistresses, and his bag of conquests
was distinguished by the superb Teresa Pickler, whom the poet
Monti married.

At the sight of Martial's love affairs, Romain Gagnon was
reduced in Beyle's eyes to the rank of provincial roué. A gam-
bler, a woman-chaser, a social glowworm with a never-ending
joviality, Martial took his flabbergasted cousin into his confidence concerning his love affairs; and this casual epicurianism,
seasoned by Parisian sophistication, was a revelation to Henri
Beyle. He looked upon Martial as his ideal of elegant living.

He admired that eclecticism which could conquer without passion and detach itself without theatrics—never placing the "search for happiness" on an inaccessible level. Beyle's rather crude antics in his first amorous adventures may well have been only an awkward parody of Martial's sophisticated prowess.

From this moment on the active life would ravish him, mold him, enrich him, delay the hour of his first publications, and prevent him from falling into mawkish sentimentality and romantic verbiage. Upon this primitive canvas would be painted the new themes which life was to offer him.

In 1800, delighted by the prospect of travel, Beyle abruptly decided to train for the Army of Italy. He was seventeen years old and he had a horse—like Fabrizio at Waterloo—and a uniform with a sword completed his fine array, although the uniform was still a bit ill-fitting! It was in the company of a certain Captain Burelvillers, a rather rough character whom he encountered as he left Geneva, that he attempted to cross the Alps: "My pleasure was so keen, so profound, that he was *pensive* about it."

Instead of sighing over her for long years before actually seeing her, like Goethe and so many others, instead of embellishing her with all the ardors of desire and contemplation before possessing her, instead of marching upon her with the secret intention of reporting back to his native country with noble lamentations about beautiful, dead cities, Henri Beyle experienced the revelation of Italy without the intrusion of any deforming prism. The memory of Juliet and Desdemona, a few passages from Ariosto, might well have left a touch of romantic fancy in his mind, but his vision could not have been very seriously harmed by them.

He did not know a word of Italian and had only a few memories from the classics concerning the Italy of the past. He was totally unfamiliar with the Italy of his own time, possibly because he could imagine nothing but the fulfillment of his heart's desires. He abandoned Paris without regret, a Paris he had scarcely known, in which he had found nothing but bitterness and disgust, while he had imagined he would find there that "understanding soul" which was the object of his life's

quest. Sorrows he could hardly have foreseen awaited him in
Italy, but he was to forgive her for all of them. He would spend
there, in various short or prolonged stays, about fifteen years of
his life. Italy was to be the subject of over half of his entire
work. How did he make his discovery of her?

It delighted him to ride as far as the Grand Saint-Bernard;
he climbed with the troops, shocked that the foot soldiers, bent
beneath the weight of their packs, envied him his mount. The
scenery moved him to tears. The joyousness of the Rolle clocks,
muffled by Lake Geneva, gave him a feeling of overwhelming
fullness—"a ravishing music, accompanying my ideas and giving them a quality of *sublimity*." The thought of military glory
hadn't entered his head: "I thought of myself as Calderón did
when he was waging his campaigns in Italy . . . like a spectator, attached to the army in order to observe but destined to
write comedies like Molière . . . I asked only to see great
things."

"To see" much more than "to do!" The army and the war
were for him, as for Vauvenargues, P.-L. Courier, and Vigny,
an occasion for meticulous observation, for reflecting upon himself and upon mankind. He was already a "moralist." The profession of arms could not hold him for long. But how eagerly
his spirit strained toward its first encounter!

The baptism by fire came as the army passed the fort of
Bard, where it was held in check: "What! Is that all there is
to it?" he cried. He had already sacrificed his life in his own
imagination, but this first contact with danger was hardly very
dramatic. Always sincere with himself, Beyle did not exaggerate
the importance of it. Most disappointing of all, however, was
rubbing shoulders with the troops. Vanished were the heroes of
Ariosto and Tasso, in which he had seen what he thought was
a prefiguration of life!

Still another revelation awaited him in the Po Valley. One
evening, either in Ivrea or Novara, he attended the theater and
heard there for the first time Cimarosa's *Il Matrimonio segreto* [2]:

2 *The Secret Marriage*, a light opera by Domenico Cimarosa (1749–
1801).

Suddenly my two great deeds . . . to have crossed the Saint-Bernard . . . to have been under fire . . . disappeared. All of it seemed gross and base to me. . . . Everything was sublime in Cimarosa. To live in Italy and to hear this music became the basis of my every reasoning.

Stendhal made this confession almost thirty years afterward; he was still unsatiated, and he had heard *Il Matrimonio segreto* more than a hundred times!

The lesson that Henri Beyle sought from Italy, which was always to be "an opportunity for sensations" to him, was, first of all, a lesson of the sensibility. With music, the revelation was sudden. This future proponent of "crystallization" watched his career of melomanic dilettante opening like lightning before him. Italy was to further seduce him, through her scenery, her arts, her literature, the amiability of her customs, and her women—the Lombards, above all, whose smooth, velvety skin had a certain Leonardian nuance. Beyle loved music, as one loves a more sensible and faithful mistress. He spoke to her of love, and she answered him. His memories of La Scala would later appear to him in the depths of Russia or Germany, and they would move him to a poignant nostalgia. "In this ocean of barbarism not one sound that answers my soul," he was to cry out from Smolensk on August 24, 1812. In his *Life of Haydn* he risked the following admission: "Good music does not deceive; it goes straight to the depths of the soul to seek out the grief which is consuming us."

Stendhal's work, which is occasionally judged to be rather dry, is "completely impregnated by a kind of musical vapour," allowing the slow perception of this muted accompaniment which lulls "the passions" or "the weariness of passions." His parched dream of feminine devotion fed on this inner music. A veritable idolatry would one day inspire this regret: "I am often angry over not having left Paris to apprentice myself to Paisiello [3] in Naples." His main condition for musical bliss would always be "to love and be unhappy." He was not unaware of the fact that his love for Italy had begun through his love for Italian music.

3 Giovanni Paisiello (1741–1816), composer of operas and church music, the most noted of his works being *The Barber of Seville*.

Milan completely conquered Stendhal and was to become
his spiritual homeland. This enthusiasm, transposed in 1796,
is still evident in the opening passage of *The Charterhouse of
Parma*. To be honest, it could be because he adored Milan in
his years of maturity that he had the illusion of having loved her
immediately. The Casa d'Adda on the Corsia del Guardino,
where he used to compose from *paperasse*, the Casa Bovara on
the Corso di Porta Orientale, where he lodged—these were certainly a far cry from the cramped houses of old Grenoble! Discovery of architecture! Discovery of La Scala, in a rapture of
sounds and voice and a radiant burst of beautiful shoulders! He
was fascinated. But his shyness, his embittered adolescence,
caused him to stay his young wolf's hunger, despite the example of Martial Daru.

The novelties of his trip from Paris, the distraction of a new
environment, the revelation of the lakes and the opéra bouffe—
these were soon not enough for the young greenhorn who had
strayed into the army. Although he was soon promoted to second lieutenant, sporting the black-plumed helmet and the wide
green cape of Davout's Sixth Regiment of Dragoons, he had
too tender a skin for saber-wielding and prolonged rides on
horseback. His secret fancy awaited no less than a Juliet or an
Héloïse. In vain! Before long, he fell back again into his melancholy. To stave off his friends' ridicule, he flaunted the principles of a roué, which he clearly kept himself from putting into
practice; while the whole of Milan was giving itself to pleasure,
while he watched the beautiful amours of plumed generals passing in brilliant array—Mme. Ruga, Mme. Arese, Mme. Gher-
ardi, and a host of others!

One has to imagine this almost cherubic esthete, with "grace
at hand," in the midst of a bantering, rough soldiery in order
to understand how he could have allowed himself to be swept
into a questionable love affair—for which he had such repugnance. And one cannot ignore this circumstance, because it
contributed more than is usually realized to making Henri
Beyle what he was because of the withdrawal it imposed upon
him. As Paul Arbelet has stated,

There was undoubtedly a modicum of risk in this affair. The choice
was not a happy one. Beyle was the victim. This tender dreamer,

Virginie Cubly's platonic lover, was treated crudely by love from the outset. This shy and melancholy lover deserved more.

The reasonless melancholy, which might possibly have led him into the *mal du siècle*,[4] thus ended in a tangible disease. Shut up in his room "like a sick lion," humiliated in his flesh, overwhelmed with disillusion and anxiety, saddened almost to death, Beyle brooded on suicide, particularly in the morning, when he was forced to remind himself of the ailment he had forgotten during the night. He was clearly suffering great pain. The psychological repercussions on the writer were such that the true meaning of the following remark from his *History of Painting in Italy* is generally agreed to have applied in its real sense to Beyle himself: "A part of any famous man's autobiography should be conveyed by his doctor."

He would enjoy periods of respite; he would forget, or seem to forget; but from this moment forward he had lost all inner peace. Even though he sometimes joked about his misfortune with his friends who were acquainted with it, how many bitter confessions must there have been when he was alone in the face of his own despair! How many visits—to Dr. Prévost in Geneva, to Dr. Chomel in Paris—down to that final allusion, in the face of the trembling that made his handwriting illegible, to "all the passed mercury!" Such was the origin of his forty years of suffering, desires, disgusts, and always renewing fears; also, basically, of the stoicism that lay beneath his assumed mask, and that was destined to make him appear to be the exact opposite of what he was. Whence also, in some part perhaps, arose the vagabond life which was to be his—a life filled with passions, most often hopeless, spent in the pursuit of consolations, distractions, and diversions. Whence also might have arisen the egocentric nature of his literary works, which were filled with secret echoes and never precisely fulfilled his juvenile aspirations.

There was in Henri Beyle's early experience in life a certain warping which decisively marked him. The *Journal* of 1811 testifies to this:

---

4 The "romantic agony" which began at the end of the eighteenth century, characterized by melancholy, despair, and hopeless love.

Of course, if I had been loved in Milan my nature would be quite different. I would be much more the ladies' man. . . . Those two years of sighs, tears, transports of love and melancholy, which I spent in Italy without women, in that environment and at that stage of life, have undoubtedly given me this inexhaustible source of sensibility which today, at twenty-eight years of age, makes me feel everything down to the smallest details.

"This inexhaustible source of sensibility" was never to run dry. Although he wanted to be taken for a roué, he was basically sentimental and preferred Werther to Don Juan.

Beyle soon tired of the military life. With the help of the Daru prestige, he managed to worm his way into General Michaud's staff as an aide-de-camp, although he was only a second lieutenant. He made only two brief appearances in his corps, barely participating in the Mincio campaign, and such a citation as the one he received several years later is unreliable. He was no great warrior; the military profession was never particularly respected in his family. Not that he feared danger— he feared boredom! But his irregular affectation of the general staff was dashing Pierre Daru's hopes for Beyle's career in the Intendance. Beyle was forced to rejoin his regiment, constrained and coerced into an obscure Piedmontese garrison. He had everything to learn. Ill and homesick for France, he took a leave of absence and ultimately resigned, without any regard for his erstwhile benefactors.

He carried away from Milan an image that was to be with him for twelve years, "twelve years, not of faithfulness, but of a kind of constancy"—the image of Angela Pietragrua, to whom he had never spoken his love. Exquisitely beautiful, plump, gay, more sturdy than delicate, she was actually rather unworthy of such adoration. But her poignant memory, with the help of his own imagination, was to haunt Beyle for many years. He looked upon her as one of those "women of great capacity" who alone might make him happy. This prolonged reverie was to disclose that type of energetic, unprejudiced woman who epitomized an aspect of his ideal, although perhaps not the most attractive one.

A draper's daughter, Angela had married one of her father's employees, who seemed to take very little exception to her love affairs. In 1800, her favorite of the moment was Joinville, a Commissary of War, rather ordinary looking but quite lively, who happened to be a close friend of Beyle's. Although Beyle, at this time, played the part of the sighing suitor whenever he was near her, Angela noticed none of this. There is something touchingly comic about his enthusiastic assurances when he was alone, his fits of impatience, his complicated plans. Methodical, even then, in all of life's undertakings, he was still basically completely guileless.

What impression did he have of this first sojourn on the other side of the Alps? He had not been able to form any concept of the whole of the country, as too many regions remained unknown to him; his impressions were clashing and contradictory. Certain traits of the Italian temperament surprised him, without his being able to define what they were. He was overwhelmed by the enchantment of a voluptuous music. He carried away from Milan, where La Scala had prevailed over every delight, a secret love which he would unveil ten years later. From Milan, above all, where his secret pleas remained without an echo, he brought a painful feeling of emotional emptiness. But he had loved this Italy, from which his destiny was to keep him for a long time—loved the climate of it enough to think of it as the homeland of his dreams.

In 1802, Henri Beyle fell back again upon the Paris streets, freed of all constraint in a France which was slowly coming to life again. The Jacobins were pacified; the emigrés were returning; and social life was "taking up where it had left off," in that thirst for pleasure which commonly follows troubled periods. He tried to play a role in society. The Palais Royal, the Tuileries, the Champs Elysées, the Ranelagh—these were the fashionable haunts. Despite his meager resources Beyle longed to play the dandy. He took great pride in his nankeen breeches, his waistcoat quilted with swan feathers, his dark brown coat, his bronze and walnut cane, his carrick. At night he strutted about in silk breeches and hose, his neck swathed in a triple jabot, his hair blowing in the breeze. He learned to dance. He learned English in order to read Shakespeare. He was captivated by the theater; tragedy, fostered by the heroic times, was all the rage.

Great ambitions were flourishing—military ambitions, as well as other less glorious and more lucrative ones. Without a *sou* to his name, Beyle would soon dream of founding a banking house with his former classmate Mante! Such were his major concerns at the time of Austerlitz. At the moment, he wanted to become a great man, but he was constrained in this because of the allowance his father supplied him, with a parsimony which irritated him. In 1803, he declined an invitation to dine with Mme. Daru, because he had only twenty-six *sous* in his pocket and might possibly have been put "in the position of paying for a *fiacre*" to escort his relatives, Mme. Rebuffel and her daughter Adèle, home. His lack of assurance often stemmed from this habitual lack of funds: "When I am in need, I am bashful wherever I go. . . ."

As early as his first arrival in Paris, he had been struck by Adèle Rebuffel, at that time still a child. Returning from Italy to find her a young woman, he considered marrying her although he was without a position. Before long, though, he began to notice that she had a "dry nature . . . occupying herself chiefly with little displays of vanity." A lock of hair tendered, a kiss furtively exchanged—these were hardly enough to hold his attention for long. Furthermore, Beyle's ardors seem to have been diverted at that time toward Adèle's mother, the piquant Mme. Rebuffel, who was neither unsociable nor prudent.

He next became infatuated with Victorine Mounier, with her delicate face, framed by a high collar, and her almond-shaped eyes. But it was to her brother, Edouard Mounier, that Beyle addressed his epistles, filled with chaste declarations, taking as his model the strategy of *Liaisons Dangereuses*. Victorine was a musician, of the same age as Beyle, whose family had emigrated between 1790 and 1802. He had met her only rarely, since her father had been named prefect of Ille-et-Vilaine. Edouard Mounier seems not to have seconded Beyle's passion. But never had the writer been more abandoned to lyric romanticism, completely inspired by his model. He brooded too much; he lacked simplicity; but never had he been more sincere.

On Victorine's return to Paris for the coronation, Beyle did

not dare to risk a confession. Little, however, did his frustration
matter to the indifferent Victorine.

Such violent love as I felt for her, from June 3, 1803, to January
13, 1804, subsisting without being fed, can only persist through an
ardent and vast imagination. I loved her very much, and I had seen
her only seven times in my life; my every other passion has been
merely a reflection of that one.

Thus Henri Beyle early discovered the power of the imagination in love. He had made of Victorine a Beatrice. This love,
which fed on itself for two years, finally died of starvation.

Between 1803 and 1805, Beyle proceeded with his intellectual
"second education," plunging into the study of Ideology [5] and
establishing the foundations of what was eventually to become
"Beylism." One is struck, however, by his complete indifference
during those years toward his previous military life and toward
the events which were then unfolding on the European scene.
He lived in an intellectual oasis, in love with the theater and
infatuated with Helvétius and Destutt de Tracy. Deciding to
rid himself of his Grenoble accent, he took a course in elocu-
tion with Larive, and then with Dugazon of the Théâtre Français. He learned the part of Orestes, made friends with Talma,
was admitted to the dressing room of Mlle. Duchesnois, and
took the latter's part against Mme. George in a controversy that
was raging between the two actresses at that time. He played in
private theatricals and did his best to shine in them. But he
was as unsuccessful as he was obstinate in his profession of
comic bard, although he took the keenest pleasure in the rather
easy society of the women who frequented Dugazon's.

It was there, in 1804, that he came to know Mélanie Guil-
bert, whose professional name was Louason, an actress three
years his senior. He found her "a heavenly figure," with "an
air of intelligence about her smile." She pleased him. The labors
of his approach were slower than Mélanie had expected,
although she had managed to remain sentimental throughout
several love affairs. Once again Beyle became the victim of his

5 Tr. note: Ideology is here used to describe the early eighteenth-
century school of philosophy based on the teachings of Condillac.

own discretion and his too tender nature, although he exhorted himself to boldness. Ultimately, the two enjoyed many lovely hours together. "She is a very beautiful woman, with a Grecian profile, severe, immense blue eyes, and a graceful body, although she is a trifle thin," he wrote to Pauline. This last trait, however, was far from displeasing to him. As she had an engagement at the Grand Théâtre in Marseilles, he accompanied her there in August, 1805; this was a part of the reason, doubtless, for Beyle's decision to learn business in the wholesale grocery firm of Charles Meunier, where his friend Mante, already installed in Marseilles, found him a position—which he heartily disliked.

The first phase of this love affair delighted him. Together the lovers explored the city and its environs. Mélanie went bathing in the Huveaune, a living embodiment of that picture which had so enticed the adolescent Beyle in M. Leroy's *atelier*, where he had studied art: "This scenery, with its charming lushness, became the ideal of happiness to me. It was a mixture of tender and voluptuously sweet feelings. To go bathing this way, to see women so lovable!"

Beyle wanted to adopt Mélanie's little girl, the issue of one of her previous affairs. He tried to persuade Dr. Gagnon and shouldered every responsibility. He wanted Pauline and Mélanie to become friends. But the actress was enjoying very little success, business had reached a crisis, and the theater was no longer able to pay the company. The engagement ended and Louason went back to Paris. They saw each other again, made several attempts to resume their relationship, but satiety had come upon them. This was the break. And Mélanie played her role with gusto.

Mélanie, whom he would later see as a "more graceful Mme. Rolland," with "the extreme delicacy of the artistic soul," had revealed to him a noble soul. She had given his heart, for a time, that feeling of fullness for which he was so avid. But it would take him twenty years to persuade himself that he had been happy! In 1806, he harshly noted:

I am beginning to find Mélanie stupid. I can remember a thousand and one traits proving little intelligence; after her departure, there was immediate joy over my liberty; forty or fifty days later, there were a few slight impulses of regret. Actually, to evaluate fairly,

I believe, there was a great deal of friendship, of love even, if only she hadn't wanted to dominate me and hadn't always complained. *Ecce homo.*

Or again: "I wanted desperately to be loved by a thin, melancholy woman, an actress. I have been, and I did not find continued happiness." Was he possibly, as has been suggested, one of those who stops loving the moment he is loved? In an access of barrenness, he felt himself incapable at that time of presenting anything but a "lifeless skeleton"—"of the loveliest hour" his soul had experienced, and one doubt assailed him: "Perhaps I shall always believe that happiness is there, where I am not. . . ."

3 · On German and Austrian Roads (1806-1809)

AFTER this second escapade, it was a matter of climbing back into the saddle. Dr. Gagnon interceded on Beyle's behalf; Pierre Daru allowed himself to be moved; and the prodigal son entered the Bureau of Reviews. In October, 1806, he was attached to the Grand Army as secretary to Martial Daru, and then as Provisional Deputy Commissary of War, and finally as a regular in the latter post. He was present at Napoleon's triumphal entry into Berlin. He stayed there for two weeks following the battle of Jena, with a satisfaction which had nothing to do with his own merits.

In February, 1808, Pierre Daru entrusted Beyle with the Intendance of the Properties of the Department of the Ocker. His duties were to keep him in Brunswick for a total of two years. He studied German, although with no particular haste to learn the language. Southern lands had, by this time, left too great a mark on him; he would never understand this language, which he regarded as simply "the cawing of crows," and what little he learned of it he soon forget "through contempt." Why familiarize himself with German literature? He remained impervious to the philosophy from across the Rhine.

The picturesqueness of the city escaped him. Indifferent to the past of the House of Brunswick, he ignored even the Duke of Brunswick, who had once thrown himself against revolutionary France and who had just been defeated and mortally wounded, while commanding the Prussian army at Jena and Auerstadt. He mentioned nothing about the "resistance" of this princely family during the French occupation. Henri Beyle accepted the decisions of politics—without either discussing them or philosophizing on their cause.

He dedicated the leisures which his duties allowed him toward observing this new society. Official toil was monotonous, but he did it conscientiously; a smattering of the Daru prestige began to rub off on him: "I am," he wrote to Pauline, "the secretary of a Prefecture six times as great as that of the Isère." Before long, he was charged with the duties of Intendant of the Properties of the Duke of Brunswick, Attached to the Imperial Domain, a post that opened the way to the Council of State, which he was to enter in 1810. This must not be regarded as the doing of favor alone, as Daru demanded a great deal from his colleagues; Stendhal was revealing himself to be an administrator of considerable initiative, with a talent for command.

He neglected the society of the French, rather common in his opinion, but willingly frequented the home of General Rivaud de la Raffinière, Divisional Commander, and that of Prefect Henneberg. The social life of Brunswick, above all, attracted him; it was of the "highest quality," having renounced none of its activities under an occupation it had ceased to fear. The French were welcomed into it without umbrage. After all, had they not added a certain air to the city—the air of a European capital? Brunswick society quickly mastered the French tongue; it had not been so long since Voltaire had been the guest of Frederick II or since Rivarol had triumphed at the Berlin Academy. German patriotism, however, had not yet been awakened by her historians and philosophers. Little did Stendhal suspect that a silently seething Germany was secretly forging the thunder of its revenge. At formal balls and gala dinners the two societies mingled, equally eager to shine; each forgot its respective status, with neither condescension on the one side nor humiliation on the other. It was still a long way to Leipzig.

Beyle was no longer timid, feeling that his fortune was made. He was prominent in society and this pleased him. Soon he began to call himself Monsieur *de* Beyle in the manner of an aristocrat, and he even began to dream about a *majorat* [1] and a baron's title. He solicited prints of the family arms from

1 Tr. note: Property conferred on the eldest son.

Pauline: they were of silver, with crossed gules, accompanied by three roses; the gules were crowned by three silver stars.

Stendhal was a particularly frequent guest at the home of the von Strombeck family. Herr von Strombeck was a jurist, a humanist and a student of astronomy, who had done some traveling in Italy. He lacked any sign of "philosophical leaven," possessed little outward distinction, and was a trifle slow-witted; but Stendhal was later to write him from Erfurt, in 1813: "You are my only friend in the language of 'ja!' . . . Nothing will make me forget the Brunswick days." Although Stendhal set little store by Strombeck's wife, he admired the beauty and wit of her sister, Philippinschen von Bülow, or Philippidion. But it was with Wilhelmina von Griesheim, or Minette, as she was called by her friends, that he next became infatuated. She was the youngest of three daughters and he met her on his introduction into the home of General von Griesheim, her father.

This gathering danced, dined, played cards together, acted in amateur theatricals, and proceeded in bands to their country estates on horseback, where they hunted hare, duck, partridge, and deer. Although Beyle had little talent for the sword, he was highly proficient with a pistol. He took a dandy's concern for his appearance, and was more than a little pleased with himself, although they used to call him *der Schwarze Franzose*— "the black Frenchman." He drank with his friends in a *gemütlich* atmosphere at the sign of the Green Huntsman (*zum grünen Jäger*), situated at the edge of a wood beneath the arbors, while the gypsies languidly strummed their guitars. There were outings. He went as far as the Harz mines; he climbed the Brocken; and, in the course of a stroll to Wolfenbuttel, von Strombeck disclosed to him that German was the land of sexual fidelity.

Stendhal already had a taste for German beauty. He was attracted by the regular and noble features of the "sublime Philippinschen," with their touch of dreaming melancholy. He prized her sensitivity, her honesty, her measured religious feeling. Although she was almost thirty, he saw her as the kind of woman who could make a husband's happiness. But it was the blond Minette with whom he fell in love, "that northern soul" whose memory would always be associated with an image of freshness, delicacy, and sweetness. This was his discovery of passionate love *l'amour-passion* and that process of "crystallization" which was later to absorb him so intensely. He found himself in the same situation as had Werther: Fraulein von Griesheim was engaged to a Dutchman named von Heerdt, somewhat reminiscent of Weimar. Beyle underwent the same raptures and agonies as had Goethe's hero, in the Wertherian setting of the Green Huntsman, which he would later transfer to his *Lucien Leuwen*, to the sound of the same music—"sweet, simple, and a little slow."

Minette von Griesheim was not altogether indifferent, but to what degree did she return his love? In order to ascertain this and to arouse her jealousy, he paid court to another young lady, Minna von Treuenfels. Whereupon Fraulein von Griesheim demanded explanations. She had little interest in her official fiancé, it seemed. But the flame of passion was soon extinguished. Beyle's state of health, which was undergoing new anxieties, may possibly have been the cause of this. At any rate, he had no intention of marrying Minette, and she would certainly not have become his mistress. Once again, he pursued the delights of being in love with love. The bond slackened. Minette's father had incurred the displeasure of Jerome Bonaparte, king of Westphalia, by refusing the rank of brigadier general in the new Westphalian army, and Minette followed her father into disgrace. Beyle never saw her again. She ended her life as a religious recluse at Sainte-Marie in Preussisch Minden, after her fiancé was killed in battle.

The image of a certain type of German of simple virtue was incarnate in this young woman: "Everything that pleases me about Germany always has the look of Minette." This idyl exalted in Beyle that poetic idealism which was always the sincerest part of his nature.

Secretly, however, he enjoyed other, more physical affairs, with the earthy Charlotte Knabelhüber, a waitress at the Green Huntsman, for instance, but he never confused the two kinds of women. Much later, in 1832, he would despondently remember Minette von Griesheim, as he stood in front of San Pietro in Montorio—love, in his opinion, being "the greatest affair in life, or rather the only one."

Stendhal's lack of curiosity about the movement of ideas was actually not so astonishing. The works of William Schlegel had not crossed his path. Brunswick society was extremely Gallicized. It was not within the capabilities of his German teacher, Kochi, a professor at the city school, to act as his intellectual adviser. Under the direction of Herr Emperius, another professor at the school, he pursued his study of English, devoting himself particularly to Shakespeare, whose excesses no longer shocked him. His taste for French tragedy had its repercussions in this love of Shakespeare.

He never forgot his beloved Italy for long. He immersed himself in Gozzi's *fiabe* and Goldoni's comedies. He had by no means exhausted Tracy's *Logic*, which was his bible, nor Helvétius' *On Man*. He fed himself on the historians, whom he vilified and then plundered with a ready hand. He discovered Sismondi and Ancillon. His intellect was constantly in motion, and he was never a man to let his duties absorb him completely. It was in Germany that he became an enthusiast of Mozart. He studied the score of the latter's *Don Juan* and sent it on to Pauline. This passion for Mozart gradually insinuated itself, until finally it rivaled his passion for Cimarosa.

He drafted *Notes on the Duchy of Brunswick*, awkwardly trying his skill in a genre that was to create such illustrious works as *Rome, Naples and Florence, Memoires of a Tourist,* and *Promenades in Rome.* But this flat and gloomy, "sometimes Ossianic" country had committed the sin of not having been situated four or five degrees further south! Beyle, who had fallen under the spell of a "land where the oranges bloom," yearned for that land. And although he regarded the Germans as an honest and virtuous lot—if basically rather dull—Germany was, even less so than France, a country for the "pursuit of happiness" in his opinion.

In Germany, however, Beyle tasted satisfactions which had given him confidence in himself: "I owe it to the offices you have conferred upon me," he wrote to Pierre Daru, "that I am not a more or less ridiculous little *bourgeois*, and that I have seen Europe and enjoyed the advantages of rank." This stay in Europe also afforded Beyle direct experience with man.

The emotional satisfactions of this period of his life must

not be minimized, either. Although often attended by boredom, he nevertheless enjoyed in Brunswick one of the pleasantest periods of his life. With Minette and her friends, he had lived in the shadow of several blooming young ladies. And despite certain severities, he would always keep a sincere affection for Germany—with just a touch of condescension.

But Beyle would always be an insatiable man. The "pursuit" was always to appear far more fascinating to him than the "capture," and in his search for happiness he was far more touched by the "memory of happiness" than he was by the moment of happiness: "It has been four years since I was in Paris, with one, lone pair of worn-out boots, without heat in the dead of winter, and often without a candle," he wrote in 1808.

Here I am a celebrity. I receive a good many letters in which the Germans call me "Monseigneur." Great French celebrities call me "Monsieur l'Intendant." Arriving generals pay their respects. I receive petitions, I write letters, I lose my temper with my secretaries, attend ceremonial dinners, ride a horse, and read Shakespeare; but I was happy in Paris! I was in a desert upon which I occasionally found an oasis. . . . Here, I am at a banquet covered with dishes, but I have not the least appetite.

The point of satiation had arrived; Beyle was longing to rejoin Martial Daru, who was with the active army in Spain. At last, in November, he was recalled to Paris. He left Germany without a regret, not suspecting that he had only known rather superficially a Germany which was in the process of vanishing, a Germany which was about to be emancipated.

One can find a good many traces of his adventures in Germanic lands in his *Haydn, Mozart and Metastasio, On Love, Racine and Shakespeare, The Life of Henri Brulard,* the first part of *Lucien Leuwen,* in the unfinished short story "The Rose and the Green," and in "Mina de Vanghel" and "Memoires of a Tourist."

Between 1806 and 1814, Henri Beyle crossed Germany four times. In the spring of 1809, he followed the armies that marched against Austria and remained more than six months in Vienna, tasting its delights. It was there that he became infatuated with "the Countess Palfy," or "Madame de Bérulle" (only two of the various pseudonyms by which he referred to the Countess Pierre Daru). He was present in uniform at Haydn's obsequies, where he heard Mozart's *Requiem,* the orchestration of which struck him as excessively harsh.

If we try to calculate what Beyle owed to this stay beyond the Rhine, in terms of experience with war and with human nature, the Austrian campaign comes into perspective.

Why should he be censured for having exchanged the uniform of the Dragoons for that of the Intendance? Had he been confined to an active corps, he would have observed less of everything; but because he circulated among the ranks, he achieved a much wider vision of the war.

It was after combat that the horror was most gripping. The *Journal* is most enlightening on this subject, and it discloses, in advance, the impressions of Fabrizio.

There was a burned-out bridge, where there had been fighting the previous day, on which remained the bodies of three *kaiserlicks.* "These are the first," he noted. Between Pfeffenhausen and Landshut "in a little square field," he encountered a few more corpses, together with numerous abandoned helmets. He was struck by the chaos of a hospital, left in the hands of a single Austrian surgeon. Throughout the night an officer, "wounded between the shoulders by grapeshot" and destined to die, constantly cried for water in a "nasal voice." At Ingolstadt were assembled three or four thousand wounded men. He noted the devastation of a little village, deserted by its inhabitants—"completely vulnerable, completely crushed, completely filled with straw and uniforms of every color"—and "the good German peasants, stolidly drawing the cart to which they have yoked their horses."

War, made up of contrasts, never allows one to forget, even in the face of beautiful scenery: "a superb road on a plain, bordered by lovely hills but otherwise rather flat, leading up to a post; beside the post, a dead man." The bodies of men and horses were piled upon a bridge: "in the middle . . . was a horse, erect and unmoving, a singular effect." They were forced to push all the bodies into the river: "On the bridge was a brave German, dead, his eyes wide open; courage, faithfulness and German goodness were etched on his face, which expressed

only a touch of melancholy." Finally, Beyle's carriage was forced
to pass "over bodies disfigured by the flames. . . ."

Visions of fire are the dominant note in these impressions,
which are related coolly, with great concern for the tiny, true
detail—the gruesome juxtaposed with the picturesque. Stendhal
relates the burning of an Ebersberg château, in which one
hundred and fifty corpses were about to be consumed. Ebersberg
itself, filled with wounded men, was finally set afire by Austrian
shells:

No one was concerned about putting it out; the entire city burned,
as well as the unfortunate wounded located in its houses. . . . The
commissaries say that the spectacle of Ebersberg is a thousand
times more horrible than any possible field of battle, on which
one only sees men being cut down on every side and not these
horrible corpses with their noses burned away and the rest of their
faces recognizable.

When one undergoes such an experience in the full flush of
his youth, he is no longer able to look upon mankind or the
world with the same eyes. Stendhal was to be sheltered from
the sentimentality of the *mal du siècle* by the realism of the
years just evoked. One could hardly expect him to experience
"the anguish of the eaglet at the edge of its eyrie"; this was to
be the heritage of children "conceived between two battles,"
for whom such battles would be "history" and not "reality."
A chimerical vision of the world was not to be his lot.

4 · Henri Beyle in the Council of

State * The Italian Voyage of 1811 *

Toward the Catastrophe (1810-14)

AFTER THIS TRIAL, an official communiqué informed Beyle that he had been appointed auditor to the Council of State by a decree of August 1, 1810. He noted the date in his *Journal*: "I have opened this fine letter at 11:22 in the evening. I am twenty-seven years, six months, and twenty days old. . . . If someone had told me two years ago that I was never to be Commissary of War, I might possibly have been distressed." On August 22, he became, in addition, inspector of accounts, furniture and property of the Crown. This happy juncture brought him back to Paris.

During the interval between appointments, Beyle comfortably devoted himself to a life unruffled by metaphysical anxieties, if the following police report is to be believed:

He is a heavy-set young man, aged thirty-one years, born in Grenoble. . . . He goes very rarely to the salons. . . . He attends the theatre a great deal and always lives with some actress. When he is not on a mission he works four or five hours a day on certain *Historical Extracts* and on notes from his travels. . . . He never misses a performance of the Opéra-bouffe, and spends his evenings at the Français. He always lunches at the Café de Foy and dines at the Frères Provençaux. He buys a great many books. Every evening at midnight he returns home.[1]

---

1 M. François Michel (*Le Divan*, August–June, 1941) has established that this police report on M. de Beyle was plainly written in Stendhal's hand! It was probably at the request of Count Beugnot that he filled out this report. It was on official stationery and was undoubtedly destined for the Ministry of Foreign Affairs.

A life deprived to this degree of the sublime could give the impression of material success, and this is the impression Beyle tried for, although only in retrospect, for at the time he felt sated with it. He was dreaming of his beloved Italy, which he had not seen since 1802: "Italy is a homeland to me; everything that reminds me of her moves my heart."

No one leaves the army and adapts to civilian life without a certain amount of trouble. Beyle was no exception, as the *Journal* of 1811 testifies: "[They speak much of war with Russia.] [2] It would be charming, on my return from Italy, to go into a very active army." No matter if, two years later, on his return from Moscow, he laconically added: "That has taken place. 'Charming' is hardly the word for it—25 February, 1813."

He was living in "an extremely convenient apartment [for me and for my position of ambition] [3] and beyond that, one of the gayest in Paris," but it was no use. He was overcome with dissatisfaction:

This capital of the greatest of modern empires is exhausted for me; I am sated with its pleasures. I have gone beyond most of them; that is to say, I did not have them when they might have given me pleasure, and now that I am able to attain them they seem insipid to me. Obviously I do not have the frivolous and vain nature one needs in order to enjoy Paris in her entirety.

How disenchanting are the days following war, when the memory of great events makes the mediocrity of what follows doubly painful, when one doubts oneself and one's future! There was a taste of ashes in Beyle's promotion. He believed himself incapable of loving: "It seems to me that since I have been Auditor I have lost my sexual desire. Perhaps it is feeding the fire of my intellect"—(It was at about this time that the words "Beylism" and "Beylist" were appearing under his pen)—"I believe I could easily lose the habit of women. The talent for possessing common women is almost totally lacking in me."

During a short vacation with his friend Grozet, in Le Havre, Beyle was reminded of Marseilles and Mélanie by the smell of tar, and he wondered with anguish: "Is it, then, completely

2 Words enclosed by brackets written in Beyle's English.
3 Words enclosed by brackets written in Beyle's English.

impossible for me ever to fall in love again? Sad result of voracious passions and of the misfortune of having been plunged too soon into the maelstrom!" He would have been completely happy, he thought, "with a heart like Mélanie's." At last he possessed the things he had lacked in Marseilles, when love was making him happy, but through a just compensation he no longer possessed what he had had in Marseilles. His timidity was by no means defunct. Disgusted with "human rabble," he was never "more content" than when, shut up in his room, he could no longer hear "even the sound of a doorbell."

His imagination, nevertheless, continued to weave the most intricate plans of attack concerning the Countess Pierre Daru, although he dared not go beyond the bounds of the "searching looks" he had cast in her direction in Vienna—and to which she remained utterly indifferent! He hazarded squeezing her hand and composed long declarations of love which he always prevented himself from sending. He composed an oriental fiction, in the style of the eighteenth century, in which Alexandrine Daru became the Sultaness Fatima, and in which thickets of roses bloomed upon the walls of Amasia, but he timidly kept it to himself. Another work, *Advice for Banti*, revealed a precise and logical plan of attack: "If Banti wishes to possess her he must attack immediately." But "D-day" and "H-hour" never struck on any clock.

He realized that he was too sensitive "ever to have any talent in Lovelace's art." [4] Although he used military terminology in affairs of the heart, all of his courage vanished at the sight of the enemy: "One degree more," he confessed in 1811, "and I will blow my brains out rather than tell a woman who perhaps loves me that I love her. And I am twenty-eight years old, and I have roamed throughout the world, and I have a certain character! . . ."

In spite of his comfortable income, Beyle lived beyond his means, drowning his heartaches in love affairs. He was receiving 8,800 francs income and spending 15,000 francs. He was living on the fashionable rue Neuve du Luxembourg and continued to insist on being referred to as M. de Beyle. Chérubin, how-

4 Tr. note: Seduction. Lovelace is the libertine hero of Samuel Richson's *Clarissa*.

ever, was giving him some anxieties concerning his future inheritance and refusing to grant him a *majorat*—"something every father does"—which would have allowed him to advance himself at court and sheltered him from need forever. He envisioned, as if it were a suicide, "marrying some good-natured and pleasant nonentity," and, in a fit of ill humor and depression, he confided his thoughts on the matter to Pauline.

Every day, however, was not so morose. The salons of Mme. Lebrun and Mme. de Baure, Daru's sisters, were open to him. He frequented the fashionable haunts and gadded about in a stylish cabriolet, in which he was hardly ever alone. On January 29, 1811, the "little Jewish singer" from the opéra bouffe Angeline Bereyter, became his acknowledged mistress. He used to call her "the little angel," for she knew how to be a docile friend and was never burdensome. For him alone she sang the airs of Cimarosa and Mozart that so delighted him. On one occasion he returned to Paris from Saint-Cloud just to hear her sing one act of *Il Matrimonio segreto*—a dangerous test!— and then dined with her on cold partridge and champagne.

We touch here on a delicate point in Beyle's amorous psychology. Reality was paring away a part of the dream, and it was the dream, at heart, which Beyle preferred. Thus the following confession seems not so ambiguous: "It seems to me that my physical happiness with Angeline has robbed me of a great deal of my imagination." How he dwelt on the thought of seeing Angela Pietragrua again! When Pierre Daru granted him a leave of absence, his imagination was already planning the attack: "I am in love with my journey, or rather, I should say that I have practically no inclination left for the opéra bouffe [and the amiable girl with whom I lay every night!]" [5] His longing for Italy was further crystallized by his reading of Mme. de Staël's *Corinne* and Simonde de Sismondi's *History of the Italian Republics*.

With what feelings he looked forward to again seeing the lovely Milanese, although she had hardly noticed "the Chinaman" before. Her image had been with him every step of the way. With what fanciful dreams had he envisioned their happy reunion in the "millions of castles in Spain" he had built for

5 Words enclosed by brackets written in Beyle's English.

her: "I imagined myself returning one day as a colonel, or
with some other promotion superior to that of M. Daru's
employee, throwing my arms about her, and bursting into
tears."

But at the moment of triumph Beyle suddenly underwent a
change of heart. Those "lively," "charming" memories that
had transfigured Milan and Angela herself in his eyes for ten
years suddenly metamorphosed themselves into "reality" and
he was paralyzed: "A thousand little streams of happiness in
my memory, little streams that made up a river, dried up in an
instant." A "horrible blackness" filled his soul, which his passion had overcome with timidity. His memory "of the tender
and melancholy feelings" he had once experienced at La Scala
totally vanished. And, what was worse, he foresaw for himself
"no great pleasure in being in the arms of Mme. Pietragrua!"
He could no longer see anything except what could feed or do
harm to his budding passion.

Henri Beyle, nevertheless, finally became Angela's lover,
in spite of his burdensome past. The grave and sensual expression of her features, the splendor of her waist, her brunette
loveliness, were doubtless not quite what they had been in 1800,
but she was extremely fascinating, even in the ripeness of her
thirty-fourth year. Her favorite at the time was a Venetian pa-
trician, whose liberal ideas had led him to Lombardy, a man
named Widmann. Wise in the ways of love, Angela used the
supposed jealousy of her husband to keep Beyle at bay when
she wished. Although Pietragrua's charms did not hold him
in Milan for the entire duration of his leave, little was lacking,
obviously, or he would have strayed further! He carried out
his first "grand tour" of Italy: Florence, Rome, Naples, and
most important, Parma, where Correggio's frescoes, already
witnessed in Dresden, enchanted him. He haunted the museums; he translated Lanzi's History of Painting. This was the
beginning of his artistic initiation. The hour of his real leisures
had not yet struck for him, however. The last act of the imperial
epic was about to begin!

On his return to Paris, Beyle was greeted by the rather chilly
welcome of his superiors. Before long, he was embroiled in the
events that preceded the fall of Napoleon. Sent into Russia

as a messenger to the emperor, he first paid a visit to the empress at Saint-Cloud, saw the king of Rome, and was loaded down with parcels. Heavily, his *calèche* rolled across the flatlands. After he left Königsberg the effects of pillage began to diminish his speed. After Kovno there was uninhabited wilderness and he was forced to continue on horseback. He was present at the battle of Moskva and the capture of Smolensk. He watched the Kremlin burn. Then came the looting—during which he rescued a volume of Voltaire from the flames. Finally there was the disorganized and horrifying retreat. On the 16th of October he left Moscow "with three million eleven hundred men," crossed the Berezina River, and took fifty days to reach Vilna. Throughout this entire drama he kept a cool head, remained "simple and unaffected," and flattered himself that he had furnished the army its only day of rations on the return route. "I have lost everything," he said at this time, "and I have only the clothes I am wearing. The best part of it is that I am thin." There is a pluck in these words which gives an indication of his character: "I made my escape by dint of determination; I was often on the verge of complete exhaustion of my strength, and of death itself." This attitude caused him to claim that he had taken the retreat from Russia "like a glass of lemonade." He had even had the meticulousness to shave every day in the midst of the confusion. But he was shocked to the core at the ugliness which surrounded him: "Everything is gross, dirty, stinking, physically and morally." He knew very well that "within two years it will be an outmoded claim to have been in the battle of Moscow." His soul was decidedly created for Cimarosa, for an exalted love, for the arts. He had brought with him a large green notebook containing the first draft of his *History of Painting*, on which he had been making corrections. How he deplored having lost it in the debacle!

On May 8, 1813, he set out again for General Grand Headquarters in Dresden. Following the battle of Bautzen, during which he saw "everything that can be seen of a battle, that is to say, nothing," he directed the Intendance of Sagan for a month and then fell gravely ill. Nursed back to health in Dresden, he subsequently took a convalescent leave which

brought him back to Milan, where he resumed relations with
Pietragrua.

Almost immediately after his return to Paris, he was sent
with the senator Saint-Vallier to reorganize the defense of the
Dauphinois frontier in Grenoble. But the decision was to be
won on another front. Stendhal proved himself to be active
and zealous, and even found time to court a friend of Pauline's,
Sophie Gautier, in Vizille. But he was hardly a prophet in his
own country—his fellow-townsmen laughed at his affectation
of nobility—and after two months he left M. de Saint-Vallier
in order to petition in Paris for reinforcements. He arrived there
just in time to witness the triumphal entry of the Russians into
Paris. Eight years earlier he had witnessed a similar spectacle—
the triumphal entry of the French into Berlin. Such things as
these cause one to regard the vicissitudes of history with a
philosophical eye. His health, in addition, remained precarious.

The death of Dr. Gagnon came on September 20, 1813, and
a deeply grieved Beyle received news of it in Milan. With
Napoleon's fall came the collapse of his good fortune, and
Beyle found himself "cleaned out from top to bottom at the
very moment that everything was being demanded for him"—
an important prefecture and the Legion of Honor. He accepted
the blows of fate without grumbling. He had seen too many
corpses on the battlefield to exaggerate the importance of life's
reverses: "Ten or twenty years of poverty have just descended
on my person"; "Alas! I shall sell my furniture and run out in
two months!"

Like so many others who found themselves on the streets
at the time, he tried to turn circumstances to account, as he
had approximately 37,000 francs in debts. He subscribed to
additional acts of the Senate and swore allegiance to the august
House of the Bourbons, without expecting any great advantage
from it. Still, all was not lost. Count Beugnot, who was allied
with the Bernadotte clique, had just been appointed Minister
of the Interior, and Beyle was a favorite of the Countess Beugnot. Unfortunately, however, her greatest favorite was Louis
Pépin de Bellisle, Beyle's literary confidant at that time and
his neighbor on the rue Neuve du Luxembourg; and it was the
latter who eventually became Master of Requests and then

Prefect. Count Beugnot tried to obtain for Beyle a post in the diplomatic corps; there was even a momentary possibility of his becoming the director of Paris' revictualment; but not one of these projects materialized.

Henri Beyle, who was no born petitioner, was absorbed, in the midst of his insolvency, by other concerns: "I have been working since the tenth of May on *Metastasio and Mozart.* Ultimately, this work gives me a great deal of pleasure; it mitigates all the pain of seeing M. S. D(oligny)—(that is, Count Beugnot)—fail to appoint me Secretary to the Florentine Embassy." He was by no means obstinate, and persisted no further in his attempt to ingratiate himself with the new regime. Undoubtedly he had a certain premonition that "black" would eventually succeed "red." But he was not to be one of those who groveled at the feet of the new masters, ruled only by the thought of protecting their interests.

5 · Arrigo Beyle, "Milanese" (1814-21)

THE FORCED leisures now given him permitted Beyle to belatedly begin his literary career. His decision was made: he would go and "live like a poor devil" in Milan on his *demi-solde*'s [1] income, a total of about eight francs per day.

The excitement of the Hundred Days did not tempt him in the least; the beautiful eyes of Angela Pietragrua were calling him to Lombardy, where they would once again entice him. Furthermore, it is from departures that one makes new beginnings.

Did Beyle, who henceforth refused even to consider Chateaubriand a Frenchman, harbor bitter thoughts against the France he was leaving behind? Or did he, perhaps, have some premonition that partisan reaction was about to render the air of his homeland unbreathable? His exile from Paris was to last until the day Austria's mistrust of him would force his return. For, although the Austria of the Holy Alliance ruled Lombardy, Sarau and Metternich ruled with a gentle hand for several years. Beyle was very well able to respect Austria and to sympathize with the patriots who, through "romanticism," pursued the liberation of their country. It was not until after the troubles of 1820-21 in Turin and Naples that Austria adopted a really harsh line and the specter of the Spielberg haunted the liberals. And at that time Henri Beyle would prudently become a Parisian again.

1 *Demi-solde*. Half pay. An officer on half pay, in this case those who fought under Napoleon.

In 1814 Beyle nourished the resentment of all *demi-soldes* against the Restoration. The return of the Bourbons in their foreign carriages, the excesses of the White Terror, the role played by the *Congrégation*,[2] all of these things aggravated him to such a point that he sided with the rebels in disgust. Now it would be his turn to be an *émigré*. His eyes well opened to the world, his critical spirit on the alert, he was dominated by a single concern: the cult of the self, or "egotism." He took up "his passion as a profession."

On August 10, 1814, he arrived in Milan, where he was to remain for several years, with the exception of a trip to Paris and through England in 1817, a brief stay in Paris in 1819, and a few brief appearances in Dauphiné. He occupied a modest house overlooking the Corsia del Giardino. This interval completed his emotional naturalization; by the end of his stay he was able to boast that he was a true Milanese. As early at 1811, he had said: "I have only an Italian heart; had I mingled in the society of 1800 . . . I might have taken on Italian ways." Much later, in 1835, writing to the Neapolitan lawyer, Di Fiore, who had fled to Paris when he was condemned to death for contumacy in the fall of the Parthenopian Republic, he would proclaim: "I adored and still adore, at least so I believe, a woman whose name is a thousand years old. This passion was almost a madness between 1814 and 1821. . . ."

Broken and impoverished, but always proud, Henri Beyle settled in a city in which poverty was no disgrace. La Pietragrua regarded him as no longer worthy of her attentions. Although he had once considered her "a woman of enormous genius," now realizing that she had made a fool of him, he referred to her as a "sublime whore in the Italian manner, like Lucrezia Borgia," an epithet that actually bore a touch of respect! She was using the same dilatory tactics with him as she had previously used. A loose-tongued servant aroused his suspicions; there followed several scenes and subsequent reconciliations; finally he managed to acquire most farcical proof of his misfortune by concealing himself in Gina's closet. Deciding to play his role of comic lover no longer, he ceased his sport with Gina once and for all; but this type of female, without scruples and without

2 A secret order presided over by the Jesuits.

prejudices, would later appear again in his novels, usually serving as a foil for and complement to his tender heroines. Thus ended the amours of Henri Beyle and "the Countess Simonetta."

It was a hard life; he considered "abandoning society," and hid his distress under a mask of epicureanism and dilettantism. In actual fact, he was beginning to accustom himself to material mediocrity and to a life in which he was no longer prey to administrative tasks and official drudgery; a life of idleness, but extremely rich in emotional and intellectual terms, in which this *demi-solde* was at last able to become what he had never really ceased to be from the depths of his heart—a writer—and a writer who scorned the public: "I might create a work which would please only myself and which would be considered beautiful in the year 2000," he noted in 1804 in his *Journal*.

He browsed through the museums, haunted the theaters, and became a critic of art and music: "By dint of being happy at La Scala I had become a sort of connoisseur." He was refining his tastes, sharpening his understanding, frequenting liberal circles, and winning his place in society. These were wonderful years. Forever ended were the wartime forays. He was living at last in his chosen environment, not with all the display he might have wished for, but at least wholly according to his heart.

Sensuous Milan, of La Scala, the opéra bouffe, and the ballets of Viganò, where on a certain evening in 1817 the future author of *Racine and Shakespeare* met Lord Byron and Vicenzo Monti in Ludovico di Brême's [3] box, on the threshold of that romantic battle aroused by Mme. de Staël even in Italy! Milan, with its social life, mingling luxury, and joviality! It was here, in the corner of a drawing room at about two o'clock in the morning, that Métilde Dembowski loaned Stendhal "a fifteenth edition of *The Letters of Jacopo Ortis* [4]—"following a discussion of Dante, love, Saint-Preux, and the letters of the Portuguese nun." It was here that Maddalena Bignami, who had tried to poison herself over a love affair, gently regaled him with the amours of Foscolo and Isabella Roncioni! It was here that several strikingly beautiful women sought with the tips of their tongues

3 The editor of *Il Conciliatore*, the liberal romantic periodical.
4 A novel in the genre of *Werther*, by Ugo Foscolo.

—unfashionably but not ungracefully—a few grains of candy from the box tendered them by a gallant hand.

Lombardy—of the lakes and the Brianza, where Beyle rediscovered, "with an exquisite sensibility, the sight of beautiful landscapes"—was slowly to impregnate his soul with an enchantment which would one day find its pure expression in certain flights of *The Charterhouse of Parma*. This barrier of snow-capped Alps, long contemplated, would bring the aging Stendhal "a freshness through memory," expressed through the instrument of the imprisoned Fabrizio.

There was no longer any question of a cabriolet, as in the days of his Parisian splendor. Milanese simplicity delighted him, however, and he was always able to slip away to some favorite spot. Ideology had already marked him; now Italy would stir his intellect.

Upon material patiently accumulated with an eye toward his artistic education he was to impose a form which would be the *History of Painting in Italy*. The music of 1814 inspired his *Lives of Haydn, Mozart and Metastasio*.[5] His Italian *Journal*, altered and enriched, was to become in 1817 *Rome, Naples and Florence*, a second version of which would be published in 1826. In 1817, he began a *Life of Napoleon*, to which he would return several times, but which was to remain unpublished. His interest in Napoleon became keener and the Empire more beautiful in the light of the Restoration.

With the liberal uprisings of 1821, Austria would turn against the carbonarists, and Beyle, feeling his safety jeopardized in Milan, was to return again to Paris. His departure, however, had another still more urgent reason—the most total disappointment in love, a crucial point in the history of his sensibility and his evolution as a writer. A cherished image dominated this period of his life—that of Métilde Viscontini Dembowski, who was insensitive to the worship of her idolater: "And he came and his own did not welcome him."

We can think Métilde Dembowski for having produced on Beyle such an everlasting impression, by her beauty and her nobility of character: "One could never forget this sublime brow when one had once seen it; it must be said, however, that

5 Referred to elsewhere as simply *Haydn, Mozart and Metastasio*.

none of these vulgar and prosaic beings had ever seen it." We can thank her for having kept alive in Stendhal, long past her premature death in 1825, "that passionate sensibility" which was never dulled and "without which one does not deserve to see Italy."

Métilde, who felt neither love nor pity for him, was both fearful and haughty, proud and melancholy. For several years she lavished on him a majestic sadness, reminiscent of Racine's Bérénice; she inspired in her idolater an enormous need for sacrifice and surrender and possessed the best part of Stendhal's heart.

Stendhal compared the very birth of this love to a melodic resonance: "The Madness of Dominique: dated March 4, 1818, *the beginning of a great musical phrase. Piazza delle Galline.* That never really ended until May of 1824, on the *rue du Faubourg Saint-Denis.*" This "great musical phrase," in fact, from which was born *On Love,* reechoed again and again in his works—*The Red and the Black, The Life of Henri Brulard, Lucien Leuwen, The Charterhouse of Parma*—as touching, as inexhaustibly creative as that "little phrase of Vinteuil" in Marcel Proust's book.

Métilde was an aristocratic Milanese beauty with a touch of *"espagnolisme"* which delighted Beyle. Her presence intoxicated him with a "sudden enthusiasm . . . for real and total simplicity." She gave him the concept of "perfect beauty." Although not basically cruel, she tortured him to protect herself and preferred to regard him as a seducer with base motives. She would always remain in his memory, like "the greatest pain."

In 1807, at the age of seventeen, she had married Jean Dembowski, a Polish officer twenty years her senior, who later became a general in Napoleon's army, a man of great courage and quick intelligence, but of a grasping nature. Although quite gallant toward the ladies, Dembowski was brutal to his own wife, who had borne him two children—whom she idolized. Dembowski's jealousy had been aroused once, in 1809, by the poet Ugo Foscolo. To escape from her husband's ill treatment, Métilde had fled to Switzerland, where Foscolo was then living, and saw him on the eve of his exile to England. Their meeting was purely by chance, but gossip about it sped to Milan and created a scandal. Theirs was no more than a pure and deep friendship, just as Métilde's letters testified. Although she might have been aroused some years earlier by the poet with the red hair, who alluded to this subject as "one fatal afternoon," Métilde's marital disappointments and maternal anxieties had absorbed her completely since then—to say nothing of her political activities, for she played an active part in liberal circles and had had a brush with the Austrian police in 1822.

Beautiful but slightly thin, Métilde had "an aquiline nose; a perfectly oval face; tiny, delicate lips; huge brown eyes, shy and melancholy; and the most beautiful brow, from which hung the most gorgeous hair, of a dark chestnut color." She reminded one of those "Lombard creatures so charmingly reproduced by da Vinci in his Herodiades." (Stendhal was doubtless thinking of the dreaming "Salome" of the Uffizi Gallery, today attributed to Luini.) Her worshipper compared her to "an orange tree which dared not bloom for fear of sinning."

Although Beyle met her ten years after the Foscolo incident, he had heard the contemporary gossip. Regarding it, he said: "She was highly dishonored; meanwhile, she had never had but one lover." Although discretion was rare enough in the Milan of that era, it was Métilde's abandonment of her conjugal roof which had so scandalized society. Stendhal wanted to see in the young woman's first fall some hope for himself. In reality, however, by the time Stendhal became acquainted with her, Métilde's life had weathered the storms and gained a measure of stability through complete renunciation: "There is a kind of serenity even in misfortune," she wrote to Foscolo.

The fervor of Stendhal's despairing passion is known. Through it he came to know the delights and pangs of "crystallization." Although Métilde's beauty seemed to him "like a promise of happiness," she remained forever out of reach. A labor of spiritualization took place within his soul, which "experienced" this passion as a poet experiences a "sweet, new form." For three years he remained completely insensible to other, less austere charms—even to those of the actress Nina Viganò, who might have welcomed his attentions, as well as to those, perhaps, of the sublime Countess Cassera! [6] And he confessed, with winning candor: "In 1821, love gave me a singularly comic virtue: chastity."

Before long, the persistence of her suitor began to exasperate the beautiful Milanese. "Ah, if only it were midnight!" she exclaimed one evening, when he was becoming particularly wearing. Decked out in a pair of green spectacles, he followed her to Volterra, where she had gone to visit her children, who were at school. This compromising indelicacy outraged her, and on her return to Milan she practically barred him from her drawing room. Henceforth he was to be received there only every fortnight. He was in despair! He entreated her to relent. At last he meekly submitted: "A white satin hat . . . which he saw at a distance from the street stopped the beating of his heart and caused him to lean against a wall." Dante, in his *Vita Nuova*, had suffered the same inhibitive effect at the sight of his Beatrice. Every fortnight took on the color of the welcome he had just received. He paced the streets beneath her window; he left Milan in order to curtail his own suffering and meditated over Lake Maggiore. He found a little peace in the church of Madonna del Monte, not in the prayer which his heart was unable to shape, but in the memory of "sublime music" he had once heard there. "I am going away from Milan one of these days so that I might receive one of your letters," he said, "for I believe in your humanity enough to think you would not refuse me a few lines, so unimportant for you to scribble, but so precious, so consoling, to a despairing heart."

When he was suddenly recalled to Grenoble by his father's death in 1819, even the news of his worthless inheritance could not touch him. Métilde alone mattered to his heart: "Everything on this earth has become completely unimportant to me, and I am indebted to this thought which ceaselessly absorbs me for the complete and astonishing insensibility with which I have gone from rich to poor." His amorous devotion, beyond all jealousy, at last attained the serenity of renunciation: "Adieu Madame, be happy; I believe you can only be so by loving. Even if you must love someone other than myself, be happy."

6 The Contess Cassera was the woman to whom he went at night when he left Métilde. At the latter's reproaches, he ended the affair.

A suspect in the eyes of Austria, which regarded him as an "extremely dangerous man," he felt distrust surrounding him in the salons, where he was suspected of being a secret agent of the Bourbons. Fearing his eventual arrest, he resigned himself to "bitter separation" feeling that it would be a unique pleasure to blow out his brains.

After three years of intimacy, I left a woman whom I adored and who adored me—(oh, the power of self-delusion!)—and who never gave herself to me. After a period of so many years, I am still trying to divine the reasons for her behavior. . . . "When will you come back?" she asked me.—Never, I hope. There would have been one last hour of equivocations and useless words; one alone could have changed my future life; alas, not for a very long time. This angelic soul, hidden in such a beautiful body, departed this life in 1825.

When he learned the sorrowful news, he inscribed in English, beneath the date, in his copy of *On Love*—a book inspired by Métilde—these revealing words: "Death of the author."

Hours so ardently, so painfully, experienced transform a man and his vision of happiness. The "grand passion" became more meaningful than ever to him. To love was, first of all, to have the capacity to suffer. He was elevated to a mysticism reminiscent of Raymond Lulle's definition of happiness: "a great suffering endured for love." Because she had rejected him, Métilde, who was to die at thirty-five, became the very essence of love to him, and this notorious roué could be seen renouncing the joys he might have seized in order to acquire "in God's eyes" the qualities which might make him worthy of this ineffable passion.

He crossed the Saint-Gothard by horse, secretly hoping that he might break his neck, and set out on the following day for Altdorf "in very bad company"—with several of Louis XVIII's Swiss officers of the guard. Many times during the years to come, Métilde would appear to him "like a tender, profoundly sad, phantom whose image disposed 'him' to good, just, tolerant ideas." She would never leave his heart. As late as 1841, Stendhal was to conjure her image in the dust of the Forum.

Why wonder, then, at the melancholy which was to mark the characters of Stendhal from that time forward? The memory

of an often bitter life, and above all that of Métilde, the most
beloved, was transmitted to them with delicacy. It is for the
reader to surprise the transparency of the confession.

The feeling of despairing weariness which thus arose in him,
when he had torn himself free of Milan, prompted him to
sketch pistols in the margins of his manuscripts and inspired
him to write the following epitaph:

> Enrico Beyle
> Milanese
> Lived, Loved, Wrote.
> This soul
> Adored
> Cimarosa, Mozart and Shakespeare
> Died at the age of _____
> On _____, 18_____.

6 · The French Years (1821-30)

HENRI BEYLE was to remain in France for the next ten years. He returned there with a prostrate heart, bringing back his first published works, a beautiful sheaf of materials on art and history, some specific experience with social customs, and a taste for great souls. He had "an Italian heart," if not its customs. Actually, however, this abrupt renewal of contact with Paris would force upon him an immense self-constraint. Dreading that the emotions which were making him miserable might be detected, he wore a mask of gaity, of *esprit*, and balked at every confidence. He became the sparkling wit of the salons.

He installed himself in the Hôtel des Lillois on the rue de Richelieu near the Louvois and Favart theaters, where the Italian company was then performing. He chose the same lodging as Pasta—then at the height of her triumph—so that he might spend his evenings near her, listening to the language of his beloved on her lips, mute in his delight, watching the faro games, and always on the alert for some news of Métilde.

He became a frequent guest at the home of Destutt de Tracy, who, with his Countess, flooded Beyle with attentions. He had known them since 1817. In their salon, where social lights mingled with political liberals, artists, and writers, he became friends with Victor Jacquemont. Introduced by de Tracy into the home of Mme. Cabanis, he met Fauriel there. Renewing his amiable friendship with the Beugnots and their circle, through them he met Duvergier de Hauranne. In 1826 he was seen at the Museum of Natural History with Cuvier, but it was really the naturalist's daughter-in-law, Sophie Duvaucel—tiny, slim, and delicate, with her intelligent and simple distinction —who attracted him. But although she was somewhat shocked by Beyle's paradoxes, she was by no means taken in.

Wednesday evenings brought him to the home of "Ancilla" [1] after 1828. The Ancelot menage had as much literary fecundity —if not talent—as it had good spirits. Jacques Ancelot was a popular playwright and an Academician who, like his wife, had a certain taste for coteries; their colorful circle was to provide material for some biting observations. Brilliant, paradoxical, and arrogant, Beyle was an object of admiration to some and of scandal to others, for he was a devil-may-care enigma. At the Ancelots' salon he met Augustin Thierry, Miss Clarke, Mme. Belloc, and the aging Lafayette. He was also a regular visitor at the home of the painter Baron Gérard, whose circle was one of the most amiable and intelligent in Paris. There it was that Stendhal became reacquainted with Talma, Mlle. Mars, and such young friends as Prosper Mérimée and Victor Jacquemont, with whom he enjoyed brutal frankness. He also struck up a friendship there with Abraham Constantin. Gérard's flexibility in the face of successive regimes was surpassed only by that of Cuvier, and it offended Beyle, who often reproached Gérard as well for a certain charlatanism and malevolence toward his rivals; but he prized the painter's urbanity even more than his talent.

The most glittering of all the salons was that of the Countess de Castellane, to which noted foreigners sought admittance and diplomats flocked, but in which literature reigned supreme. Patronized by Count Molé, Beyle was first received into this salon at the beginning of the July Monarchy. It was later to aid him in the depiction of certain social circles in his novels. Since 1822 he had been attending Mme. d'Aubernon's salon, where he met Victor Cousin, Louis-Adolphe Thiers, Auguste Mignet, and Pierre-Jean de Béranger.

Nothing at the time, however, could rival the assemblages of Delécluze, the art critic of the *Journal des Débats*. Between two and five young gentlemen were invited every Sunday to the

1 Tr. note: The nickname with which Mérimée and Beyle patronizingly favored Virginie Ancelot, whose dilettantism they sometimes mocked.

latter's *grenier* (loft) on the fifth floor of the rue Chabanis. This was the headquarters of liberal romanticism, and the author of *Racine and Shakespeare* cut a vivid figure there, plunging energetically into the pursuit of ideas and also retaining a good many ideas of the others. Etienne Delécluze, who was not prone to assert himself through his wit, found Stendhal's nature incomprehensible. The latter, however, had an affinity for Paul-Louis Courier whenever the pamphleteer made an appearance. Also remembered as habitués of Delécluze's were Mérimée, Jacquemont, and Vitet; nor can we omit Albert Stapfer, former Ambassador of the Swiss Republic to Paris, in whose home could be found, in addition to the habitual frequenters of these various salons: Humboldt, Maine de Biran, Benjamin Constant, Simond, Bonstetten, Cousin, and the editor Sautelet. Stendhal also met at the Delécluze gatherings Loeve-Veimars, the dandified translator of Hoffman, a humorist who leaned slightly toward the philosophic, and Charles de Rémusat, a veritable *princeps juventutis*.² Beyle again became friends with J. J. Ampère, son of the great physicist and deputy of Fauriel, who was then a professor at the Collège de France, where he wished to see a chair in art history awarded to the author of *Promenades in Rome*. Ampère had a beautiful, idealistic nature—his long love affair with Mme. Récamier proves that—and, in certain profound ways, he was very much like the worshipper of Métilde. As for Sainte-Beuve, Stendhal was not to meet him until after 1829.

Such is the hastily summarized picture of the world in which Stendhal was evolving and in which his reputation as a "man of great wit" was established in a decisive manner. He undoubtedly cut quite a different figure in society from the one he had cut at the outset! But we know the unfathomable sorrow which lay beneath this deceptive façade.

There was a significant, twofold gap during this period, from the standpoint of social contacts, which should not be so astonishing—Beyle knew nothing about the way to the Arsenal ³

2 Leader of men.
3 The Arsenal was the second of the great French libraries established by the Marquis de Paulmy. One of its early curators was Nodier, who was the nucleus of one of the earliest romantic *cénacles*.

or the Abbaye au Bois.[4] Nevertheless, he met Musset and La-
martine, and in 1830 Mérimée arranged a meeting for him with
Victor Hugo, seeing the two men as heads of a school.

Among his intimates and fellow-guests at the Hôtel de
Bruxelles, rue de Richelieu, there was Baron de Mareste, squat,
broad-chested, stocky, myopic, and miserly, who had often been
his proxy with the bookstores. There was Barot, a Lunéville
banker with a noble bearing, master of a plump fortune, an
amiable but rather unimaginative man. Finally, there was
Poitevin, a retired soldier decorated at Waterloo, with no more
wit than imagination, but with an excellent education, who
"had had so many women that he had become sincere as to
the actual number of them." Among Beyle's other friends must
be mentioned Romain Colomb, the punctilious functionary of
indirect taxes, with his dog's faithfulness, who was one day to
become Stendhal's tireless executor. Also among his friends
were Eugène Delacroix, who shared Beyle's horror of philistin-
ism, and Joseph Lingay, who furnished timely pamphlets to
successive ministers and who—thanks to his police connections
—could furnish Beyle inside information on the underworld of
Restoration politics.

Stendhal, who flattered himself at having arrived at the heart
of Cosmopolis, naturally counted among his friends a host of
foreigners. There was the Prussian, Dr. Koreff, devoted to
hypnotism, who had a curious but slightly prying mind. There
was Sutton Sharpe, a London lawyer who used to come to
Paris with his gambling cronies to squander the fees he made
in London. There was Domenico Di Fiore, a Neapolitan exile,
as majestic as a *Jupiter mansuetus*, and Andrea Corner, a descendant of the Venetian doges, who was drowning his melancholy in drink.

Henri Beyle experienced no little pleasure in his rediscovery
of Paris, where he found every day the "three or four cubic
feet of new ideas" which were indispensable oxygen to him. Although he was without a paid position and had to live by his
pen, he spent about two years away from Paris between 1821
and 1831. Most of this time was spent in Italy, where he could

4 The Abbaye au Bois was the convent to which Mme. Récamier retired, which subsequently became an important salon.

be discovered with Delécluze, J. J. Ampère, and Duvergier de Hauranne, strolling through Rome on a sightseeing tour or chatting with his newly discovered friend, the pharmacist Manni. In Florence he paid a visit to Vieusseux's bookshop, the center of new literary theories. Returning to Milan in 1828, he was forthwith ejected. Austria had an excellent memory!

In 1821, Beyle went to England to watch the celebrated Kean perform Shakespeare. There he met a diminutive young woman of easy virtue, who had lovely chestnut hair, and who lived in a veritable doll's house. Timid, impressionable, very pale, and actually quite modest, she graciously furnished him the "first real and intimate consolation for the unhappiness which was poisoning his every moment of solitude." In 1826 he returned to London for the third time.

Although the skylines of Parisian buildings shocked him, and despite an extremist government which sickened him, he was at least able to live in Paris without fear of the police and the *cabinet noir*.[5] He was a regular guest at the Café Lemblin, rendezvous of the *demi-soldes*, and he received a pension of 900 francs, plus a very small income. Occasionally, he dined at the Rotonde, or the Café Anglais. Although he continued to applaud Pasta at the opéra bouffe, the music—even when it was gay—most of all when it was gay!—plunged him anew into his lovesick despair, and after 1824, the date of Métilde's death, into a mourning for her soul.

Despite the alertness and depth of his gaze, he had never been a handsome man, even in his youth. A contemporary caricature depicted him as short-legged, paunchy, well groomed but not particularly elegant in appearance, with a delicate hand on which gleamed a signet ring bearing a stone. The forties were upon him. In his portraits one is struck by a bitter line at the corner of his mouth: "How many experiences for an ironic twist of the lips!" He sported a newgate frill and a *perruque*, which he wore up until his death.

Monetary anxieties plagued him. Concerned about his intellectual liberty, he refused to bow and scrape either to the new government or to "John Q. Public." His contemporaries dedicated several, not always eulogistic, articles to him. Deter-

5 The secret censorship bureau established by Louis XIV.

mined to gamble his work "in posterity's lottery," he was appalled by certain tricks of vulgar literary fare. His books were often published at his own expense. Following the publication of *The Red and the Black*, one editor offered him an advance, counting on manuscripts to come; but he regarded this gesture as an infringement on his liberty: "That horrified me and would have disgusted me with writing." In the same way, he refused to sacrifice his integrity to popular taste. Such stringency is worth mentioning. He was no less reticent in regard to those who, lacking talent, built their fortunes in business.

Although he was not prevented from going to the salons, where he shined, Beyle darkened into despair and drafted will after will—six of them in less than six months—during the year 1828! One of them expressed his desire to be buried in Andilly, in the valley of Montmorency. For it had been there, "in the middle of a wood, just to the left of la Sablonnière as one ascends," that he had corrected the proofs of his treatise *On Love* in 1822, with death in his soul, haunted by the mad idea of returning to Milan. In Beyle's *Armance*, Octave leaves the courtyard of the Andilly château "with the feeling one might have on marching to his death." The Civitavecchia copy of the novel bears the signs of Beyle's great disappointments, noted in English:

> July 7, 1828—Yesterday Ermenonville [6]
> Three great despairs
> Abandon of Gina 1817
> Impossible of Métilde 1830
> Abandon of Manti 1826
> all my love.

For here a name must be added to his list of amours: Clémentine Curial, the daughter of Countess Beugnot, variously referred to as Manti, Menti, or Menta. In 1824, just as his pain over Métilde was subsiding, he fell in love with her. Menti's husband was a general who had covered himself with glory during the Empire, and subsequently thrown in his lot with Louis

6 Ermenonville, Rousseau's last retreat, was the site of an overnight journey Beyle made with Mme. Daru and a party of friends at the height of his infatuation with her. He convinced himself that she would have been his that night had there not been others present.

XVIII. On May 22, 1824, Henri Beyle achieved "an astonishing victory," as he put it. Although not particularly beautiful, Menti had a pleasant face, with magnificent eyes; she was witty, cultivated, and of a restless and tumultuous nature. Their ardent love affair, alternately tender and violent, lasted for two years . . . moving from Paris to her château at Monchy, where it occurred to the Countess to hide her lover in the basement for three days. Totally abandoned one minute, overwhelmed with tender reproaches the next, sensual and changeable, Menti was not altogether immune to the presence of officers in her entourage.

She valued Stendhal for his originality of wit and his amorous subtlety. In June of 1826, as he passed Saint-Omer on his way to England, Stendhal observed that there was "a cloud over San Remo." This word, mysterious for a long time, was an anagram of Saint-Omer, where Menti had rejoined her husband for an official celebration. On Beyle's return from London in September, the break with her took place, "a horrible crisis" which put him "very near gun point." Although he fought to renew their affair, and although Menti was compassionate, she had written him during the course of a similar estrangement in 1824 the following prophetic words:

Your love is the most dreadful misfortune that could befall a woman. If she has happiness, you will take it away from her; if she has health, you will rob her of it; the more she loves you, the more harshly and barbarously you will treat her; as soon as she has said "I adore you," then comes the device with which you will so refine her pain that it will be even more than she will be able to endure. How painful to find that the person one loves is infamous!

One must make allowances, in this disturbing tirade, for the exasperation of the moment. However, several traces of the sentiments he was then experiencing can be detected in his *Armance*. The relations of the two were not so badly shattered, though, and friendship followed love. Beyle went back to Monchy in 1833, this time in broad daylight! Between 1836 and 1839, he had a fleeting hope of seeing *veteris vestigia flammae* [7] revived. But Clémentine was then about fifty. During

7 Old vestiges of the flame.

the period of their estrangement she had lost a daughter, Bathilde, whom Stendhal had greatly cherished. The remorses of Mme. de Rênal over her son Stanislas, with their alternating hopes and despairs, recall those of the Countess Curial at the bedside of her daughter.

Toward the end of his stay in Paris, Beyle experienced yet two more passionate affairs which were to mark his work as a novelist.

In the spring of 1829, he became enamored "briefly, but to the point of madness" with Alberte de Rubempré, whom he dubbed "Mme. Azur" because she inhabited the rue Bleue, and whom he always referred to under a mysterious pseudonym —"Sanscrit." This twenty-four–year-old woman, "the least mannequin-like Parisienne" he had met, was the daughter of a certain Boursault-Malherbe, who had managed his affairs in several fields—theater, politics, and business. Alberte was a cousin of Delacroix, who had been infatuated with her for some time, and who consequently became jealous of Beyle. Alberte de Rubempré, "an extraordinary woman, exceedingly witty, lovely, and separated from her husband," was created "to understand whatever genius possesses of the most elevated." Stendhal prized her for her "most penetrating and most surprising wit" . . . "she discussed everything like a man" . . . "with a perfect frankness and the most good-natured gaiety." At first jealous of some young rival, probably Mérimée, whose mistress of the moment she was, Stendhal paid assiduous court to Mme. Ancelot in order to provoke the attentions of the one he wished to conquer, gaining the advantage over her. Alberte, by no means prudish, took account, *urbi et orbi*, of the exploits of a partner who set little enough store by certain qualities, but who had quite a need for rehabilitation, compared with his friends, ever since his misadventure in 1821 with a certain Alexandrine.[8] Meanwhile, Stendhal left for Spain and remained absent for three months. This was too much for the ardent

8 Tr. note: The author refers to an incident related in Stendhal's *Souvenirs of Egotism.* During a night on the town with friends, Beyle was unsuccessful with the young lady, Alexandrine, who betrayed his failure to his friends. They ribbed him unmercifully and circulated the story. Thus arose his reputation for *babilanisme,* or impotence.

Alberte. On his return he discovered that Baron de Mareste had made the conquest—"See Sanscrit for the first time in 85 days and see, alas, the bar[on]," he noted in English. The place Alberte occupied in Mareste's life from that time until her death is well known. The relations of the two men considerably cooled. Beyle abandoned the Café de Rouen, where he met every morning with Mareste and Colomb, for the Café Lemblin, also located on the Palais Royal. Although he rarely had the art to conquer, despite all his battle plans, he had an unfortunate talent, on the other hand, for making his friends fall in love with his mistresses and his mistresses fall in love with his friends. He was thus left with the meager consolation of enigmatically signing the abbreviated name of his lost love— Alb. Rub.—in the *Promenades in Rome,* to a learned article from the *London Magazine,* "The Story of the Last Conclave" (1823), borrowed from the *Revue Britannique,* by which, for once, Henri Beyle reclaimed his own, for the article was his. So ended in "black on white" what had actually been a fugitive sensual frenzy. They did not break with each other, by any means, any more than Beyle broke with Mareste. In spite of Alberte's wit, she was only mildly interested by the author's *The Red and the Black,* considering the character of Mlle. de la Mole—which owed more than one characteristic to herself— unbelievable and attributing to its author, which he denied, the malady that she believed Julien to have.

His other affair came very close to taking a matrimonial turn. During Beyle's estrangement from Menti, he had met at Cuvier's a young Italian of the Siennese aristocracy, Giulia Rinieri de' Rocchi, who was born in 1801 and did not look her age. She had come to Paris with Daniello Berlinghieri, a commander of the Order of Malta and a resident minister of Tuscany. Berlinghieri, with a ludicrous physique but a tender soul and cultivated mind, had once been Giulia's mother's cicisbeo. When the girl's mother, whom he had adored, died in 1824, this feeling transmitted itself to her children, and most particularly to Giulia, whom he had taken under his wing—arousing some little scandal about himself—before officially adopting the girl. Beyle first presented himself at Berlinghieri's salon early in 1827.

Giulia was a brunette, with tousled hair, delicate features, and fierce, burning eyes; it was almost inevitable that Stendhal should be attracted by her. She relished the brilliance of his wit, if not the attractiveness of his appearance, and after three years she declared her passion for him in a classic manner: "I see clearly, and have for some time, that you are old and ugly; and thereupon she kissed him." Prudently, he imposed a period of reflection upon her. At the termination of this odd novitiate she gave herself to him. During the July Revolution, Beyle spent the night of the 29th at the Legation of Tuscany on the pretext of reassuring Giulia. The very day of his departure for Trieste, the 6th of November, 1830, he formally asked her tutor in writing for her hand in marriage. He was politely sent packing; and he did not insist further. But he saw her again in 1832 and 1833, three times, being at that time a guest of Berlinghieri. In a letter dated April 1, 1833, Giulia confessed to him that there was danger of another man's entering her life, with a frankness that proved her trust: "My dear friend, you would not hold my honesty against me; you have often told me that you wanted me to open my heart, isn't that so? Let us hope that it will remain closed."

This "fatal letter" moved Stendhal more than he wished to admit. He renewed his plea for marriage on May 13, 1833, with no greater success. Berlinghieri felt he was too old. A month later Giulia married Giulio Martini, a cousin, who joined the Tuscany legation in Paris. Between 1836 and 1839 Beyle saw Giulia again in Paris. She always gave him the warmest welcome. In 1840 he saw her again in Florence and in Rome. Their tender relationship endured intermittently for no less than eleven years. A little of Giulia's nature transmitted itself to Mathilde de la Mole. In his will Beyle left his copy of Rousseau to Giulia.

Henri Beyle's long Parisian sojourn, interspersed with trips to England, Italy, and Spain, came to its end in 1839. The July revolution served to put Beyle back in the saddle, politically. The shamed Restoration had ignored him—not completely, however, if it is true that during the period of Chateaubriand's ambassadorship Amédée de Pastoret had officially requested a confidential report from him on the papal cardinals,[9] and that there had been envisioned for him a mission to Rome on the death of Leon XII. But nothing at all had come of this. Therefore he had turned his leisures to profit and passed through a second stage in his literary career. The tentative gropings of youth had produced the first fruits—his *Haydn, Mozart and Metastasio*, written in Paris in 1815. The Milanese years had brought their harvest with the *History of Painting in Italy* (1814) and *Rome, Naples and Florence* (1817). The Parisian years, during which there appeared *On Love* (1822), *Racine and Shakespeare* (1823 and 1825), a *Life of Rossini* (1823), the second edition of *Rome, Naples and Florence* (1826), *Concerning a New Plot Against the Industrialists* (1825), *Armance* (1827), and *Promenades in Rome* (1829), were crowned by a masterpiece: *The Red and the Black* (1830). Thus it was that a Stendhal at the height of his powers set out again on the road to Italy, as Chief Consul to Trieste. Although the general public had been most often cool toward his works, the "happy few" had loved them. And since Beyle, aware of the uniqueness of his contribution, had not really expected fame until much later, he had some reason for a certain contentment. Beyond this, he had also been contributing to the *Journal de Paris* and to several English periodicals for a few years.

His material situation was hardly brilliant; by 1828 the income from his position as a retired soldier had been reduced to half, and he had also ceased to write for the English journals, which had been paying him irregularly up until the day Colburn, his English publisher, had declared bankruptcy and stopped all payment. He had then petitioned for a post at the Bibliothèque Royale, which had been refused him. Therefore, the consulship of Trieste, accorded him by the July Monarchy through the intercession of Count Molé, Mme. de Tracy, and Domenico Di Fiore,[10] must have filled him with joy. (He later

9 Tr. note: Beyle himself says that Pastoret "sent me to Rome on a secret mission in 1829," but the author was often prone to embellish the truth, and thus his statement cannot be trusted.

10 Tr. note: Di Fiore had by this time become an official in the French Ministry of Foreign Affairs.

requested again the prefecture he had once sought during the Empire, but Guizot, a doctrinaire who mistrusted Beyle's wit and sarcasm, his reputation for amorality, and his dilettante's renown, refused his candidacy.) [11] His means of subsistence had thus become much too precarious. There was no salvation except in an exile far from the Paris in which he could have lived so contentedly "in a fourth floor apartment, writing a book or a play."

Thus it was that Italy recaptured him, if not completely reconquered him. One last time he crossed the Alps. The period which followed was to be one of meditation, "remembrance of things past," and preparation for death.

11 Tr. note: Guizot, François Pierre Guillaume (1787–1874). A minister who headed the Conservatives, opposing Molé, and who also served in other official capacities. He later accorded Beyle the greatly coveted Legion of Honor.

7 · Henri Beyle, French Consul *

Arrigo Beyle, "Romano" (1830-42)

HENRI BEYLE took up his new post in November, 1830, "like a singing cricket." It assured him a salary of 15,000 francs, and although hardly fascinating, it did shelter him from need. The title was flattering. His administrative competence permitted him to look forward to his new duties without trepidation. Unfortunately, Austria was not unaware that Stendhal and Henri Beyle were one and the same, and the Milanese chief of police pointed out his passage to Vienna's prefect of police, who notified Metternich. His report emphasized "both the degree of hostility which animates this Frenchman in regard to the Austrian government and the dangerous character of his political principles."

His liberal ideas were, in fact, hardly as dangerous as Austria believed; carbonarism [1] seemed to him an extremely "poetic" movement. Although he saw quite clearly that Italy—or rather, one enlightened part of Italy—was envious of a certain "lilac robe" worn in England and France, namely the two-chamber system, he did not regard Italy as ripe enough yet for a representative government. The excesses of the French Revolution had made him a convinced partisan not of the "cascade" but of the "gentle slope." His sympathy was thus a platonic one. He had never been tempted to compromise himself and follow Alexander Andryane into the Spielberg. But the *Ballplatz* sus-*exequatur* and protested to Paris against his nomination.

1 Tr. note: A secret revolutionary movement that began in Italy and took root in France around 1830. It involved much symbolic ritual.

67

His stay beside the Adriatic lasted from November of 1830 to March of 1831—time to test Ovid's impressions in exile: "I made a voyage to Fiume; This is absolutely the last outpost of civilization." He was dying "of boredom and of the cold." The "bora" which blew from the north aggravated his already jangled nerves. He was "poisoned" by the indigestible cuisine, "given a headache" by the stoves which had no draughts, and condemned in his mortal boredom to read even the advertisements in the *Quotidienne*, or daily paper. After having believed his advanced years secured, he began to envision himself on the streets again. He nevertheless set to work with great energy: "I am quite absorbed by my profession; it is good, pected his good will to quite a degree! Metternich refused him honest, agreeable in itself, and wholly enjoyable. . . ." What was to be done about him? He would have loved some smiling city beside the Mediterranean—Naples, Palermo, Nice, or even Cádiz: "I feel more and more that the heat is for me, with my forty-five years of living and with passed mercury one element of health and good humor. . . ." He therefore proceeded to obtain a post in Civitavecchia, which paid less and whose sole interest was in being twenty leagues from Rome and the Alban Mountains.

This was simply going from Scylla to Charybdis: "Had the pontifical police read the notes, which included a copy of *Promenades in Rome*, that he carried in his trunk," suggests Jacques Boulenger, "Henri Beyle would not even have entered Civitavecchia." Austria had not failed to point out to the government of His Holiness that the consul who had been dispatched to them was the author of *Rome, Naples and Florence*, already placed on the Index by a decree of March 4, 1829. (He was to enjoy this privilege a second time, by a decree of June 20, 1826, for *The Red and the Black*, "and at the same time, of similar authors.") It was certainly not owing to the "magnanimity" of the Roman Curacy that his presence was tolerated in the consulate of the Papal States, but to the flexibility of papal diplomacy, which was only waiting for an opportunity to rid itself of the miscreant.

As a matter of fact, on August 5, 1832, Count Hartig, the

governor of Lombardy, received from Saint-Siège the following reply to an official communiqué concerning Henri Beyle:

The government of His Holiness proposes in good faith, as soon as it shall have a free hand, to rid itself of this agent of revolutionary propaganda, as well as his worthy colleague, the provisional Vice-Consul Quillet, in Ancona.

This was during the days following the occupation of Ancona by French troops, ending the revolt of Romagna (February 23, 1832). Appointed by his ambassador, Saint-Aulaire, to direct the finances of that expedition, Beyle carried out his mission "with a great deal of talent and wisdom." Without illusions as to the eventual future of liberalism in Italy, he kept himself from any propaganda, through conviction, through obedience to his hierarchical superior, a man of the "old guard," and through his own prudence. But he was mistrusted all the same.

This was a misunderstanding of the restraint that maturity had given him and the delicacy he had always possessed, further strengthened by his "official tie." He had definitely decided not to publish anything while in consular uniform, as much through regard for the government "which had given him bread in his old age" as for the government which had proven itself, in reality, more generous than Austria had been: "I might not, perhaps, be able to speak well of the Roman government without lying, and if I should speak ill of it I would seem to be ungrateful." To which he quietly added these disillusioned words: "The July Revolution, finding that I had been in Moscow, Vienna and Berlin, had given me a small position in the environs of Rome."

This suspicion in regard to him was not to be allayed, even a score of years later. For in 1840 a report of the Department of high police, otherwise reassuring in regard to him, would again concern itself with his comings and goings! Confidence reigned supreme, as one can see. It must be recognized, however, that Beyle scarcely suffered in the Papal States, except for certain postal indiscretions.

In his new post Beyle was to have thirteen vice-consuls, or consulary agents, under his jurisdiction. During his journey from Trieste to Civitavecchia, as he crossed the Apennines, which were infested with robbers and insurgents, he made a few observations on the state of Italy's spirits and addressed to his minister a report filled with "the juice of facts." Other reports followed, without passing through official channels. Paris soon gave him to understand that he did not have to amuse the ambassadors! This was indeed regrettable, as what Frenchman of the time was better equipped to paint the political and social picture of the Papal States? He took it for granted. Having become the *bête noire* of the Foreign Office, and despite the lovely, gold-embroidered, blue jacket which he donned for important occasions, he confined himself to his bureaucratic duties. And these he accomplished with a greater sense of obligation than they realized: "I would like to do the job conscientiously; unfortunately, it seems to me that it must be done otherwise. Our agents are isolated and see nothing . . . as for me, I've learned a thousand things in my travels." Nevertheless, he escaped to Rome on innumerable occasions, from which place his ambassador sometimes invited him to return to his post.

But how could he be expected to bury himself in Civitavecchia? This "abominable hole" was composed almost entirely of Neapolitan fishermen; steamships from France landed only four times per month. Built on an arid, rectilinear shore, it was one of the most oppressive landscapes in Italy. There was, of course, a certain nobility in the "fiery beacon built by Trajan" [2] and in the circular fort which had been designed by Michelangelo, but one soon tired of it. The city's houses looked like army barracks, and the only thing in the entire place that Stendhal found "poetic" was the convicts' prison.

Immediately after his arrival he paid his respects to the governor, Cardinal Galeffi, a little old man of exquisite politeness. Next, he contacted the liberal circles. Among his friends in Civitavecchia were Donato Bucci, the antiquarian, in whose residence the offices of the consulate were located; Benedetto Blasi; and the courtly Manzi, who "spoke Greek" as well as the Neapolitan Di Fiore, and who used to unearth tombs and Etruscan vases in Cerveteria and Tarquinia. Beyle became very

2 Alludes to the lighthouse in Civitavecchia, built by Trajan.

fond of these men, to whom he owed what rare conversational pleasures he enjoyed during his exile. He had been very unwise, however, in retaining the services of young Lysimaque Caftangioglou Tavernier. As an unpaid student secretary, Tavernier had been admitted to the service of Beyle's predecessor, Baron de Vaux, who later became dissatisfied with him. Tavernier's liberal ideas appealed to Beyle and so he kept him. He was to become titular secretary in 1834, to be naturalized in 1836, and to receive the Legion of Honor in 1841. He saw to the management of the consulate during the absences of his wayward employer, whom he was extremely anxious to succeed. Jealous, an informer, servile, he was as vain as he was muddleheaded, as obsequious as he was insolent. His malicious nature rebelled at no dishonesty, and he literally poisoned Stendhal's consular life.

Henri Beyle's soul was "a flame which suffers when it cannot burn"—how could he possibly have resisted escaping from Civitavecchia as often as possible, even to the point of staying in Rome five days out of ten?

Stendhal loved Rome, not with the adolescent fire that had attracted him to Milan, but with that touch of melancholy fitting to a disappointed heart which had known much and suffered much. He found "in the city of tombs and memories" the best setting in which to await old age with serenity, the country which might best stimulate him to plunge into "the remembrance of things past."

Within the Stendhal who had fallen in love with Milan there always remained something of Fabrizio del Dongo and his enthusiasms; and into the Stendhal now tenderly attached to Rome there entered something of Count Mosca's both tortured and indulgent heart—no longer expecting from life the things it might have given him. We have already mentioned his confession to Di Fiore concerning "the woman whose name is a thousand years old," for whom he had tasted a passion which had almost been "madness." He went on to say:

I obtained for my part her older sister, whose name is Rome; she has a grave, stern merit, without music; I know her intimately and completely; there is no longer anything impassioned or romantic

between us after four years of *matrimonia*; I would abandon her
with pleasure. . . .

Already, this same year, on the first of November, 1834,
Beyle had given vent to the following heart-rending protest:
"What! To grow old in Civitavecchia, or even in Rome! I have
seen the sun so long!" Or again:

I am bored to tears; I am becoming stupider every day; I can find
no one with whom to enjoy those games of the racket and shuttle-
cock which are called "having wit" . . . Must I die, stifled by
idiots? . . . I am utterly stupified here. How can I amuse myself
when I am old if I allow the candle that lights the magic lantern
to die?

These confessions reveal the dominant tone of his feelings
during the last ten years of his life, in the course of which the
Milanese imperceptibly became a Roman.

To retrace this period of Stendhal's life one must present his
evolution in the Eternal City, rather than in the somewhat
ignoble setting of Civitavecchia. He restrained himself from
publishing so long as he was a functionary. He was not prevented, however, from filling innumerable notebooks with his
illegible writing. In 1832 he composed the liberated *Souvenirs
of Egotism*, in which he relived his recent years in Paris. After
the brief vacation that brought him back to Paris by steam
packet in 1833, he began a major novel, *Lucien Leuwen*, which
was to remain unfinished. In *The Life of Henri Brulard*, he
undertook a biography of the most meticulous detail, dealing
with his life through his adolescence. His leave of absence between 1836 and 1839 interrupted a short story which was never
taken up again. But in the course of this period, during which
he enjoyed a tender affection for the "amiable Jules"—Mme.
Jules Gauthier—he gave us in return *Memoires of a Tourist*
(1838), *The Charterhouse of Parma* (1839), and *Italian Chronicles* (1839), all of which were published during his lifetime.

His *Novels and Short Stories*, composed between 1826 and
1839, the text of *Voyage in the South of France* (1838) (a
companion volume to *Memoires of a Tourist*), and a rough
draft of *Lamiel* (1839–42), his last attempt as a novelist, were
to remain unpublished, as well as *Intimate Collections* and

Marginalia. The latter pieces were deciphered little by little, having intrigued many a seeker after their enigmas, and are only now fully assembled; they have enabled us to adjust our image of the writer, which had been for some time merely approximate.

Such was the intense and diverse activity of a being ceaselessly involved with noting down the "sounds" of his soul. But although his spirit remained alert, his body became singularly corpulent—he was forced to order a chair built to his size from Paris—a cruel irony! Nature had been extremely unkind in housing a soul so avid for beauty in a body so ungainly.

Except for the important works commissioned by Napoleon and those more modest ones executed by the papacy and Prince Demidoff, the Rome of Stendhal's time was rather similar to that of Goethe. It rose up in the heart of a country which Henri Beyle always forbade himself from evoking in the vein of the *Letter to Monsieur de Fontanes.* The "austere Roman," whose affliction he felt very deeply, provoked no lyricism in him. So it was that in this open setting, in this light so reminiscent of Poussin, the idea of death began to impose its unrebellious peace: "This is undoubtedly one of the most beautiful places in the world to die." So it was that Henri Beyle, dreamer, one day traced with his cane in the dust of the road from Albano to Castel-Gandolfo, the initials of the women who had filled his life—and even more, his unsatisfied imagination.

He had dreamed of living on the Pincio, which Napoleon's administration had fashioned into a beautiful garden. He had loved the view of Saint Peter's from the via Gregoriana, where the painter Salvator Rosa lived. But reality was harsher to him. He was forced to confine himself to several less august dwellings (except for a brief sojourn in Quirinal in 1811), much closer to the "odor of rotten cabbage" which was ruining the Corso: The Hotel Cesari on the via di Pietra (1816–17), and the Hotel Franz Roesler (1827). Between 1823 and 1824 his friend Agostino Manni, a pharmacist and learned chemist with whom he shared many a discourse on poisons, found him a small lodging, with no view, near the Piazza Colonna on the Largo dell'Impresa alla Lotteria. In 1831 he shared an apartment on the via di' Barbieri, and a servant, with the miniature painter

Abraham Constantin, a reliable friend, kind and trustworthy, with the faithfulness so characteristic of the Swiss. Between 1833 and 1836, he could be found on the Piazza della Minerva, near the Pantheon of Agrippa. Finally, in 1840 and 1841, there was his last asylum—between the Corso and the Piazza di Spagna—48 via dei Condotti, where he was cared for by a servant named Barbara, who stole from him; he did not protest, however, "being liable to be very ill in her care. In any case, this would not be to die in a wayside inn." It was here that he experienced the first alarming symptoms of his impending death. On April 19, 1841, he addressed his pathetic farewells to Di Fiore: "I hope very much to come back, but still I want to bid you my adieus in the event that this letter should be the *ultima*. I really love you, and there aren't a great many I love. Goodbye, and take these events cheerfully."

It was in 1831, and after, that he found himself near the Eternal City for good. He had to evaluate the intellectual bases which had constituted his *Promenades in Rome*. He intended to correct them. For twelve years he was to think about a second edition.

In Rome, as everywhere else in Italy, he was more interested in human nature than in the fine arts and music. He wanted to learn more about the "social habits" by means of which the various strata of society sought their "daily happiness." For some time, he had perceived that "society, with the Italians, resembles the masterpieces of their country." Although attracted by history, he preferred to it memoires, short stories, and chronicles: "there are a great many things for which history is not detailed enough, and which she is consequently unable to illuminate for us."

Roman history held little excitement for him; there was nothing of the humanist about him. Only a few allusions to the grandeur and decadence of Rome disturbed his thoughts. If he permitted himself an occasional fleeting thought which might have resembled a yearning for classic antiquity, far from all dry asceticism, it was because he never suspected about Rome what André Suarès so penetratingly discerned about Athens: "The great advantage of Athens over Paris for the good life is simply that I am in Paris and that Athens is no more."

He was fascinated by the history of the Middle Ages, and particularly by that of the Renaissance and the church. He pursued historians with an interest that was all the more lively because he had absolutely no memory for history and could reread the same treatise every three years with the same pleasure. Nevertheless, how much more did he prefer the very vivid *Life* of Benvenuto Cellini, the richly colorful narratives of the *novellieri*,[3] and the tragic histories that he had copied in libraries and in private archives. These latter were to become one of his most revealing books: *Italian Chronicles* (1839). It may perhaps have been because he had not the historian's gifts that he finally renounced, after having returned to work on it, the overwhelming subject of the *Life of Napoleon*, which he had had the audacity to attack in 1817.

Always infatuated with the arts, Stendhal was beginning to acquire more maturity in his judgment, more experience in his vision. Just as Cimarosa and Mozart had stirred his soul above all other composers, so Correggio had created his delights above all other painters; and it was undoubtedly because of the many wonderful hours he had once spent before the Correggios in Parma that he decided to center the action of his *Charterhouse* in that charming city.

He was a little cut off from music in Rome; this was no longer the chosen land of that opéra bouffe which had given him, in addition, an idea "of the perfection of comedy." Stendhal amused himself by going to see the satirical marionettes. There was a strange gap in his musical taste: "I have absolutely no taste for purely instrumental music; even the music of the Sistine Chapel and the Choir of Saint Peter's Chapter gives me no pleasure. . . . Vocal melody alone seems to me the product of genius. . . ." It had also occurred to him in the *Promenades*, while evoking the *marchesina* Métil (de) Dembows(ki), to transfer to Rome some moving memories of La Scala.

In that Eternal City whose moral tone he captured so well,

3 Tr. note: Tales of gossip, as opposed to *novella*, or novels.

like the President de Brosses, Henri Beyle was not equally
attracted to every social class. The bourgeoisie offered, in his
opinion, only a mediocre interest. He went elsewhere, from the
society of diplomacy to that of the nobility, from that of the
high prelacy to that of the foreign colonies; but his pleasure in
these milieus died down over the years. He still placed the
Romans at the head of all Italian peoples for their strength of
character, their simplicity, their intelligence, the precision of
their artistic sense, and their gift for satire—despite the profound abjectness they permitted themselves and their innate
tendency toward ferocity. Twenty years of the Napoleonic regime had made them the greatest people in Europe. Beyle was
once again confirmed in his idea that "the human plant springs
up more robustly here than anywhere else," and not even the
customs of Transtevere, whose energy he admired so much,
could change his mind. He saw in Roman *virtù* a constant of
the Italian temperament, and a veritable contamination established itself in his mind between the Italy of the Renaissance
and the Italy of his own time.

It is not so strange that this disciple of the Ideologues, this
restive student of the Abbé Raillane, so acute in his judgments
concerning the church's political activity and civilizing influence, proved to be unable to penetrate to its profound spiritu-
ality. Is it so shocking, then, that Beyle did not march on Rome
like a pilgrim?

Anything that was of a mystical or merely spiritual nature
escaped him, although he felt with rare delicacy all the idealism
of such sentiments. Stendhalian egotism would probe very
deeply into the knowledge of the "self"; we must accept the
fact this author divested the self of any metaphysical prolonga-
tion, and we must accept him as he was, with his blind spots
and his obstinacies, balanced by his psychological penetration
and his ironic wit. The adolescent Beyle fresh from the École
Centrale did not carry a seminarist's aspirations into Italy.
And forty years later the devil was not transformed into a monk.

There was none of M. Homais' vulgarity, however, in Beyle's
reservations about the Church, the dogma which he ill understood, or the government of Saint-Siège, which he understood
only too well. On the day following the Conclave of 1823, al-

though he remarked on the interested concern of the Roman
people and the plots that were thickening about the body of
the dead pontiff, he was far from sharing the sarcasm of a man
like de Brosses in the face of the same spectacle. With a wave
of compassion, he regarded the moribund pope as simply "a
poor old man, alone, without a family . . . a suffering and
abandoned man." We must note to this libertine's credit his
avowal of sympathy. Over and above a certain mocking wit
inherited from the eighteenth century and an irreverence that
was more diverting than malicious, he possessed nothing of
Voltaire's malignant impiety. He observed the externals of Catholicism, while remaining impervious to its inner spirit. He
did, however, display a certain admiration for the vigorous
political activities of the great popes, the wily capacity of Sixtus
Quintus, and the Curacy's artfulness in managing human nature: "These people have no peer in the world for the management of men." He had a certain gratitude toward Julius II and
Leon X for having played the role of Maecenas. But he sympathized with the cardinals who—present at the arrival in
Saint-Siège of Adrian VI, elected pope when no one in the
Conclave knew who he was—turned to raise their hands to
heaven, even though he perceived that they were antiques:
"*Sunt idola antiquorum!*" [4]

For the Rome of 1830–41 was, in his opinion, still very much
the same Rome upon whose streets "Caesar and Brutus had
marched"; still the Rome of Michelangelo and Raphael, of
Julius II and Leon X, much more than of the martyred Saint
Peter. Then why concern oneself with catacombs? Let us admit
his failings, but without allowing ourselves to forget what André
Suarès said of him: "More than anyone else, Stendhal admires
the Church of Rome as an empire, a political party, an incomparable order. To him the popes are princes filled with force and
talent. Therefore he is Roman in the widest sense of the word."
It is commendable when one has not been touched with spirit-
uality to be able to understand and feel the beauty and temporal
grandeur of the Church and proclaim it. Eternity was not in
his province.

Although the years between 1831 and 1842 were not the

4 They are the idols of antiquity.

most impassioned ones Stendhal had ever known, they were
perhaps the most delicately throbbing. The echo of a whole
adventurous destiny was reverberating there in the silence, from
which gushed forth in 1839 all the unique and fascinating
lyricism of *The Charterhouse of Parma*. In it were appeased the
last ghosts of love through a kind of gradual renunciation,
touched with a certain stoic bitterness. In it Stendhal's egotism
reached the end of its melancholy course and contemplated
itself, with more sadness than complacency. In it one can hear
the last accents of a harsh existence, but one can still hear,
at length, the secret echo of that same tender musical accompaniment.

Stendhal divided his time between Rome and Civitavecchia.
In his official residence, when he was not plagued by stomach
pains, migraines, colic, gout, and kidney stones, he sought the
company of the liberals to kill time. But what was the friendship of a Donato Bucci to a soul as avid as Beyle's? At other
times, between irksome consulary tasks, he would go out hunting, striding along the deserted coastline in meditation, but
without much enthusiasm. For the pursuit of quail is a baga-
telle to a man who has built his life around the pursuit of
happiness, particularly when the years are advancing and he
has not yet attained it.

He both detested his employment and dreaded losing it. His
periodic escapes continued. In Sienna he saw again the lovely
Giulia Martini; in Florence he visited Vieusseux's bookshop;
he bought in Naples a bust of Tiberius which had just been
unearthed and which he later presented to Count Molé, on
the latter's departure from the Ministry. He had a certain debt
of gratitude, after all, to the man who had always closed his
eyes to Beyle's desertions of his post, and who had kept him
on a paid vacation for three years!

In 1833, M. de Latour-Maubourg succeeded Saint-Aulaire in
Rome's Colonna palace, and the consul of Civitavecchia joined
in the official celebrations: "Never have I seen so many di-
amonds," he said of one sparkling soirée offered by the new
ambassador. But Beyle, who had taken such pleasure in the
witty, urbane conversation of Saint-Aulaire, soon tired of these

unexciting ceremonies; he still had a taste for social life, but his refinement now demanded a more sober setting.

He haunted the Café Greco, a rendezvous of the artists and writers. He dined at the home of the banker, Torlonia, whose residence stood facing the palace of Venice. He was a frequent guest at the beautiful historic palaces, particularly that of the Cini family, on the Piazza di Pietra, and the Caetani family, on the via delle Botteghe oscure. The Princess Caetani was a patron of artists and intellectuals; she had had a great affection for P.-L. Courier, in his day, and her three sons were extremely fond of "Dominique," as Stendhal sometimes referred to himself.

"Cini—*cinis—cendre!*" [5] The young and beautiful Countess Sandre Cini, only twenty, coquettish and gay! How wonderful it would be to make love to her, if only she would let herself be loved! Even if one did wear a wig—even if one was a bit paunchy! Why did the young and handsome Don Filippo Caetania have to be in love with her? A frank discussion took place; an agreement was reached between the smug young Roman and the sighing quinquagenarian. Their friendship was saved—but Stendhal was forced to surrender arms: "Sacrifice made—Countess Sandre—February 18, 1836." How could he have renounced those amiable soirées that staved off his intellectual asphyxiation, to say nothing of the outings to the Roman castles, where our consul sometimes played blindman's buff! During his prolonged absence in Paris the following year, Beyle, alarmed at the growing rumors of epidemic in the Eternal City, counseled the Countess Cini with a tender and sober concern: "Go to Lucques, so that Rome might be less the murderer." This was a loving friendship, which had just missed becoming love!

Rome, which had been abandoned by travelers in 1831, was again overflowing with the most brilliant cosmopolitan society. The writer's thoughts turned faithfully toward his welcoming friends, and even toward their children, by whom he did not want to be forgotten: "Every now and then, buy a few little

5 Tr. note: Through a multilingual play on words, the Countess Giulia Cini was referred to by Beyle as "Sandre."

cakes, give them to the children, and tell them that M. Beyle has sent them from Paris." This passage displays that tenderness for children which this confirmed celibate was to again express. The child would be no intruder in either *The Red and the Black* or *The Charterhouse of Parma.*

Despite the interest of his Parisian vacation, which renewed friendships and social circles of former days and brought with it new friendships—above all, that of the Countess de Montijo and her two young daughters; despite the diversion of a trip through France which occasioned his *Memoires of a Tourist,* one could sense that he was recalled in spirit to the Eternal City, Roma, which he inscribed in his marginal notes as *Amor* (a transparent anagram!) and sometimes as *Omar,* in a naïve attempt to mislead the reader, *mutans Romae nomen* (oh, changing name of Rome)!

Returning to his post after an absence that resembled desertion, Beyle could boast to himself that he had become a truly Roman personality. He did not fail to take a turn about the Piazza Navona by *calèche* on the day of Mardi Gras, inundated on the occasion by the Bernini fountain. When an art exhibition was held at the Porta del Popolo, a portrait of Stendhal by Sodermark, a Swedish colonel and an artist, was hung to the right of the cyma: it was the "king of the exposition." This was almost the same as an honorary citizenship!

Friends from France sometimes came to visit him in Civitavecchia. Among them were Adrien de Jussieu, J. J. Ampère, and the Grenoblois Rubichon, a former émigré and a tireless traveler, whom Barante referred to as "the madman of the Royalist party" and whom Mme. de Boigne described as "the most extreme of the extremists." During the course of a trip to the excavations of Tarquinia, he chatted with Stendhal for six hours. Thus, it often happened that Stendhal served as a cicerone, albeit sometimes over his dead body.

In Rome he met Berlioz, who did not particularly care for him. How could the future composer of *The Damnation of Faust* have possibly appreciated this stubborn adherent of the opéra-bouffe?

Beyle also visited the French Academy, where he met his compatriot, the painter Hébert; he also visited the art exhibition given by Horace Vernet, and that of his successor, Ingres. But he had little use for academies, whatever they might be.

Several men of intellect who met him in Rome have borne perceptive opinions concerning his character. In 1831 Saint-Aulaire's private secretary, Louis Spach, after complimenting Beyle's fascinating conversational powers, could also discern the fact that he "loved to appear more evil than he actually was," hiding "the idealistic yearnings of his soul beneath a mask of irony" through a kind of modesty, and creating a "shield of banter for his wounded heart."

Alfred von Reumont, author of *Roman Letters of a Florentine* and secretary to the Prussian Embassy, bore witness to Beyle's keen intelligence, his boundless frankness, his knowledge of Italian subjects, and his urbanity. In the Roman salons, where his interlocutors were sometimes afraid to tangle with him after hearing him, there were lively discussions during which he often offended people because of the freedom of his opinions and the sharpness of his wit.

Among the celebrities he introduced to Rome must be mentioned a certain Russian whom he met in 1832 at the home of Mme. Ancelot—Alexander Turgenev. The latter gave evidence, once again, of the discerning intellect, the utter competence, of a certain Stendhal, who was as well acquainted with ancient as with modern Rome: "They dislike him here because of the truths to which he subjects them and the bon mots with which he seasons them, but in my humble opinion it is he who is right.

When M. de Rigny succeeded Count Molé as minister, Beyle was forced to spend more and more time in Civitavecchia, for he had lost his protector. His new minister recalled him to his duties in menacing terms: "If you find it in your heart to preserve the post his Majesty has entrusted to you. . . ." One could hardly ignore such a disconcerting remonstrance! But the "sirocco" that blew in from Africa, the "foul air," made his solitude still more oppressive to him: "What a prospect, to see the witty people in Paris only two or three times more before I die!" Also, what despair! "Must I live and die here on this solitary shore? I am afraid so. In that case, I shall die utterly stupified by boredom and the non-communication of ideas."

Was this, perhaps, the reason he began to feel the weight of celibacy pressing on him, urging him toward marriage, in that very Civitavecchia? This was an odd affair! Convinced that henceforth his high hopes concerning his career were useless, M. le Consul de France deigned to cast his eye upon young Mlle. Vidau, the daughter of a laundress. She was related to a French family, which had come to be bizarrely stranded in that somnolent port. But the young lady had a wealthy uncle, alas—who was, furthermore, a monk. He made certain inquiries and subsequently refused to give his niece, and more specifically his money, to a miscreant and a Jacobin. Moreover, our tarnished suitor, in order to pay court to the young lady, had further offended him by attending mass in an embroidered blue jacket.

This interlude, which could only be compared in its comicality to his break with Angela Pietragrua, brings us to his last mysterious affair—"The Earline Campaign" (*la guerre Earline*, as he called it)—the last amour of a disillusioned heart, and one that no longer had the strength to reach its tragic rending in 1821.

There is no point in lingering here over Mme. de Saint-Aulaire, whose charms attracted him and who was his inspiration for Mme. Grandet in *Lucien Leuwen* and the Duchess de Vaussay in *A Social Position*, an unfinished work. She was blond and gracious, with delicate and charming features; born in 1791, of Dauphinois origin, she was again to have served as a model of the heroine of Part III of his *Lucien Leuwen*, which was never written, but which was to have depicted the life of an ambassador to Rome. Nor need we dwell further on Stendhal's last fancy, "Mme. Os," whom Robert Vigneron recently presented with his inimitable style in a most diverting issue of *Divan*.

For to spend these last pages elsewhere would be to betray Stendhal's secret soul, which was always with Métilde. As for Earline—[the last romance] [6]—she was the final, subtle musical accompaniment in Stendhal's Roman life.

6 Words enclosed by brackets in Beyle's English.

Who was she? Some have supposed her name to have been nothing but a version of the Italian word *contessina*, combining the English root word "earl" with the Italian ending "ina." The only certain fact is that she was a young woman of the aristocracy, whom François Michel has perceptively identified as the Countess Cini.

In a disconcerting mixture of French, English, and Italian, and even an occasional word of German, Stendhal retraced the stages of a "crystallization" which he believed he was observing in the young lady's heart. However, although he once again spoke of "war" and might have wished "to do battle," he had only a few slight urges toward audacity and very little hope. He regarded himself as having lived longer than he had lived— longer than he had any wish to live. But he could not rest his unoccupied heart in that pathetic little city, and *la guerre Earline* was not so much a love affair as a sentimental pastime with subtle inner repercussions. The aging Stendhal—it was 1840—always had the same agitated sensibility. It was now simply a matter of killing boredom, not so much by loving as by dreaming of love. The Dominique of the heavy, wrinkled brow was definitely out of the game: "What prevents the birth of a flame in Dominique [is the lack of hope]" [7] For hope was no longer in season.

The most touching of his marginal notes contained an unconscious return to his tenderest and most painful past:

The moon's pale light and the moon's dark ghosts, every fortnight at 8 and 11 o'clock, produce exactly the same delicious effect on me as they did in Milan [during Met's time]; [8] all that is lacking is the stroke of the clock, every five minutes, which used to echo in my heart.

Thus, at the heart of his passion what a timidity there was! It was the sound of the little clock in Métilde's apartment, heard from the street at the time of his exile, to which he attached the memory of what had been for him "the greatest pain"; and yet twenty years had passed, and it had been fifteen years since Métilde's death.

During the period following Beyle's last return to Italy a

7 Words enclosed by brackets written in Beyle's English.
8 Words enclosed by brackets written in Beyle's English.

surprising change occurred in his feelings toward Civitavecchia, possibly because his sixtieth year was upon him, or because he began to feel the need to take up his winter quarters. There is a last confidence in regard to this which must be mentioned:

[I have seen this sentiment].[9] [I] prefer the stay at C. V. (Civitavecchia) [to] that at Lutèce. The view of the sea, the thought of contemplating it as one walks—(sic) on the pretext of hunting—have strengthened this feeling. Lutèce, in fact, [without Pakit and Eouki and their mother, was rather insipid.] [10]

These words make sense if one recalls a note accompanying the Waterloo episode on Paul Hazard's copy of The Charterhouse of Parma: "Para Ud Paca y Eukénia" (For you, Paca and Eugénie). Paca-Pakit, Eukénia-Eouki, and "their mother" —and there appears the image of Mme. de Montijo and the splendid youngsters who were her children. Had not their friendly salon been a haven for Beyle between 1826 and 1839 since Mérimée had introduced him there? Had he not recounted his exploits in battle to Paca and the future Empress Eugénie, who was always to keep her faithful affection for him? Had he not accompanied the young Spaniards in their carriage, with a strange tugging at his heart, when they returned to their own country? Paul Arbelet has even suggested that the appearance of the fourteen-year-old Clélia Conti at the beginning of The Charterhouse of Parma, of no great necessity to the plot, was a tribute of the author—always rendered to beauty—to Eugénie de Montijo. "For you, Paca and Eugénie" —thus was dedicated that ingenious account of the battle of Waterloo that Sendhal loved with a special relish.

These were the last feminine phantoms to haunt the soul of Henri Beyle in Civitavecchia and in Rome. He had just created Fabrizio's immortal story, after forty years of egotism and the vain pursuit of happiness. What beautiful, inaccessible feminine images, what sweet yearnings floated above the Eternal City—just as they had once floated above the city of Milan!

The impassive features of a certain beautiful Roman had

9 Words enclosed by brackets written in Beyle's English.
10 Words enclosed by brackets written in Beyle's English.

always struck him: "What happiness," he said, "to render such a woman mad with love!" He had certainly not attained his goal. But in the climate of Rome his sentimental past arose again from the ashes: "Seated on a little bench behind the Stations of the Cross . . . near those two beautiful trees, enclosed by a little circular wall" on a journey from Albano to Castel-Gandolfo, a pensive Stendhal traced in the dust the names of the women he had loved, who had most often not honored him with their bounties, but who lay at the heart of his works.

Bitter is the decline of those beings who always set their sights too high, who always have the ill luck to displease those very persons whom they want too much to please! In 1830 Stendhal wrote to Sainte-Beuve:

I am shocked that you others who believe in God imagine that because a man despairs for three years over a mistress who has left him he lacks belief in God. Just as a Montmorency imagines that in order to be brave on the battlefield one must be called "Montmorency."

According to the Pascalian formula, Henri Beyle had been adjusting himself for some time "to enduring the sickness of the soul." This must not be overlooked.

"The self is detestable," stated Pascal. But he had "tears of joy" with which to console himself. Such was not the case with Beyle, who had neither the feeling nor the thirst for infinity. He found himself thus condemned to cling to his ego, ceaselessly probing into it through analysis which, although at first a source of enjoyment, little by little created a void in the haven of his egotism and banished the happiness it pursued: "I do not know myself, and it is this which devastates me when I sometimes think of it during the night." Such was his confession to himself in the twilight of life.

From that time forward, the regrets were more numerous than the desires, and this unregenerate epicurean was finally condemned to stoicism and wretchedness. Furthermore, he had been prepared fairly well in the Grand Army and might easily have passed from one stage of existence to another, without grumbling over his bad fortune or cursing himself. However, as André Suarès has said, Beyle was one of those energetic men "to whom life gives back almost nothing of the immense treasure they have placed in it, and which they have lost during its course." This was as much posterity's gain, however, as it was Stendhal's loss, and somewhere within himself the writer knew very well that a more understanding posterity would some day render him justice. And he had no wish to survive in any other way.

He wrote for himself and for the "happy few." [11] A century after his death, he was still conquering audiences in the farthest reaches of the world. One of his last joys was to read Balzac's enthusiastic article on *The Charterhouse of Parma*, which made him burst into laughter. But although he was flattered, this devotion arrived too late.

In his quest for the "self," he was ultimately certain of only one thing, the evidence of his sensibility: "I only know that I am: good, evil, clever, stupid. What I am completely is whatever gives me pain or pleasure, whatever I desire, whatever I hate." And when one considers how difficult it is to fix in one's memory that most delicate and fleeting expression of the face—the smile—one is struck by this remark from a lover who banished time and safeguarded for his entire earthly life the very essence of his love: "The only thing I remember, after so many years and events, is the smile of a woman I used to love."

On the 15th of March, 1841, he "came to grips with nothingness." This first attack left him stricken with intermittent aphasia. For a long time his writing was no more than a trembling hand—and he had filled so many pages! Then came his own admission, to all "this passed mercury!" His attacks of aphasia lasted from eight to ten minutes, and they left him spent and exhausted. At other times he would search in vain for the simplest of words—the word "glass," for instance. A constant heaviness of the head was broken by violent migraines; he suffered from fits of suffocation, fits of dizziness; they bled him, but it did no good; his tongue was coated and he stammered badly.

"I have sacrificed my life a hundred times over, going to bed firmly believing that I would not awaken. . . ." No daring in these words, no blasphemy; simply a matter-of-fact resignation,

11 Stendhal ended his works with a quotation: "To the happy few."

a fatalism that was instinctive, reasoned and voluntary. However, as he considered the thing that had become his major preoccupation, he added, in sober homage to his shame and his torment: "I have hidden my illness fairly well: I find that there is nothing ridiculous about dying in the street if one does not do it deliberately."

These, then, are his last succinct adieus to Di Fiore. "Despairing songs" were never Henri Beyle's forte. One was more discreet in Delécluze's *grenier* than at an Arsenal salon.

Stendhal's swan song was probably his letter of June 9, 1841, to Romain Colomb, which betrays him. It is difficult to read these three lines without emotion because they reveal with exquisite sensitivity the destitution which was his. Crowning forty years spent in the "pursuit of happiness," the creator of Mme. de Rênal, Clélia Conti, Mme. de Chasteller, Mathilde de la Mole, la Sanseverina was reduced to the following: "I have two dogs whom I dearly love; one of them is black, an English spaniel, beautiful but sad and melancholy; the other is a young wolf, café-au-lait color, gay and spirited, in a word the young Burgundian; I was sad because I had nothing to love."

He sensed that the end was near. Without weakness, without any hope concerning the beyond, he waited that death which he compared to a rapid and perilous passage by steamboat along the dangerous waters of the Rhone, under the central arch of the Pont Saint-Esprit. There, on a certain day in 1833, he had been the traveling companion of the "Venetian lovers," Georges Sand and Alfred de Musset, a little against their will. Perhaps he was not at all sorry, at heart, at escaping what Michelet defined as "that great torture called old age." He was nevertheless seized by a sudden urge at that time to leave Civitavecchia and Rome, to return to the place which was his real homeland—and which had never really ceased to be so—France.

His leave of absence in his pocket, he started on his way on October 21, 1841, knowing full well that it was over for him, that never again would he return to the Eternal City which, although it had not converted him, had nevertheless revealed to him "perfect beauty."

Five months later in Paris, on March 22, 1842, he was seized at dusk by a lightning attack of apoplexy, at the corner of the rue Neuve des Capucines.

They carried him home—or rather, to his hotel—and at two o'clock in the morning he expired without ever having regained consciousness. He had come very close to dying in an inn, if not a "wayside inn," as he had predicted.

Through the efforts of Romain Colomb, a funeral service was held in the Church of the Assumption. He had definitely not required it, any more than he had declined it; although he had held a seat at Saint-Caroline's for several months in 1806.

Three people—Romain Colomb, Mérimée, and Abraham Constantin—accompanied him to the cemetery in Montmartre, where today reposes the poet who quested throughout his life— had Stendhal ever done anything else?—"The tear that was never shed." [12]

12 Heinrich Heine.

Part Two

The Work of Stendhal

All that which takes me away from
knowledge of the human heart is without
interest to me.
Journal 1811

NOT ONE of Henri Beyle's books did the author inscribe with his own name. He had a penchant for pseudonyms, even in his private life. When he presented his public with *Haydn, Mozart and Metastasio* in 1814, he jokingly signed it Louis-Alexander-César Bombet.[1] In 1817 the *History of Painting in Italy* appeared with the initials M. B. A. A. (M. Beyle Ancien Auditeur).[2] His ravenous hunger for literary glory brought with it no accompanying desire to immortalize the surname of the ill-loved Chérubin Beyle! With *Rome, Naples and Florence* (1817), there appeared an astonishing pseudonym to which he held from that day forward: M. de Stendhal, Officer of the Cavalry. He later put the title aside, and kept the name of Stendhal for the two editions of *Racine and Shakespeare* (1823 and 1825), the *Life of Rossini* (1824), *Concerning a New Plot Against the Industrialists* (1825), *Promenades in Rome*[3] (1829), *The Red and the Black* (1831), and *The Abbess of Castro* (1839). Only his first novel, *Armance* (1827), appeared without any author's name. *Memoires of a Tourist* (1838) and *The Charterhouse of Parma* (1839) were published as: By the author of *The Red and the Black*. This was in order to focus attention on the latter book, which had not received the success

1 The second presentation of the work in 1817 no longer bears any indication of the author's name.

2 M. Beyle Former Auditor.

3 Tr. note: A present translation of the work is entitled: *A Roman Journal* (New York, 1957).

it deserved. The author thus made himself known through several important works under the name Stendhal; under the same assumed name his posthumous work therefore appeared.

Could this Germanic name have been in homage to his tender memories of Brunswick? Actually, Beyle himself produced the key to this enigma in a quip: "That babbler, Winckelmann, *born in my fief.*" Winckelmann had, in fact, been born in Stendal in the old Brandenburg Market; the writer assumed the name of that town to pique his audience's curiosity. The addition of the "h" accounts for its German pronunciation, with the accent on the last syllable and the "d" slightly aspirate. It is known that he pronounced it "Standhal."

A cursory view of his work and an examination of its chronology comprises a major investigation. In the face of the fourteen books that appeared during his lifetime, the nineteen works revealed after his death, through the diligence of the "Stendhalians" and the "Beylists," take up a great deal of room. These posthumous publications are: *Correspondence*[4] (1800–42); *Journal*[5] (1801–23); *Thoughts* or *Filosofia Nova* (1802–1805); the rough drafts of *Theatre* (1797–1834); *Molière, Shakespeare* and *Comedy and Laughter* (1803–23); *Italian Schools of Painting* (1811–15); *Pages from Italy* (1818–38); *Napoleon* (1817–38); *Miscellany of Politics and History* (1822–29); *Literary Miscellany* (1797–1841); *English Courier* (1822–29); *Miscellany of Art* (1824–37); *Novels and Short Stories* (1826–39); *Souvenirs of Egotism*[6] (1832); *Lucien Leuwen*[7] (1834–35); *The Life of Henri Brulard* (1835–36); *Voyage in the South of France* (1838); *Lamiel* (1839–42); and finally, *Intimate Miscellanies and Marginalia* (1804–42). The selection of these titles was, to be sure, occasionally the editor's doing. But the piety of posterity, succeeding the indifference of his contemporaries, was

4 Tr. note: Selections from this work are published in *"To the Happy Few"* (New York, 1952).

5 Tr. note: A version of the Journal is published in English as *The Private Diaries of Stendhal* (New York, 1962).

6 Tr. note: Published in English as *Memoires of Egotism* (New York, 1949).

7 Tr. note: An incomplete three-part novel, the first two parts of which have been published in English as *The Green Huntsman* (New York, 1950) and *The Telegraph* (New York, 1950).

greater than even Stendhal had hoped for. Since one cannot read everything, the choices most often made among his works —*On Love, The Red and the Black,* and *The Charterhouse of Parma*—present an incomplete picture of the writer, with whom the wisest approach is an autobiographical one. For, with Stendhal, the man is always behind the author. Scorning the invention of subjects, he transposed his own life in his novels, far more than is realized. His "dream of life" was always more "real" to him than his own life. For Henri Beyle, who dedicated his life to the creation of his "self," was as fascinating as the heroes he created.

Since his work was not published until his later years, it is partially contemporary with early romantic works; he is, in fact, more closely linked to the preceding generation. His "Napoleonic" years delayed his output and displaced him in time; and had he achieved the career to which he had really aspired, we would have had even fewer of his beautiful books. We must also take into consideration his strictness with himself and his unswerving conception of the writer's dignity. Although he certainly plagiarized shamelessly in his first books, his demanding sincerity and his keen concern "to see clearly into what is" imposed upon him a fundamental honesty which makes these works special. Situated at a pivotal point between two epochs, torn by the disparity between two heredities, living at a time when the newest vogue risked substituting, for the logic and liberty bequeathed by an exhausted eighteenth century, a wave of passion for romantic fancies, his early experience introduced into his life the tragic element that was to be the ballast of his sensibility and thought. Because of this—and without denying the spiritual gap in his thinking—he reached for the psychological depths of human nature, rather than delighting in surface impressions. Thus arose his disdain for the factitious humanity of so many of his contemporaries. His generation was too embroiled in the violence of events to fully explore its capabilities in the arts and literature. And it was this which protected Stendhal from the despair of the children of the century. Rousseau had left a profound mark on his thinking. Rationalism and sensualism had further marked him. Through Locke, Condillac, Cabanis, Helvétius, Destutt de Tracy, and the philosophy of the Ideologues he became a carry-over from the eighteenth century, although with him the "sensitive man" was never a negation of the "honest man." Imbued with the ideas of the past century, which satisfied his intellect, only romanticism and its effusions could fill his heart—which had reveled in beautiful scenery ever since the time he had first discovered Rousseau's *Reveries of a Solitary Stroller*. For, sensitive as no one else was, he held his sensitivity in check. The complexities of his nature fused the finest logic with the most acute powers of observation in a delicately passionate soul. He resembled no one and expressed a unique moment in time. During the richest period of his output he was a contemporary of the romantics. His *Racine and Shakespeare* presented the first definition of the word "romanticism." He proclaimed himself a romantic; his novels offered romantic situations; and yet he was not a romantic in the style of the Cénacle [8] and the Arsenal, where genius was *de rigueur*. He was always faithful to Delécluze's *grenier*, where the clear and incisive intellect was respected above all.

In discussing Stendhal, one must not lose sight of the basic opposition between the *two* schools of romanticism: that of Nodier, which reflected the tradition of the Middle Ages, verse, drama, lyricism, music, Catholicism, and every now and then a certain affectation for elegant dress; and that of Delécluze, which regarded romanticism as neither legitimist nor devout, but, on the contrary, the very basis of a liberalism which held that literature should change, precisely because morals and ideas were changing. In his bout with formal romanticism Stendhal even went so far as to head a "romantic school" opposed to that of Victor Hugo; but he eventually took his leave of it, never terribly concerned with schools, for he was too occupied with being himself. He did not abuse the word "infinite" nor the word "ideal," which poorly concealed the vagueness of intellects and the emptiness of hearts. He confined himself to the *real*, maintaining that a banker "has the qualities required to make philosophical discoveries: that is, to see clearly into what is, which is a bit different from talk of shining fancies."

8 Tr. note: The Cénacles were small coteries of romantics, most important of which was the group referred to above, which was formed in 1823 and included Nodier, Vigny, and Musset, among others.

But this vision of the real world in no way prevented Julien Sorel from claiming the right to his "ideal life"; such was the secret domain in which Stendhal took refuge. It was in his worship of the fiercely individualistic hero that he would be most profoundly romantic. Analyst, psychologist, clear-sighted critic, refined dilettante, penetrating observer, in love with energy and *virtù*, in love with love, always and vainly in search of "the understanding soul" who might appease his torment, Henri Beyle, European pilgrim, raised a monument to the glory of the *individual* through the study of his "self," without any sacrifice to the style of the Empire—a monument that time cannot change. His work was to take wing through great labor and would be at last crowned by the unparalleled success of *The Charterhouse of Parma*.

1 · False Start * Birth of Egotism

IT IS a venial sin for the beginning writer to deceive himself as to his aptitudes. Henri Beyle was no stranger to this error, and he persisted in it for fifteen years. Whatever the subject may be it is the author, first of all, whom his books reveal. Stendhal's work seems less to obey a concern for esthetics than a concern for truth, which borders on an art. In considering his books, "hastily composed, crowded in pell-mell, and hardly reviewed," bearing the mark of "a superior and *manqué* genius," Paul Arbelet sees in them "that *je ne sais quoi* of incompleteness and unripeness, that original flavor of an aborted fruit, that rare and disturbing taste, that special dish for satiated and curious minds, of a troubled and unprecedented mixture." They bring us, still further, a priceless lesson in frankness toward oneself. Untutored in verse, which he considered "a disguise for hoak," Stendhal chose a prose that was able to express his precise analyses and sharp observations. How can it be doubted that he realized his deepest aspirations? The hard work he imposed on himself, and by which he at last conquered himself, was like the internal effort of a fir tree suddenly denuded of its terminal growth and painfully beginning its reascension through a slow torsion of its every fiber. After the defeat of his tentative dramatic efforts and before his first published works, one has the impression that he developed himself against his feelings and against his heart. This is because his youth had nourished two dreams, both of which were aborted: to compete with Molière and to rival Cimarosa.

Oh, the misfortune of having been born "in a basically inharmonious family," when one wants to be understood "only by people born for music!" Oh, the misfortune of having no gift at all for singing, nor the violin or clarinet, which Beyle practiced time after time, with no success: "I had begun too late . . ." But what does a performer's talent matter if one believes he has the soul of a composer because "a charming little air" comes to mind with the words "dear sister" on writing Pauline! It is regrettable that Henri Beyle had never heard as a child those airy melodies so beloved at the end of the eighteenth century—those gay and nostalgic tunes which give the soul a vision of gay and dulcet happiness, at first poignant, as if lost, and then progressively searching, as if on an anxious quest, a quest for the twin soul that Beyle's desires were so fixed on. He came very close to having become a composer rather than a writer! *The Life of Henri Brulard* bitterly confesses this:

Fate had it that I should seek out the sounds of my soul and note them on the printed page. Laziness and the lack of opportunity to learn the techniques of music, the stupid side of music, to be able to play the piano and note my ideas, bear most of the responsibility for this decision, which might have been quite another had I found an uncle or a mistress who loved music. As for the passion, it has remained completely.

Stendhal always carried within himself this regret over his early renunciation, and this tenacious delusion.

Like Ariosto, he was moved "to the point of feeling" only after a comic passage in the opéra bouffe. As animated as the Commedia dell' Arte, as spontaneous as Goldoni, it was the quintessence of comedy to him. This music of the late eighteenth century, "filled with song and fancy," so frivolous and so delicate, a bit thin orchestrally, but so filled with melodic invention, expressing a world of voluptuousness, was like the harmonious fresco of a ceaseless "pursuit of happiness." Beneath the brio of the song there appeared sometimes the melancholy of an accompanying theme that spoke to the heart in secret at its moment of greatest joy. He took a psychological interest in the sonorous painting of characters and feelings, which revealed to him, even in the opéra bouffe, the resources of the best analytical novel. Augmenting the spirited effect of Italian gaiety,

which could permit itself "the most daring innuendos," the
maddest and yet most significant jests, this music—over and
above the intrinsic pleasure it brought him through its expression of the tender passions—brought Stendhal back to the study
of man. And it was the study of man that he had wanted to
undertake from the beginning, in order to rival Molière. His
Filosofia Nova clearly states his viewpoint: "I speak only of the
comedy of character; I despise that of intrigue."

Responsible to himself alone for his future fame, Beyle did
not have the "foolish temerity" to take up classical themes. He
would describe nature as he saw it before attempting the classic
themes, and he forthwith entrusted his very noble resolutions to
his *Thoughts.* At the end of his road, however, what a stinging
defeat he confessed in *The Life of Henri Brulard!*

The infinite vulgarities of mind for the treatment necessary to
make a play actable prevented me from doing so quite despite
myself; and not a week passed but that I suffered odious remorses
over this. I outlined more than twenty of them, always too detailed, too profound, too unintelligible for the stupid public . . .
with whom the Revolution of 1798 peopled the loges and the pit.

This kind of intellectual inhibition, which prevented him from
writing successful plays, might well have had another cause:
having mischanneled his talents from the start. In a more
reasonable moment, the writer bemoaned the time lost in waiting "nonsensically for the moment of genius, a bit like the
voice of God speaking to Moses from the burning bush!" In
spite of his enormous labor, Stendhal never went beyond the
stage of outlines, peppering his sketches with numerous reflections on dramatic art and on his work methods. At eighteen he
was already dissecting famous theatrical works, watching them
performed again and again. He was observing those about him
and studying himself. He filled notebook after notebook, accum-
ulating a treasure of psychological notations which was to constitute the primary material from which he would later draw
for his novels.

Molière, Goldoni, Beaumarchais, Regnard, Collin d'Harleville, Corneille, Voltaire, Alfieri, Racine, Shakespeare—these
writers were the constant objects of his scrutiny. But his mind
left his pen behind. A simple name, a few prefatory lines, and

he was already caressing in his imagination a work destined never to be born. His raw curiosity was less concerned with direct observation than with the study of human nature through books. Convinced that there was new material for humor every time he moved two hundred kilometers to the north or south, he possessed a certain talent for reflecting on theatrical art but absolutely none for theatrical writing. A dramatic theme was never anything but an equation to him.

He was everlastingly occupied with two themes: *The Two Men* and *Letellier*. But the issue of so many of his efforts was to be that curious *Treatise On the Art of Creating Comedies*, in 1813, in which he codified his critical observations. "Never was there a man of that age," stated Henri Martineau, "more able to deal with poetics and less able to realize a work of the imagination." *The Two Men* is an occasion for endless experiments, in which the author paraphrases Helvétius' theories and Rousseau's humanism, enlivening them with Alfieri's turgid republicanism, and finally attaining as his result an exceedingly lachrymose comedy. *Letellier* or *The Interior of a Journal* is a play of multiple plots and outlines, a satire on the Chateaubriands and the Genlis, the Goeffroys, the La Harpes, and so forth, "and on the capons who clip the wings of genius." He went on to say: "This altogether comic and passionless play will be in the style of *The Deceits of Scapin*, *The Imaginary Cuckhold*, or *Pourceaugnac*,[1] extravagantly comic under a monarchy, excellent in a newborn republic." He avoided straying very far from his model, dressed the stage with "five or six times as many characters as a play can present," and ended with nothing but a platitude in its most cumbersome form. Originally a political play, it gradually became a satirical comedy. His mistake was in assembling such an exhaustive dossier on its characters and their possibilities for action that he checked the flight of his own imagination. He later noted in the margins of his *Promenades in Rome*:

What is necessary to move the vulgar shocks the well-born. Whence arises the difficulty, perhaps the impossibility, of drama in 1834, and the reign of the novel. Idea for meditation: When Dominique

1 Plays of Molière.

used to create plays they always said to him: "That is too delicate. The spectators will not understand anything about it."

He wrote further, on a copy of *The Red and the Black*: "Since democracy has peopled the theatres with a gross crowd, incapable of understanding the finer things, I regard the novel as the drama of the nineteenth century."

When asceticism was not sterilizing his wit, he gave it a sharp edge; the novelist Stendhal was later to make use of these tentative efforts. His study of human nature, begun through books, was pursued throughout the world and enriched by his worship of the self. This second education, begun in 1802, was to reach its culmination in 1814. And although he published nothing at all during this interval, he wrote ceaselessly, even if only such works as his *Correspondence*, his *Thoughts* (or *Filosofia Nova*), and his *Journal*. Such was his attraction toward the autobiographical vein, which would be continued in *Souvenirs of Egotism* and *The Life of Henri Brulard*.

Stendhal noted the day-to-day events of his own life and the discoveries he made, with a mind bent on probing into the same problems; first of these was How to become a writer of genius? The spectacle of man and the world and his reactions to his own reading diversified this examination of himself. In *Filosofia Nova* (1802–1805) he gathered his thoughts together, although without erecting a system from them, and he inscribed them in his *Journal* (1801–23) and *Correspondence*, but it was always Henri Beyle who stood at their center. He regarded the ideas on these lucid pages as storehouses, and they present a most accurate picture of his ambitions, his work methods, his epicurean habits, and also his blunders. Not all of this is original. But his precocious maturity can be seen clearly, plus a certain boldness and sharpness of judgment. Stendhal's view of life was beginning to form; unmindful of the merely picturesque, he had such perceptive views of the human soul as reveal exceptional gifts. Imagine a novelist, long before Joyce, and his *Ulysses*, registering twenty-four hours in his hero's life! We face here that "torment of the instantaneous" which must be transcribed at its moment of feeling, but which must also be filtered by technique, lessening the speed of its transcription. These random reflections were to be developed later. The theory of "crystallization" was germinating here, as well as such literary propensities as would be affirmed in *Racine and Shakespeare*. Stendhal sensed what was agreeable to his own nature: "My moral life was instinctively spent attentively examining five or six principle ideas, and trying to see the truth about them." He wanted to acquire that "power of analysis" which would enable him to understand "the mind" and "the passions," which he would transform into some "immortal work." He was interested only in human nature. It was not long before even history books would be regarded as "an introduction to understanding of the human heart." The facts furnished in the *Thoughts* and the *Journal* corroborate each other and offer an image of the writer which *The Life of Henri Brulard* tends to somewhat blacken. They indicate how he formed, through books, his first understanding of man and the world.

The *Journal* is a "mathematical and inflexible record" of his way of life and a pure and severe statement of what he believed he was. He saw it, nevertheless, as only a fraction of his inmost consciousness: "What is most valuable about it, and what has been felt in the sounds of Mozart's music, in the reading of Tasso, on being awakened by a street organ, on giving one's arm to one's mistress of the moment, is not found in it." This disorganized document is of an even keener interest because it is so spontaneous. Beyle's family hardly appears in it; much more prominent are his fellow-students and the Daru circle. In it the writer was schooling himself in a forthright style. One of the book's key passages relates the Italian journey of 1811. The pages dealing with the Austrian campaign are gripping. He tends to retain "only those things which depict the human heart." He has discovered that the Revolution did not, perhaps, deserve his earlier enthusiasm: it had "exiled the *allegria*[2] of Europe for perhaps a century. Elsewhere Stendhal affirms his gratitude toward Ideology: "It explains me to myself, and thus shows me what must be strengthened in myself and what must be destroyed." There is more. In 1811, Stendhal felt rising in him that "inexhaustible source of sensibility" which made him likely to "dictate fifty pages of artistic observations on crossing

2 Gaiety.

the mountains on this side of Iselle, for example"; but he
resisted the temptation because "too many words would be
needed to describe it." He preferred to suggest. In his attempt
to keep the "annals of his desires, of his soul," Stendhal was
aware that "it is very difficult to depict what has been natural
within ourselves . . . the sham, the play" leave a much clearer
impression. He wanted to recapture the immediate sensation:
"To train myself by remembering my natural feelings, there is
the work that can give me the talent of a Shakespeare." He
suffered from a dichotomy between the violence or gentleness
of a feeling and the dryness of expression that characterized his
technique. Louason had said to him "with the most tender
voice . . . 'Adieu, until tomorrow.' " In his powerlessness to
transcribe his emotion, he hazarded this negative remark:

There is the lifeless skeleton of the loveliest hour, a map of the
Boromees Islands and Lake Maggiore, exactly that. That's it, and
nothing is further from what these islands meant to our enchanted
soul. The map shows us everything we saw, but the friendly beach,
the bewitching forest, where are they?

He would have a difficult struggle, both consciously and uncon-
sciously, with this deficiency. The miracle was that this least
descriptive of novelists should have acquired the most efficacious powers of suggestion. Elsewhere, in another biting frag-
ment, he passes judgment on his character; perhaps, after all,
he has absolutely none: "I seem to have some character because,
for the pleasure of testing new sensations, I love to take a
chance; but I do not master my true passion by this, in no way;
I only yield to it." He confesses without pride that he has too
much sensibility ever to have any talent for seduction. Such is
the general tone of his comments in the *Journal*. Its psychological and biographical interest is considerable.

In this way Stendhal moves on to the *Correspondence*, direct,
delicately nuanced, varied, in which this spare style affirms
itself, with certain exceptions. How many correspondents followed, after that initial exchange of letters with Pauline, whose
torpor he was trying to shake! Theirs was a close friendship. He
wanted not to distort her—for he advises her to goodness and
frankness—but simply to channel her into the conquest of the

self and the pursuit of happiness (which can include a certain practical hypocrisy). The enthusiasm that he intended to inculcate in her for Ideology sometimes gives his letters a pompous and naïve tone; but they contain a number of reasonable ideas on the education of women, whose intellectual education should be equal to men's, he claimed. The *Correspondence* deals with the same ideas as does the *Journal*, but with a greater emphasis on the writer's social life, his cosmopolitanism, his ambitions, dreams and disappointments, and that world of feeling he hid from those around him. It is marked by his personality, with all its force of penetration and all its limitations. He confesses his financial embarrassment, his arguments with editors, his amorous disappointments, his illusions, and his constantly recurring fears. Although discreet and timid in his books, Stendhal dared with his friends to use trivial, spicy, even obscene words—not through any taste for barracks' language, but as a mask; and also because certain other of his correspondents, Mérimée particularly, often expressed themselves in such language. On the other hand, how many of his other pages seem to be delicately drawn for sensitive souls—and without imitating *La Nouvelle Héloïse*! The best of his letters compare favorably with the veiled nuances of his later *On Love* and the subtle evocations of *The Charterhouse of Parma*.

2 · The Stage of Plagiarism:

Haydn, Mozart and Metastasio (1814) *

The History of Painting in Italy (1817)

AFTER FIFTEEN YEARS of vain attempts, Stendhal could no longer delude himself as to his calling. The theater was not to be his springboard! Might he, then, assert himself in one blinding book? This was beyond his powers. Nevertheless, he wanted to become a writer. His first books were plagiarisms, however, for Stendhal's genius at first seemed to be that of literary brigandage.

Montaigne, as we know, "pillaged here and there" without a scruple, to produce the "honey" that was "no longer thyme nor marjoram." Molière himself took his luck where he found it, and even boasted about it. Pascal stated: "How can they say I have said nothing new; the arrangement of the material is new." Chateaubriand outdid him in arrogance: "The original writer is not the one who imitates no one, but the one whom no one is able to imitate." And one can hardly refrain from mentioning Jean Giraudoux's quip: "Every literary man is a plagiarist except the first, and as for him, he is unknown." Stendhal made a habit of plagiarism in his first books, never suspecting that posterity would pour over his writings with a divining rod, seeking after their sources: "If my books should become popular in 1880, who would dream that a grain of gold had been found in the mud?" The reader of 1880 hardly dreamed of it, but his contemporaries who were pressed into service certainly noticed it, on occasion. Goethe was gentleman enough to find it amusing. At other times, however, there was a hue and cry. The denuded and the defeated were hardly pleased, and they complained vigorously. They were less offended by the plagiarism than they were by the casualness of the plagiarist. Stendhal had shamelessly utilized the *Haydine* of Giuseppe Carpani, for example, and in two letters printed in the *Constitutionnel*, the latter protested against the arrogance of this *"figlio dell'Isera Spumosa,"* [1] whose identity he had guessed. He was finally made a laughingstock by an alleged "Bombet Junior" —Stendhal—who took up the defense of his nonexistent elder brother and insolently accused Carpani himself of being the thief. And so the guilty man had the last laugh.

One would have preferred some more honorable beginning for the future novelist. But that era was less punctilious about such matters, and it had not actually been Stendhal's deliberate intention to plagiarize, but merely to complete his intellectual education. Before attaining his own personal style, he had to pass through a stage that was marked by *Haydn, Mozart and Metastasio*, the *History of Painting in Italy*, and *Rome, Naples and Florence*. Actually, he performed a service by rendering several unpalatable authors readable. And although Stendhal used the ideas of others, he at least chose the best of them— like the branch officer of a learned institution. Furthermore, these moments of "assimilated laziness" were followed by astonishing moments of "creative effort," to which he abandoned himself completely. His omission of the necessary liaisons gave him a casual air, by which "he who is accused of having no style proves himself to be a stylist." Paul Hazard, considering Stendhal's method of using the scissors in his game of big and little larcenies, concludes:

He so dexterously gathers the hardiest flowers from the gardens in which he works that he seems to be creating when he is taking. And, in his good moments, his plunder burdens him so little that he appears to be preceding others when he is actually following them.

Henri Beyle, always so straightforward in the realm of analysis, never had a very genuine learning. The works of the erudite relieved him of the need for the tedious research which might have stifled his impulse, often conditioned his ideas, and facili-

1 Spuming son of Isère.

tated the work of adaptation through which his style acquired mastery. These first books, moreover, contributed even more to shaping his knowledge than to creating his style. From Carpani's seventeen letters—which he neglected to mention—Stendhal produced twenty-two of his own, in which he completely did away with Carpani's pedantry. His thinking was much sounder and more precise than that of his model, whom he never hesitated to contradict, but his contradiction was undeniable proof of his imitation.

To the fraud that constituted this "corrected translation" he added a second and even a third. His *Life of Mozart* was supposedly a translation of Schlichtegroll, whom he had certainly not read. It was actually derived from a *Biographical Notice* on Mozart by C. Winckler (to whom he gave no credit), who had used Schlichtegroll as one of his sources. The book also made use of a tract by C. Fr. Cramer: *Thirty-two Anecdotes on W. C. Mozart,* translated by Rochlitz. The two letters on *Metastasio and the Present State of Music in France and Italy* owe a part of their merit to Giuseppe Baretti's *Frusta Letteraria* [2] (reissued in 1813) and to Sismondi's *Literature of Southern Europe* (1813).

Haydn, Mozart and Metastasio had absolutely no success in France; before long Stendhal himself was to regard this first book, composed with "a great deal of pleasure," as only a "spurt of tepid water." Throughout the book are already scattered several of his favorite ideas. Should we mercilessly condemn the plagiarist? Why not recognize, with Henri Martineau, that "by utilizing" several texts which would have died without his intervention he created a book that would always live—if not a masterpiece."

Stendhal's laudable habit of noting excerpts from his reading must have been chiefly responsible for his plagiarism. The most striking of all his books in this respect is the *History of Painting in Italy*. The idea for it came to him in October of 1811. During the periods of waiting imposed by Angela Pietragrua, he was deepening his knowledge of the fine arts. His artistic contemplation, above and beyond problems of pure technique, plunged him into the ideas that were his chief occupation and that

2 Tr. note: *Literary Scourge,* a periodical similar to the *Spectator.*

eventually revealed his own heart to him. Expression and line were more important to him than color, for it was as a psychologist that he viewed a painting. This work of esthetic initiation presents several debatable theories; but its first chapters, "Introduction" and "Ideal Beauty," have the import of a veritable manifesto.

Stendhal's methods of composition remained the same. From whom did he "borrow" this time? Robertson, Mengs, Quatremère de Quincy, Reynolds, Lanzi, Bossi, Amoretti, Venturi, Vasari, Condivi, Cicognara, and others did more than document the work. He pilfered anecdotes from Guichardin, Lalande, de Brosses, Ancillon; he proclaimed that beauty is relative to its epoch, its nationality, and its environment, and he argued with Winckelmann's theory of ideal beauty. Cabanis, Lavater, and Pinel had revealed to him the importance of diverse temperaments and characters, as had, even more, the Abbé Dubos, whose *Reflections on Poetry and Painting* he had read very early. Stendhal, who mistrusted his own judgment and was often forced to discuss works with which he was not yet familiar, succeeded in livening an unwieldy bulk of material. As for his style, he was already a purist infatuated with simplicity. By dint of additions and corrections, through successive drafts, he created in this compilation a work that bore the Beylist stamp. It was more than a book about the arts; it was a book about human nature. He did not stop at enumeration and description. The result was that, as Jean Prévost has said, he gave "the key of plastic expression to the heart—though the movement of his phrasing, the sequence of his thought, the order of his chapters." This fascinating book presents these great figures within the framework of their age, in relation to their environment, their milieu, and their moment in time. Stendhal's concept of beauty was by no means frozen into an unalterable canon; his discourse on the arts was undoubtedly a bit too literary. In reality, he had already found his definition of romanticism: an artist must give his contemporaries the greatest pleasure possible, but in order "to express" he must have passionately felt. His *History of Painting in Italy* is the history of his own artistic initiation. He delicately took refuge in the shelter of that fervent past in which tyrants—even when their hands were bloody—

were, nevertheless, patrons of the arts. He suffered, on the other
hand, from the restrictions of the early nineteenth century: each
man lived behind a mask; political concerns outweighed emotions and drained them; civilization was deadening the vitality of
characters, stifling the arts, and enervating souls. Stendhal
already foreshadowed a theory he was to formulate twelve years
later: "Those things necessary for the arts to prosper are often
contrary to those necessary for nations to be happy." He later
noted in the margins of one of his Civitavecchia copies: "Nineteenth century civilization is leaping ahead toward nuances too
fine; perhaps the arts will not be able to follow."

His feeling for the arts disposed him to the seductions of
love; he was not at all shocked by them. To the sensuality of
his imagination was added a sensuality of the body, and even
a psychological sensuality of the eyes. The pursuit of pleasure
seemed to him synonymous with good taste; the arts were to him
a marvelous intellectual excitation stemming from his passions.
But behind the dilettante whose esthetic was outmoded stood
the psychologist. Taine credited him with having discovered the
environmental theory readily accepted at the end of the eighteenth century. Stendhal demanded that the artist experience
the passions he was depicting at the very moment of creation,
without suspecting that a passion must first be mastered before
it can be "depicted." He sought almost the same thing from a
picture as one seeks from a novel. This critical transposition,
rejected by so many intellectuals concerned with the autonomy
of every technique, permitted him to define himself more
clearly. He took the same pleasure in a beautiful painting as in
a lovely landscape on a sunny day. He had little feeling for
"pure art." However, it was his epoch that discerned what it was
that differentiated the Venus of the Medicis from the Venus of
Canova. He conceived of a happy art whose aim is the pleasure
of the viewer and whose condition is the joy of the artist. He
recognized the value of the primitives and, far from scorning
the work of nature, he claimed that only perfect imitation, which
puts a painter in possession of his craft, allows him to soar to
ideal beauty; but only if—after studying color, chiaroscuro and
design—he finds himself with a soul capable of invention. For
ideal beauty—that "powerful balm which doubles the strength

of a man of genius and kills the weak"—is by no means the pure copy of an original, but a choice within nature, plus the imagination to depart from this choice. A picture ought not to express an idea, but inspire an emotion. It was too soon for him to descry that the subject in painting is immaterial. In art, as in literature, he fled from everything declamatory; this horror of impassioned compositions had persuaded him that the role of painting was not to reproduce extreme points of passion, but rather to depict the most noble and agreeable moments. The movements of passion, he felt, were the province of the theater. As he grew older Stendhal was to become more sensitive to color; design would seem to him of a pseudoscientific barrenness, and he would then admit that composition could easily be the province of a talentless mind. He would then understand that the subject depicted and anecdotes concerning a painter's life had no relation to his real worth, and were rather like the words of a libretto to music. Only the soul of the artist mattered, and his technique. As for esthetic pleasure experienced, he was to arrive at a clear definition of this in his *Promenades in Rome*: "If I were not afraid of shocking the moralists, I would confess that I have always thought, without saying so, that a woman really belongs to the man who loves her most. I could willingly extend this blasphemy to painting."

Stendhal's feeling for the arts, most particularly Italian art, was that of a man in love, and unhappily in love. Artistic contemplation was, for him, the only always seizable prey. He owed his deepest consolation to it. Why condemn his esthetic? He did not present it as truth; he presented it as his own, and it took on a very clear psychological significance. He was prone to reach for an ecstasy by which he was dominated, without realizing that there might exist a superior delight in this domain. Let us at least recognize in his dilettantism, which certainly never confuses art with morals, a taste for simplicity and a horror of "phoebus." Rarely did he mistake the gesture for the action. And if he did not completely succeed in sensing, before André Suarès, that "art is the drama of nature" in a mind which conceives it, expresses it, and brings it into being, he might willingly say with the same author: "Art is not a copy of nature, but it is even less a rhetoric." His tastes were disputable, contradictory, and particularly curious in that they revealed the psychology that his future work was to confirm. On considering the whole, however, it is not unwarranted to draw from his opinions, and particularly from elements emphasized in his transpositions, this idea: everything takes place in art behind an innumerable means of expression, which can be reduced to one common point beyond legitimate personal preferences, all beauty in one beauty. Stendhal was one of the links in a continuing chain of art critics who have gradually brought us to the concept of "lyric" purity, which is no longer Wincklemann's *beau idéal* (ideal beauty), but an *idealized* beauty, constantly changing through a choice in nature.

The *History of Painting in Italy* confines itself to the Florentine school up until the death of Michelangelo. Stendhal did not finish this vast, projected panorama during his lifetime, although he returned again and again to the arts in his books about Italy. The enormity of the task wearied him. It was not until 1932 that Henri Martineau published, under the title *Italian Schools of Painting,* these pages whose major value is in having reassembled facts that had been scattered throughout innumerable volumes. Stendhal never took the time to add his own unique comments to this collection. The work is rough, but nevertheless it gives us some idea of the comprehensive work he had envisioned. Certain parts of it disclose a soul of dreaming delicacy. Certain passages already bear the stamp of his personality. His esthetic comments obey tendencies already mentioned. The elaboration of this work was never completed. From 1812 to 1815, Stendhal assembled this enormous mass of material, from which his memory would later draw with abandon. He felt himself more and more in sympathy with Correggio's style, even to the point of creating "Correggian" characters in his novels. It can be said, however, that after the Italian journeys of 1811 and 1813 and the Milanese sojourn of 1814-17, his years of apprenticeship in the history of art and esthetics had reached their end.

3 · Rome, Naples and Florence

(1817 and 1826) * Pages from Italy

(1818-28) * Napoleon (1817-38)

IT WAS in Stendhal's *Rome, Naples and Florence*, composed in 1817, that he was to discover a more spontaneous vein bursting within him. The book was a hymn of joy—the outcome of his feelings toward Italy: his happiness at living so close to her masterpieces, his intoxication with her music and the vista of her lovely landscapes, his contact with a society filled with spontaneity and with a nation in which the "human plant" was more vital than in any other country in Europe. This book was neither a collection of superficial impressions nor a guide. He read innumerable itineraries; this was not ordinarily food for inspiration, but Stendhal was to change all that! Scornful of description, but curious about the "moral customs" of every region, his egotism reveled in observing the art of the daily pursuit of happiness. He divined, at the same time, how impatient this voluptuous Italy was with the Austrian yoke; the latent energy of liberal circles reminded him of the *virtù* of times past: "One must seek the whole of present day Italy in the Middle Ages," he noted boldly. His taste for vigorous amorality did not stop him from sharing the vows of the patriots who were aspiring to a national unity which was justly destined to ruin the very customs that so delighted his fancy.

The first account of his voyage was bold, graceful, and concise, filled with the delight of sudden revelations. Despite its title, a great deal of the work deals with Bologna, and above all, Milan; he did not want to draw too much attention, in the book's cover, to Austria, since the author was still living in

Milan. With the enthusiasm of his phrases, the wit of his insights and jests, Stendhal swept the memories of his reading
away with his own unique memories. Anecdotes and facts were
taken from all hands. The *Edinburgh Review,* which had at
first commended the work, later discovered that it had been the
victim of several larcenies and took offense. De Brosses, Mme.
de Staël, and many others were plundered, one by one. It is
difficult to be offended, however, by a helping hand which so
vividly embellished an anecdote or sharpened a trait. Stendhal
was not attempting to present a photographic image. His insights into the Italian temperament, the feelings he noted, and
the details he retained lost nothing by having been treated with
a certain devil-may-care attitude.

Since his publisher was afraid that certain hostile govern-
mental factions might be provoked into proceedings, Stendhal
placed at the bottom of the book's title page, as a "lightning
rod," a few eulogistic emcomiums to Louis XVIII which disguised his real feelings about the Restoration. Less through his
own vanity than for financial reasons, he presented a second
edition in two volumes in 1826, retaining only a quarter of the
original composition. This second version dealt with the fine
arts in general, and not merely with music. His criticism of the
Austrian government and the expression of his own anticlericalism were more biting in it—for although he had been living
in Milan in 1817, by 1826 he was back in Paris again. This second version, which put the accent on energy, lost nothing of
that feeling of joyous deliverance which permeated the 1817
text. Through this book Stendhal decisively familiarized himself
with every nuance of the Italian character and heart; a sound
success on Italian questions was almost worth an expert's reputation to him. All he lacked was the consecration of the Index,
and that was obtained shortly after the publication of the second
edition.

The essays missing from his *Theatre* were to have their exten-
sion in *Molière, Shakespeare, and Comedy and Laughter* (1803–
23), a critical work which opened the way to *Racine and
Shakespeare* (1823–25). The *History of Painting in Italy* had
its sequel in *Italian Schools of Painting* (1812–15), written dur-

ing the period that led to the pages of *Promenades in Rome*, systematically dedicated to the arts. Likewise, *Rome, Naples and Florence* had its continuation in *Pages from Italy* (1818–28), which filled the interval preceding *Promenades in Rome* (1820).

Hardly had Stendhal published a book than he would begin to rework it. It is difficult to go into detail concerning *Pages from Italy*, as the work is a collection of rather disparate fragments. The author borrows from all sides; there continues that same inimitable process which never leaves the reader under the same impression for very long; wearisome theories are succeeded by ingenious anecdotes, pointed allusions, Voltairian sarcasms, but also the dilettante's lack of restraint. Elsewhere, veiled confidences fleetingly create the atmosphere which would be that of his later *On Love*. Such is that mysterious page, falsely dated Florence, 1818, on which Stendhal evokes the image of two women in the corner of a drawing room, without mentioning their names: "the most heroic woman" he had ever met, who loaned him the fifteenth edition of *The Letters of Jacopo Ortis*—Métilde Dembowski—and "a young woman still in all the flower of beauty, who was poisoned by love three years ago"—Maddalena Bignami—whom the poet Ugo Foscolo idolized.

What was the position of Henri Beyle—an early admirer of Brutus—toward the "usurper?" His opinions were trenchant, but he had a subtle mind. Although he was Republican in spirit, he nevertheless recognized that royalty was sometimes a surer safeguard of liberty than a popular government; strong personalities seemed to him more worthy of interest than anonymous masses, a prey to their passions or instincts. Under Napoleon "there had been a tyrant, but there had been nothing arbitrary." His intellectual liberalism did not prevent him from being extremely hard on democracy, which tended to make equality reign among unequal values. There is no doubt that he, like Goethe, would have preferred injustice to disorder. For although individual passions delighted him, whatever the crimes they aroused, he had no intention of seeing the city disturbed by them after his experience with the French Revolution. A champion of freedom of the press, he remained, never-

theless, on the side of order. He wanted to see Italy avoid
bloody convulsions during the course of its political evolution,
knowing that public opinion would ripen only with time. Although his anticlericalism—in which P. P. Trompeo saw something "artless and almost infantile"—did not permit him to
capture the profound spirit of "that great machine of civilization and eternal happiness called Christianity," it did not prevent him from adjusting himself to the pontifical government,
although he criticized it. He was basically an aristocrat to whom
the *Memoires* of the late eighteenth century had given a yearning for a certain social ideal which could be summed up as
"agreeable man" at the "quietest time of life." It would be a
mistake to attribute this attitude either to vanity or pride; it
was rather due to a quasifeminine physical inability to tolerate
a certain vulgarity. On the whole, Stendhal had come to understand that the Revolution, by banishing the power of the traditional aristocracy, had founded a new aristocracy of the
intelligence, to which he himself belonged. Should his instinctive republicanism rise up against the author of the October *coup
d'état*? After all, he had been only a child at the time. And it
was certainly not his fault that he happened to be related to the
Darus. He had therefore found himself embroiled in the Napoleonic adventure slightly despite himself.

Like P.-L. Courier, he would assuredly have preferred Napoleon to have remained a Bonaparte, but the latter's imperial
dignity was nonetheless impressive to him. Did it anger him
that Napoleon had "confiscated" the revolution for his own
ends? Stendhal's view was more balanced than that. He had a
kind of gratitude toward him for having safeguarded certain
revolutionary reforms and for having substituted order for
chaos; he admired the grandeur of the emperor's enterprises,
his military genius, and perhaps still more his administrative
genius. But he could see the other side of the coin as well. He
knew the bitter and bloody price of victories—which he did not
needlessly exalt—with true sensibility and without falling into
sentimentalism. He was fully aware of the greatness of Napoleon's achievements, not only in France but in foreign lands
such as Italy, where Stendhal was one of the first to sense what
ferments the presence of the French had left behind. On the

other hand, he was disgusted by all the baseness, arrivism, and obsequiousness he saw in the army—often even in men who were capable of the greatest courage and sacrifice. The retreat from Moscow was particularly enlightening to him; no image there of Epinal, in either his printed or his autobiographical work. The First Empire appeared beautiful and noble to him during the Restoration, when misfortune, increased by heroic glory, had humanized him, so to speak: "The misfortune of Napoleon and France was the only charm which was wanting in those sublime campaigns that engaged our youth. As an artist, I am almost tempted to rejoice in the battle of Waterloo. . . ." The disgust that the Restoration aroused in him gave him a certain pride in his position of *demi-solde* and in his campaign years.

On two separate occasions, Stendhal set to work on his *Napoleon*. Between 1817 and 1818, he began to work on a *Life of Napoleon*, in Milan, but this version was abandoned. Between 1836 and 1839, he undertook *Memoires of Napoleon*, while in Paris. The climate of the two cities was quite different. Since 1802 the "story of Bonaparte" had seemed to him inseparable from that of the French Revolution, but a project of the latter scope seemed to him too ambitious. As early as 1815, Dominique had drafted a very incomplete but judicious character profile of Napoleon. It was on his return to Paris in 1817, in the midst of anti-Napoleonic reaction and in the face of the railleries with which the Restoration was lampooning the emperor, that he became conscious of the fact that he had been eyewitness to a superhuman feat. He remembered one evening at La Scala in 1816 when Lord Byron, trembling with excitement, had urgently questioned him about the hero to whom he had been so close and whose life would henceforth strike him as "a hymn to the grandeur of the soul." Stendhal's enthusiasm was similar to that of all the retired soldiers of the Grand Army, of Béranger. He was particularly proud, in retrospect, to have made the retreat from Russia.

His base of departure was an article in the *Edinburgh Review* concerning the public and political life of the emperor, which Stendhal translated, with a commentary. He also utilized the writings of Warden, the Abbé de Pradt, Hobhouse, and even

Michaud's *Biography of Living Men*. He was impatiently awaiting the publication of Las Cases' *Memorial of Saint Helena*, whose existence he knew of, but which had then been confiscated by Hudson Lowe (the work did not actually appear until 1823). But he became weary of the work, broke it off, and then resumed it in order to "correct and complete the style." Mme. de Staël's *Reflections on the Principal Elements of the French Revolution* then caught his eye. He was indignant! Wanting to reply to this "libel," he set to work again in earnest; but the undertaking was never completed, and the manuscript of his *Life of Napoleon* remained in Milan in 1821 among his other papers, not to be recovered until after his death.

Toward the end of 1836 Stendhal returned to this subject, which had never ceased to interest him. The July Monarchy no longer nourished the ill will that had been borne toward the emperor during the first years of the Restoration. His return from the ashes was about to be effectuated in an apotheosis. Stendhal's admiration continued to go to Bonaparte, rather than to the imperial Napoleon. For he inscribed in the margins of his *Memoires of a Tourist*: "Napoleon saved the Revolution in 1796 and on the 18th of October, 1799. Before long he sought to eradicate the Revolution, and it would have been better for France had he been killed in 1805 after the Peace." By this time, Stendhal had at his disposal all of the new works on the subject—*The Memorial of Saint Helena* and the *Memoires of Napoleon* by Gourgaud and Montholon. Now he was replying to new abrasions. These *Memoires* seemed to him the surest source. He congratulated himself that Las Cases had had absolutely no intelligence, or otherwise "he would not have confused Las Cases with Napoleon." He paraphrased Thiers, Bourriene, Norvins, Walter Scott, and Jominy, interspersing his own remarks; a style both simple and brisk presented "a reasonable account" of the events. It ranks with Stendhal's best work. His account of the French arrival in Milan in 1796 already recreated that climate of gladness and wonder that would soon reappear in the opening section of *The Charterhouse of Parma*. But this second outline was abandoned, in turn, for projects of another kind: *The Rose and the Green* and *Memoires of a Tourist*.

To tell the truth, Stendhal had chosen with his heart in

gathering his material. He had neither the makings nor the memory of an historian; his dates were often erroneous. This psychologist, who had been swept across Europe on the tide of events, knew very well how difficult it was to reach any historic certainty whatever. More curious about life than about truth, not in the least fatalistic, he perceived in history a dynamism by which representative men commanded events, rather than regarding it as shaped by simple necessity. He saw Napoleon, as would Taine, in the role of *condottiere*. He could testify to that collective passion aroused by the emperor, to the spirit of emulation he had inspired in those around him, and to the "moral principle" which had supported the regime's official façade. This secondhand work was injected with original ideas and sustained by an admiring sympathy which had made him inscribe in a biographical notice: "He respected only one man: Napoleon." But these things were not enough, certainly, to earn Stendhal the title of historian. He preferred eye-witness accounts to systematic treatises, and it was in his own capacity as a witness that he had been drawn to the powerful personality of the emperor. What better example of energy had he found along the way? There is, then, nothing surprising about the "Napoleonism" of his Julien Sorel or his Fabrizio del Dongo.

4 · *On Love* (1822) * *Miscellany of*

Politics and History (1804-37) *

Literary Miscellany (1797-1841) *

The English Courier (1822-29)

STENDHAL'S TREATISE *On Love* was a secret argument with Métilde. Instead of resorting to a romantic plot, he composed a work whose first part was an ideological treatise—or rather, a "discourse on feelings"—and whose second part was a kind of illustration. Although Métilde was quite able to prevent him from speaking of love, it was not within the power of "the haughtiest little head in Milan" to prevent him from loving her in silence and analyzing his own reactions. He noted his observations from the corner of a salon; he scribbled on concert programs, scraps of paper, and even on playing cards. Little by little this material grew, assembled without order and with no definite goal. At one point he gave the manuscript to a friend. His friend had to send it from Strasbourg to Paris, and in the course of its dispatch it was mislaid. It took the anxious Stendhal, left without a single copy, a year and a half to recover it! "Lost beneath the great chestnut trees of the Tuileries," he thought ceaselessly about Métilde. When his suffering became too painful, he haunted the salons. When such worldly distractions repelled him, the solitude of Montmorency welcomed him. After an evening at Pasta's, where he had gone in order "to breathe the idea of Métilde in every sense," he set about correcting the proofs of his work, with tears in his eyes. "This book was written in pencil during my lucid periods in Milan. It made me ill to work on it in Paris; I never wanted to organize it." Unable to endure the paroxysm of near madness which the memory of his love aroused in the woods of Montmorency, he moved on to the Beugnot estate to put the finishing touches on his work.

One suspects that a "romantic," in the strict sense of the word, would have drawn upon the situation. For Stendhal it was the occasion of a modest confidence, during which the image of Métilde appeared, in filigree, at every moment. His reserve, his desire to summarize the clinical observations of a patient on his malady in order to find "a common law by which to recognize its varying stages," caused the transformation of this real-life novel into a treatise. Had Stendhal expected to move Métilde by so much sincerity, so little pride? His systematic attempts to strip his condition to its essentials prompted true flashes of inspiration, both in his feelings and in his style: "I am making every effort to be objective. I want to impose a silence on my heart, which believes it has a great deal to say. I always shudder at having written nothing but a sigh, while I thought I had been noting a truth." In this disguised confession which Stendhal always regarded as one of his most important works and in which he probed into the knowledge of that happiness on which he was so intent, theory did not do too much harm to sensibility. Not at all moralistic, by no means hypocritical, extremely chaste—except for the chapter on fiascos which appeared only in the Lévy edition of 1854—this work netted him exactly seventeen readers in ten years! His editor avenged himself on the writer with this insult: "I can say of this book, as of the *Sacred Poems* of Pompignan: sacred they truly are, for no one has touched them."

Under various assumed names—Lisio, Visconti, Salviati, Delfante, and so forth—Stendhal exposed every facet of a contradictory but lucid heart. Métilde was here Lenore and there someone else. Since his *Filosofia Nova* he had foreseen that "there is only one law concerning feeling, and that is to create the happiness of the loved one" and "at our own expense." His idealism freed itself of base appetites with little difficulty and found its refuge in memory and hope. Stendhal quickly penetrated to the very essense of courtly love: "The lover prefers to dream of his loved one rather than to receive from an ordinary woman everything she can give." On the other hand, passion seemed to him "never vulgar, for base souls are not capable of it"; but above all, "the greatest happiness love can give is that first squeezing of the hand of the woman one loves." Through that "tender reverie" which analysis brought with it, he turned once again to the musical escape which was so dear to him. As for grieving over the fact that he was not appreciated by the common public, he scarcely thought about it. He thought even less about modifying his own approach.

In actuality, *On Love* deals only with passionate love (*amour-passion*). It concentrates most specifically on the birth of love and outlines the various types of love. Stendhal distinguished four basic types: passionate love (*amour-passion*), which alone mattered to him—the love of Héloïse for Abélard; tasteful love (*amour-goût*), "which was reigning in Paris around 1760"; physical love (*amour-physique*), "which has only an inferior rank in the eyes of tender and passionate souls"; and vain love (*amour-vanité*), "the only type Frenchmen were capable of in 1822." He refers to love as "a malady which everyone pretends to have had." But although he combines these four types of love with six temperaments—sanguine, choleric, melancholic, athletic, phlegmatic, and nervous—and puts love into an equation, all this psychological exposition is basically nourished by feeling, and his psychology is extremely perceptive. He recognizes seven stages in the birth of love, summed up in three essential moments: of admiration, hope, and crystallization. The latter combines two separate periods, that of the fleeting reverie, during which are enumerated the raptures to come, until anxiety interrupts it and it quickens into despair, and that of the second crystallization, during which the same reveries reappear, with their promise of perfect happiness, interspersed with the anguished dread of losing everything.

His analysis of love puts the emphasis on the power of the imagination, which alone escapes satiation. Love is for him that state of the soul which activates the mind, after which it is the mind which activates the heart. Whence, in opposition to the also valid but rather elementary theory of love at first sight, comes the reflective theory of *crystallization*: "It is enough to think of a perfection in order to see it in the thing one loves." "What I call 'crystallization' is that process of the mind which draws from everything presented to it the discovery that the loved object has new perfections." It is, in other words, a branch lying at the bottom of the Salzbourg mines, which, when one recovers it, is completely covered with sparkling crystals. It is doubtless the special province of youth. For experience creates distrust, diminishing the power of crystallization, and in life's decline "one returns sadly to loving the simple and the innocent, despairing of the sublime."

The system as a whole is a debatable one, but what heart could fail to recognize something of itself in this delicately subtle book? His treatise *On Love* is filled with modesty and delicacy. Its author, addressing himself to an invisible and silent female interrogator, speaks with dignity and prudence, without attempting to hide his faults. The most important lesson in this book of psychology is probably one of morality and tenderness, as well as pedagogy. Beyle upheld woman's right to be treated as man's intellectual equal. Not that he could be considered a feminist, in the modern sense, for he regarded women as "lovely little beings, more sentient than reflective." He had a horror of bluestockings; but he knew that the education of women as he had envisioned it "would double the intellectual forces of the human race and—(what is even more important)— its chances for happiness." Thus, after twenty years have passed, we again encounter the ideas of the period during which Pauline was being initiated into Ideology. It is in this breviary of "Beylism," perhaps, that he best defines man's conditions of happiness: "What an excellent advisor would a man not find in his wife if she could think!" Thus it is that his analysis of passionate love leads him, whatever the barbs he might later fling at *matrimonio*, to this peaceful thought—proof enough that this erstwhile epicurean always placed the feeling of love's dream well beyond the fury of its possession:

They say that old age, changing our organs, renders us incapable of loving; as for me, I do not believe a word of this. Your mistress, having become your intimate friend, gives you other pleasures, the pleasures of old age. This is a flower which, having been a rose in the morning, during the season of flowers, changes into a delicious fruit in the evening, when the season of flowers is past. . . .

Where is Stendhal's supposed cynicism in this statement? Such was the dream he would have loved to realize with Métilde.

The first part of this anthology, which meditates on love from a subjective standpoint and pursues its subtle analysis through a passionate ideology, remains by far the most compelling. Its second part, written far from Milan, reflects on the "malady" called love from an objective standpoint. Fauriel furnished Stendhal ten pages of Arabian experiences and a chapter on love in twelfth-century Provençe; Raynouard, the appendices on love in the Middle Ages; Cadet de Gassicourt, the chapter on love in England; and Colonel Weiss, the anecdotes on Switzerland. In 1825, Jacquemont submitted his chapter on "Love in France among the Wealthy Class." The Sensualists and the Ideologues gave Stendhal the basic ideas. He had great admiration for Lavater and his study of physiognomy; the opinions Stendhal expressed on marriage and women's education echoed those of Destutt de Tracy. In this area, he was indebted to an article by Thomas Broadbent which appeared in the *Edinburgh Review* in 1810. Many thoughts of the French moralists were incorporated into his text. Stendhal marked these pages, nonetheless, with his own stamp. The precision of its descriptions never exceeds the bounds of good taste. His ideas are moving because of what they reveal about his ardent, sober, and wounded soul. Through the delicacy of his sensitivity alone, Stendhal rises to the quasimystic idealism of a "sweet new style." Although Métilde had at times exasperated him, she had also brought him a certain peace—and "her tender, profoundly sad phantom" was to soothe him even further after 1825. She had shown him that nobility of heart is necessary for the birth of an elevated feeling. And although she had remained inaccessible, it was perhaps better for the future novelist's work that she had. She was, in reality, more than a lover; she was a tender mother and a great patriot. It was Henri Beyle's misfortune to have become hopelessly infatuated with the one woman in a thousand who had lost many of her illusions, particularly concerning love. Judging from certain allusions in his *Promenades in Rome*, Stendhal experienced toward her, retrospectively and in his imagination, a kind of sensual exasperation that bordered on a fleeting desire for vengeance, last proof of the violence of his attraction.

In this treatise so prized by the discerning, the logician and the clinician is less apparent than the artist and the psychologist. A musical vapor suffuses its best pages, as happens every time Stendhal attains that degree of exaltation and proportion which is the chosen form of his lyricism. As has been mentioned, if he discusses music like a lover, he discusses love like a musician: "I have just proven this evening that when music is perfect it puts the heart precisely into the very state in which it finds itself when it enjoys the presence of the loved one." He was abandoned to images, both tender and painful, from the past. Before long, by transposing his memories and adapting them to his heroes' temperaments, he would find the fundamental tonality of a love which would remain the same in every book. It would not be the novel Stendhal had lived, but the one he had dreamed of living—truer than his own existence. This anthology of impassioned ideology contains the most delicately shaded, the rarest, and the most inexpressible individual truths, in a seemingly rather limited framework. But rarely was a masculine homage to beauty more exquisite or more total. This cavalier gift of himself has the religious taste of a veritable dedication.

The posthumous *Miscellanies* and the copious articles from *The English Courier* reveal a political Stendhal. This liberal, as we know, was an aristocrat in sensitivity and refinement; it repelled him to court the populace under a republican regime. The two-chamber system and a constitutional king were, in his opinion, the least unfortunate of governments. But the political life of the Restoration was a very platitude. The progress of industrialism had not persuaded him that wealth must bully intelligence. A born rebel, he would always stand in reaction to ideas, regimes, and men.

The White Terror was even more horrifying to him than the excesses of the Revolution. Drawn toward social order, he had lightly sacrificed a great many small personal comforts. Although he railed against the vanity of the French, he was sincerely concerned about the honor and nobility of his country, without being chauvinistic. He criticized the men who did not always seem to him to be deserving of the positions to which circumstances had elevated them; but his war experience had furnished him not only with examples of unabashed arrivism: he recog-

nized his nation's courage, the genius of its leader, and he paid
homage to the French soldier: "We who saw him at close hand
know him to be filled with spirit and delicacy." One is reminded
of Heinrich Heine's poem, "The Drum Major." This *Miscellany
of Politics and History* contains several, often critical, articles
from periodicals from across the Channel. For his Anglomania
increased proportionately as his Jacobin faith declined.

In *Literary Miscellany* are found a few, negligible fragments
of verse; here, also, is found the rough sketch, dated 1819, of
his brief and delicate *Novel of Métilde*, customarily reproduced
in the appendix of *On Love*. Here is, once again, the vain
subterfuge of a romantic confession designed to move the indifferent one.

In this collection is also found the beginning of another
novel, *A Social Position* (1832), only three chapters of which
he completed. For Stendhal could not, while he was still consul,
depict the diplomatic world of Rome. His own ambassador became M. de Vaussay; Mme. de Saint-Aulaire became Mme. de
Vaussay, adorned with several traits borrowed from Countess
Curial. The author presented a kind of "idealized Dominique,"
whom he called Roizand. This sketch would probably have
furnished him more than one element for the ending of *Lucien
Leuwen*, never written, which was to have had as its setting the
diplomatic circles of the Eternal City.

In this *Literary Miscellany*, which embraces a period of about
thirty years, are found a good many observations on morals and
society which were already the subject of *The English Courier*.
His account of a *Trip to Brunswick* brings Mina von Griesheim
into the picture. His opinions about Mme. de Staël indicate that,
at the same time, Stendhal reproached "this wit who pretends
to the honors of genius," in whom he often found common ideas
beneath her stylistic pretensions, and that he was nevertheless
impressed by her social prestige. These perceptive pages reveal
his total admiration for her *Princess of Clèves*, whose scrupulous
finesse he relished. The *Memoires of a Tourist* would once again
point out that in the French novel "the first trace of attention
to things of nature is that row of trees beneath which the Duke
de Nemours, reduced to despair by the beautiful defense of the
Princes of Clèves, takes refuge." Did he possibly see in this

some premonition of the woods of Montmorency and the "beautiful defense" of Métilde?

The English Courier, a critical profile of France under the Restoration, was a breadwinner for the author, whom it reveals as a journalist of talent. He had even entertained the thought of founding a periodical of his own—the *Aristarque* or *The Universal Indicator of Books to Read*—but where would he have gotten the money? For several years he contributed regularly to English magazines and wrote an art column for the *Journal de Paris,* before publishing a few short stories in *Revue des Deux Mondes.* The bulk of his journalistic efforts appeared in the *Paris Monthly Review,* the *New Monthly Magazine,* the *London Magazine,* and the *Athaeneum.* A number of these articles were to be translated into English by his Irish friend, Stritch, and then by a literary woman, Sarah Austin, without the author's name.

His reading provided him material with which to express himself—with a freedom he would never have enjoyed in Paris. *The English Courier* was a kind of *Gazette de Hollande.*[1] Although Stendhal doubtless tried to avoid shocking England's puritanical public, he had spirit enough to insert a few truths about the Anglo-Saxon temperament into the criticisms he unleashed against his compatriots. Through the rambling boldness of his opinions, his liberal ideas were set forth with a pamphleteer's passion. He denounced the charlatanism of literature and took issue with the uncultivated *nouveaux riches* who were then ruling society. The press's lack of freedom appalled him. Actually, as he delivered the key to his own opinions quite frankly, he was also presenting a chronicle of the Restoration, truer than the image presented by the historians. *The English Courier* is a useful supplement to his autobiographical work. It is more than that. It sketches the political outline of France in a disparate epoch during which four generations opposed in their backgrounds were existing side by side. From actual accounts emerged a picture of the customs of various social circles,

1 Tr. note: At the end of the seventeenth century and through the eighteenth, there appeared in Holland numerous satirical and often calumnious gazettes, which were usually the work of French refugees.

according to province. He predicted the end of the authoritarian regime and the advent of the July Monarchy. These pages were an excellent preparation for the political basis of the later novels.

In the same way, he outlined the literary picture of France at that time. He preferred, above everything, the natural and the simple. Although he did not hesitate to discuss the great writers of the seventeenth and eighteenth centuries, he made himself heard, above all, as an echo and an often discerning critic of a great number of contemporary publications and served as an intellectual intermediary between two civilizations. He never forgot his capacity of art critic for long. Briefly, *The English Courier* is an eclectic work; as such, it could hardly overlook Italy. For he was well aware of the intellectual interdependence of nations, and his always alert curiosity made him a true forerunner of comparativism.

5 · *Racine and Shakespeare* (1823 and 1825) *

Life of Rossini (1823) * *Miscellanies*

of Art (1824-37) * *Concerning a New*

Plot Against the Industrialists (1825)

IN HIS *Racine and Shakespeare* Stendhal played the role of innovator and protagonist in the quarrel between classicists and romanticists. This was four years before Hugo's Preface to *Cromwell*, a manifesto which rejected the classic separation of tragedy and comedy. Stendhal's very lively work, issuing from the discussions at Delécluze's, was an incursion into the literary fray which was to earn him the title, "hussar of romanticism." Stendhal, who had had in his youth certain troubles which ruined his taste for La Harpe, had an advantage over his contemporaries: when Mme. de Staël, steeped in German romanticism, had stirred the fires of the battle in 1816 with her letter concerning the manner and usefulness of German translations, Stendhal was living in Milan; and in Italy romanticism was identified with political liberalism and patriotism and had the *Conciliatore* as its spokesman. Beyle was fascinated by the debate.

His reflections on comedy had prepared him for literary criticism. The ideas he was about to expose had served as the basis of his first books. He believed that the writer should be an interpreter of his time by creating something new, that the beautiful is relative, evolving from century to century, and that the *vis comica* itself is mortal. Had he not met in Lombardy those innovators who were preparing the way for Italian unity through their writings? Literary disputes were catching fire in Milan, even under the Empire. So it was that Stendhal contributed toward introducing into France the Milanese climate

of intellectual debate and pamphleteering that was already becoming popular in Italy. He sided "with Shakespeare against
Racine, with Lord Byron against Boileau." In 1820 he exclaimed
in an iconoclastic tone: "Woe to the spiritual and intellectual
revolution of the *mezzo-termine!*" Since 1819 the value of romanticism had seemed to him to be "in administering to the
public the precise drug to give it pleasure." Such, he felt, was the
talent of Alessandro Manzoni, a *mezzo-termine* poet. Stendhal's
moderate ideas on romanticism reflected those of Giovanni
Berchet [1] and his *Semiserious Letter from Chrysostom.* He believed that romanticism, a modern literary expression of beauty,
was the

art of presenting the people with literary works which, in the present state of their habits and beliefs, can give them the greatest
possible pleasure. Classicism, on the other hand, presents them with
the civilization which gave the greatest possible pleasure to their
great-grandparents.

The question of theater had been at the heart of this debate
ever since Alessandro Manzoni's Preface to *The Count of Car-
magnole* and his *Letter to Monsieur Chauvet on the Unities*
and the polemics which these two works had aroused. The
problem of literary language—always a subject for debate in
Italy—had not lessened. *Rome, Naples and Florence* placed the
adversaries face to face: "The Florentines, partisans of the old
words, are the classicists; the Lombards hold with romanticism."
Ever since the latter part of 1817, Stendhal had been wanting
to enter the debate. The criticisms of a M. Londonio on romantic poetry had stirred him to a reply which he wanted to
have translated and published in Italian; then he improvised
another pamphlet: *On the Perils of the Italian Language,* or
Memoires of a Friend, Uncertain in His Ideas on Language.
These two arguments prepared the way for his position in the
debate, and it was the Milanese climate of that time that he
brought with him to Paris, along with the word "romanticism."
He was a "romantic" in the Italian sense. At that time, he conceived the idea for a work entitled *Romanticism in the Arts,* but
did not complete it.

1 Tr. note: One of the originators of the Italian romantic, patriotic
movement.

What a stroke of luck it was, then, to be returning to Paris in 1821 armed with such a store of knowledge! To begin with, he "talked" his books before his friends. At that time the Penley troupe was in Paris performing Shakespeare; soon politics entered the scene and the liberals began to disturb these performances; but Stendhal, who loved the liberals, loved Shakespeare more. A contributor to the *Paris-Monthly Review of British and Continental Literature,* he published for it in French his first article—"Racine and Shakespeare"—in which he took up the basic ideas of Manzoni and Ermes Visconti. A second article—"Laughter"—appeared in the same periodical. These two works, reassembled in a booklet, constituted the *Racine and Shakespeare* of 1823.

In the midst of all this, on April 24, 1824, the academician Auger took his official stand against the romantics on the anniversary of the re-entrance of the king. This attack, less literary than it was political, was approved by official newspapers and by the Minister of Education. Every reactionary force was now thrown against the new school. Stendhal felt anything but boundless admiration for the French romantics. On his return from Italy he had remarked, with some surprise, that the word "romantic" designated on the Gallic side of the Alps a group of "right-thinking" conservatives. Auger's declaration of war, however, rendering romanticism suspect from the throne to the altar, forced Stendhal to side with the liberal opposition. He decided to counterattack. Within ten months he had composed a new work, which he read at Delécluze's in front of Paul-Louis Courier, whose tone he had taken. This pamphlet was the reproduction of a correspondence between a classicist and a romanticist. The letters of the classicist, or at least two of them, were authentic ones written by a gentleman of the old guard, probably a certain M. de Béranger Labaume of Marseilles. This book, the second *Racine and Shakespeare,* appeared with some success in March of 1825. Full of zest and forcing the issue, Stendhal pushed theories to the extreme. He defined romanticism as "the living literature destined to give the greatest pleasure to contemporaries," at least to men of less than forty years of age. All romanticism, he maintained, was destined to become classic, just as all classicism had been, in its time, romantic. By this he reaffirmed his doctrine of the relativity of beauty. Our epoch has been able to speak with every right, in its turn, of the romanticism of the classics and the classicism of the romantics. By opposing the two schools completely and playing on words a little, Stendhal defined this law of transmutation, which classified the same literary current under various headings, according to whether it was fashionable or unfashionable.

Basically, he found less fault with Racine than with his poetics and with pseudoclassicism. This was a genre that no longer appeared viable to him; he felt that it had spent itself, although he conceded that it had once expressed itself in masterpieces he admired. But he had early proclaimed his aversion for Racine's character, in which he saw all the "banalities" of Louis XIV's court. This was certainly not a valid critical argument, but it bore upon his judgment. Might there have been some question in his mind of imitating Shakespeare? It would suffice him to learn "his method of studying the world" in order to apply it to the observation of one's own. These ideas, then, were in the air, but Stendhal gave them form. Long before the blistering and incisive affirmations of the Preface to *Cromwell* he placed himself in the front ranks of the history of romanticism, and Sainte-Beuve was to credit him thirty years later "with having destroyed some of the biases and prejudices which were opposing themselves in 1820 to every, even moderate, innovation." Stendhal was weary of French tragedy, which he regarded as nothing more than "a suite of odes, interspersed with epic narratives." Dismissing the use of verse in the theater, as well as the unities, he called for historical dramas in prose dealing with national subjects, like those of the Italian romantics. Could he perhaps have been thinking of the Napoleonic era? He was not in the least upset by reforms of style and verse and he scorned sentimental lyricism. But, insofar as French comedy had become "since Destouches and Collin d'Harleville, a playful, delicate and witty epistle," he wanted to see it infused again with the dramtic element which it had lost. Stendhal was never to become completely a part of that legion of his juniors who were to take their stand in the *Muse française* [2] in 1824, quite differ-

2 Tr. note: A literary review which became the platform of the young French romantics.

ently from and far more wholeheartedly than he was taking it in 1823. His style was always slightly antipathetic to romanticism. His soul was actually more "romanesque" than properly "romantic," reveling in slow and subtle analysis. How could he content himself with opposing light and shadow when truth and life were, for him, within the nuances that separated and diversified them!

This double manifesto leads us to ask ourselves exactly what the limits of Stendhal's commitment were. Had he ever pictured himself as a writer-seer, sailing high above the clouds? Or as a leader of the people, "solitary and powerful," sitting in state upon some Sinai, either leaving the crowds behind or rising above their tide? Never. He was as remote from all posturing as he was from all sentimentality and grandiloquence. He had an instinct for truth in the realm of feeling. He could quickly expose in another what was sincere and what was "veneer"—and his perspicacity also discerned that a sincerely felt sentiment might at the same time be a false sentiment: "To give free reign to one's passions is permissible, but to passions one has not . . . oh pitiful nineteenth century!" he proclaimed, in an epigraph of *The Red and the Black*. Perhaps it was simply his early baldness and his borrowed hairpiece that prevented him from playing the role of the hero wrapped in Byronic gloom. He was undeniably linked to romanticism by virtue of the violent passions he analyzed, the romantic quality of his plots, his worship of energy, his taste for strong feelings, and a certain tone occasionally reminiscent of the cloak-and-sword novel. There was also his idealization of the hero, his fanatic individualism, his egotism, his noncomformity, and even a certain rationalization of his own profligacy. But what particularly distinguished him was an unparalleled psychological insight and a style that was brisk and devoid of self indulgence. Having failed to impose his concept of romanticism on France, he became a lone rider, more concerned with writing in "French" than in "literary French." He divorced himself from the poets and was neither stimulated nor excited by *Hernani*, which he found disappointing. He wished to resemble no one. A slow maturation was taking place within him. He withdrew from critical discussion and went beyond it, placing the fine arts on a level with literature. His

Racine and Shakespeare surpassed the oratorical position taken
by the Preface to *Cromwell* His most important statement was
that the arts must evolve and that beauty is relative.

His romantic infatuation did not make him any more in-
dugent toward Byron than he had been toward Racine. Although he respected Byron, he could not forgive him for having
preferred his title to his genius, for having wanted to be both
a great man and a great nobleman, just as Racine had wanted to
be both a great poet and a dashing courtier. He regarded Byron
as "a prideful man who will end by blowing out his brains
because he cannot be king." And yet Stendhal's literary antip-
athies and sympathies cannot be exaggerated. He was, in regard
to romanticism, very much the same as he had been in regard to
carbonarism—at first, the captivated spectator, and then, reticent. He gave the debate one of its initial stimuli and took his
position; then he detached himself from this group, which was
moving from worship of the individual to worship of form, and
with which worship of form often rather poorly concealed a lack
of individual substance. Steeped in living experience and truly
curious about human nature, his rather analytical and dry
probity threw Stendhal outside of the framework of the 1830's.

Except for the worship of passion and the individual—which
he interpreted in quite a different way—he no longer had anything in common with the romantics except negations. That
psychological truth, that social truth, which he required of
literature, demanding an intellectual instrument of the highest
precision, might very well have been his reaction against a romanticism infatuated with empty souls and synthetic passions,
which was describing the external world more and more as it
had less and less to say about the internal world. It is hard to
imagine this author of the *Italian Chronicles* in the adulterated
genre of romantic drama. Finally, it must be remembered that
Sir Walter Scott was then at the peak of his popularity, and
that Stendhal, with his propensity for cosmopolitanism and his
receptivity to new ideas from across the Channel, was rebelling
against that writer, whose influence was invading France. He
considered Scott to be as poor in ideas as he was rich in historical bric-a-brac, and regarded him suspiciously as a promoter
of purely commercial literature. Stendhal was basically neither
a romanticist nor a classicist, in the usual sense of the words,

but for the generation of 1880 and those thereafter he would be considered—as Barrès has accurately defined him—a sensitive "classicist of the soul."

The *Life of Rossini*, revealing another aspect of Stendhalian melomania, enjoyed a certain success due to its energy and its timeliness. Conceived in the atmosphere of Pasta's receptions, it is completely a first draft. The work appeared while Rossini was making his conquest of Paris. Not that Rossini had won an equal place with Cimarosa and Mozart in Stendhal's heart, however; the writer would have been less disposed toward him had he merely heard him in Milan. It was because of Stendhal's opposition to French music, so mediocre since the beginning of the century, that he interested himself in Rossini. Since 1818 he had been convinced that French taste would find Rossini's *Barber of Seville* congenial. This was not a matter of blind infatuation, however. He found Rossini's music "light, sharp, never boring." He regarded him as "lively, generous, brilliant, quick, chivalrous, preferring to paint with little depth rather than become burdensome." But his musical style, a herald of romantic inspiration, appeared to Stendhal "not poetic enough." He regretted that the music of the eighteenth century had been abandoned for a composer who "wanted to approximate the roar of German music." Created to express the "tender passions," music could also express the spirit. But Rossini had never come close to expressing passion. "His love is only for the voluptuous," claimed Stendhal. He had met Rossini in 1816 through Elena Viganò and the Monbelli sisters. In Paris La Pasta, at the height of her career, impressed the musician. Stendhal begrudged Rossini his glibness and least appreciated in him a certain grossness of character and style.

Stendhal had first considered writing a history of music at the beginning of the nineteenth century. In the end, he limited himself to Rossini's early period, ending the study with the year 1819. In a casual style, as if in improvisatory haste, Stendhal employed a kind of mimicry, using the "flourishes" that might best give some feeling of the renowned composer's own talent. Why cavil at his exclusive taste for vocal music and the *opéra-bouffe*? If his lack of technical knowledge prevented him from discussing music like a craftsman, he spoke of it like an

enlightened dilettante. Berlioz and Saint-Saens thoughtlessly
mocked him for it. Berlioz mentioned a "Monsieur Beyle, or
Bayle, or Baile, who has written a *Life of Rossini* under the
pseudonym of Stendhal, which includes the most irritating
stupidities about music, for which he believes he has a feeling." Henri Prunières, Romain Rolland, and Adolphe Boschot
were a little fairer. Barrès, on the other hand, praised him for
having demanded that music above all "furnish us with a sensual pleasure." Stendhal had, in fact, rather accurately appraised
the composers of his time. His epicurean impressionism, if ever
the preoccupation of the moment was idealistic—and it often
was—exalted him to such a point that it recalls a page from the
Confessions, in which Rousseau relates that one evening in
Venice, having fallen asleep in the *Théâtre Saint-Chrysostome*,
he was suddenly awakened by "the sweet harmony of angels'
song," in a melody he would never forget; his first thought was
to "believe himself in Paradise!" Stendhal adored music like a
lover. It distracted him from his tense intellectuality. It
aroused voluptuous and tender reveries in the depths of his
being; music spoke to his heart—because his heart had a great
deal to say to music.

The success of his *Life of Rossini* won Stendhal a position
on the *Journal de Paris*, from 1824 to 1827, writing a column on
Italian theater and art exhibitions. Continuing the tradition of
Diderot's *Salons*, in his own way, Stendhal criticized the school
of David and advanced the theory that drawing is learned, like
arithmetic; this gave rise to a polemic in the extremist news-
paper, *le Drapeau blanc*; Stendhal emerged from the fray somewhat the loser. Vitet, who wrote the *Globe's* music column,
regularly took to a stand opposed to that advanced by the
Journal de Paris, not without politics being at the heart of these
armed thrusts. Stendhal's incisive review of the productions of
the Italian theatrical company productions totaled more than
forty *feuilletons*.[3] These pages, which rivaled *Rome, Naples and
Italy* and *Promenades in Rome*, comprised the remainder of the
Life of Rossini. In them was evaluated Pasta's worth as an artist;
the later *Souvenirs of Egotism* was to go into further detail concerning her.

Stendhal also presented, in the *Revue trimestrielle* of July-

3 Tr. note: Term denoting a journalistic article.

October, 1828, an extremely frank work dealing with *The Fine Arts and the French Character*. In it are discovered again the governing principles of his esthetics and his opinions in regard to his compatriots—so capable of thinking and so incapable of feeling. Henri Martineau has further assembled, in these *Miscellanies of Art*, a serious work on the excavations of the Tarquinia ruins.

There must be mentioned, in addition to the foregoing, a political and social pamphlet which appeared in 1825: *Concerning a New Plot Against the Industrialists*. It exudes rancor—the rancor of counting for nothing compared with the émigrés who were moving in the best society, compared with the imperial nobility that was accommodating itself with flexibility to its recent reverses, compared with the great middle class that was about to found an empire on wealth. Hardly had the "Saint-Simonians" unleashed their periodical, *Le Producteur*, than an acid Stendhal took issue with their doctrine, which placed industrial capacity at the peak of its scale of values. His ignorance on the subject was vast, but he was not approaching it from a technical standpoint. He was more concerned with the eternal values of the intellect, with dedication, beauty, and generosity. Sainte-Beuve paid homage to him for this in his *Causeries du lundi.*[4] Personal rancor aside, Stendhal proved himself almost clairvoyant. He also had a certain right, in his poverty, to condemn the utilitarianism of a class at the dawn of his power and to proclaim the eminent value of free thought, which always refused to prostitute itself no matter what its need. *Le Producteur* replied with an article by Armand Carrel; Stendhal answered it and found an ally in the *Globe*. Briefly, this pamphlet resounded like an alarm bell at the threshold of a century during which industrialism was to present undreamed of perils to human personality. Was the writer's individualism perhaps sensing this and rearing up in the face of imminent danger? Did he foresee that the painfully won equilibrium between soul and substance was about to be broken—that the time was near when, subjugated by the machine age, we would be forced to seek, without finding it, that "extra soul" to which our age aspires, convinced that civilizations are mortal?

4 Translated as *Monday Chats* (1851–62).

6 · *Armance* (1827) * *Promenades in Rome* (1829)

STENDHAL's first novel, *Armance*, was published when he was forty-four years old. The book is strange and disconcerting; Sainte-Beuve spoke of it as "a basically enigmatic novel, lacking truth in its detail" which displayed "absolutely no imagination and absolutely no genius." It is the story of a perfect love, complicated by excessive delicacies and continuous misunderstandings; its protagonist is a young man of somber disposition whose malady one is hard pressed to understand. The work appears to be, by turns, an indecent parody on the chaste narratives of the Duchess de Duras, a work of dry analysis in the style of *Liaisons Dangereuses* or *Adolphe*,[1] and an imaginative effort that probes too deeply into a rather common and uninteresting affair. It has earned its author additional reproaches for having depicted a world with which he was not familiar.

The subject was in the air. The era being a prudish one, it was perilous to present "the greatest of love's impossibilities." The Duchess de Duras had just successfully published in 1824 and 1825 two short novels—*Ourika* and *Edouard*—which put the accent on social impossibilities. One of them concerned the union of a young colored woman and a socially prominent young man; the other dealt with the union of a commoner and an aristocrat. In one as yet unpublished novel—*Olivier*, or *The Secret*—she presented the theme of sexual impotence, telling the story of Olivier's gradual withdrawal from the woman he loved. This novel enjoyed a *sub rosa* circulation and was known

1 Tr. note: A semiautobiographical novel by Benjamin Constant.

to the redoubtable Latouche, who forthwith published an *Olivier* dealing with the same subject, without any author's name and in the same format as *Ourika* and *Edouard*. The work which created a scandal, was generally attributed to Mme. de Duras; in the January, 1826, issue of the *New Monthly Magazine* Stendhal credited her with it. At that time he decided to enter into the game and set to work on an *Olivier* of his own, feeling that the name would give him "exposure and not indecent exposure." He changed the idea, calling his hero "Octave," and entitled the work with the name of its heroine: *Armance*. He was not interested in the salacious aspects of the case. The novel was a chaste one, concentrating almost completely on the psychological repercussions of this agonizing situation. Although a risqué letter to Mérimée of October 23, 1826, offers a cynical commentary useful in understanding it, the book is a work of delicacy which the author composed with élan in the chastest language and purest style he had ever used.

The novel's protagonist is Octave de Malivert, a descendant of the Crusaders whose family had emigrated under the "usurper." He has just graduated from the École Polytechnique. A taciturn being who typifies the disorientation of aristocratic youth, he will not permit himself to fall in love. Although he is smitten with his cousin, Armance, he forces himself to break off with her. Armance is in love with Octave, as well, but she tries to hide her love because she is without wealth. Thus there is equal scruple on each of their parts, but there is also a certain cruelty on Octave's—he is a veritable tormenter of both himself and Armance. A plan for their union arises after Octave's confession—"I am a monster." Armance believes him guilty of a great crime and feels even more tenderly attracted to him: "I sometimes have thoughts of committing a crime like yours so that you will fear me no longer." One is reminded of Dostoevsky's Sonia, as she confronts Raskolnikoff. The marriage of the two lovers is celebrated. Octave has sworn to kill himself so that Armance may have the freedom that his disgrace prevents him from impeding; a false letter, on the other hand, causes him to doubt her sincerity. At first compassionate toward his young wife, he finds he no longer has the courage to die. Finally, in order to keep his self-respect, he sets out for Greece

and at last poisons himself. Although he leaves his fortune to
Armance on the condition that she remarry within two years,
Armance takes the veil.

So it is that in the guise of an idyl which knowingly maintains mystery and bizarre intrigue, this intrigue is shared by
author and reader rather than by the characters. Twice Octave
almost confesses his secret and then reneges. There is continuous innuendo, but it is all a matter of guesswork with this
creature—alternately violent, scrupulous, and taciturn—who is
driven by his neurotic need for dissimulation. Everything is implied; the entirety constitutes what has been called "an exhaust-
ing exhibition of *delicatesse*." At the same time, the author has
attempted to deal with social morés, as well.

Everything had destined Stendhal to deal with this subject:
several celebrated cases dealt with in literature or offered by
history; his psychological curiosity about *babilanisme*, or impotence; the memory of his speechlessness with young and beautiful Alexandrine, plus the inopportunely interposed image of
Métilde herself; and finally, the state of sensual indifference into
which the refractory Milanese had plunged him, and which
had lasted for three years. Who, better than he, could present
the story of a *babilan* in love— and intensely in love? Stendhal,
who rarely experienced a fusion of the senses and the soul, always dissociated the elements of love. He did not place love's
greatest joy in possession, but in that first evidence which proves
that one is loved. Does this indicate total mastery? Might Armance not have welcomed Octave's confession? And yet he
says nothing at all, or at least postpones any attempt to en-
lighten us, until the last epigraph: "[If he be turn'd to earth, let
me but give him one hearty kiss, and you shall put us both into
one coffin.]" [2] The solution of Isolde. The solution of Juliet.
Composed directly after his break with Clémentine Curial, the
novel is filled with melancholy. This was one of the most dis-
mal periods of his life. When he commiserated with his hero
by means of Virgil's verse, he was thinking about himself: "I
have lived and broken the destiny Fate gave me." The poly-
technician Octave is Henri Beyle at twenty; they share the same
liberal ideas, the same strong aversion for their respective

2 Tr. note: Words enclosed by brackets written in Beyle's English.

fathers, the same adoration for their respective mothers. And, like Octave, Stendhal preferred his reputation for debauchery to the reality of his extreme shyness. All of his hero's misfortunes he himself had known, and Octave's passing stoicism was his own, hidden under a deceptive veil of egotism. Within the character of a protagonist to whom he gave aristocratic elegance and somber Byronic reveries, he studied every nuance of a certain psychological pathology. Why take issue with the continual preciosities that present the phases of his crystallization? One certainly cannot integrally liken the author to his hero; however, behind the façade of a transposition pushed to its extreme, Octave's enigma may well have been his own. Lacking that, how could he have depicted the agonies of his character so well? The Civitavecchia copy of *Armance* bears this note: "I have reread this chapter, which seems true to me, and to write it one must have felt it." Has the necessary attention been paid to such passages of the book? Here is one of Octave's confessions: "Almost every morning *he needed, on awakening, to instruct himself on his misfortune.* There was a cruel moment, but before long the idea of death came to console him and to bring peace to his heart." Later, in 1838, Stendhal, alluding to that youthful misadventure which we have already related, analyzed his state of mind at the time in revealing terms: "There had often been more agonizing moments, but none so close to gun point; this was when, in the morning on awakening, I would instruct myself on my misfortune. At this moment I bordered on tears." The relationship between the two statements is undeniable. From the *Armance* of Civitavecchia we have excerpted two remarks, the first of which is obviously a variant: "He had sworn a thousand times during those four years that he would never love. This obligation not to love was the basis of all his conduct and the most important business of his life." The second remark is composed in the first person and not in keeping with the text, seeming much more like one of those self-evaluations to which he was often given: "Always ashamed, disgusted with everything. I can see only one thought; outside of that fatal idea there is nothing. To forestall a pain which seems always new." Stendhal has too often been regarded as the paralyzed lover. Undoubtedly there was within him at certain times a soul that struggled against his temperament, without always conquering it, and that, in the lap of what he militarily termed "the victory," never knew a moment of tranquil abandon. This would seem to be the case, in recalling a furtive remark from his treatise *On Love*: "A man pays court to an extremely honest and sophisticated woman; she learns that this man has had certain misfortunes, physical and ludicrous; he becomes unendurable to her . . . the crystallization is rendered impossible."

From another standpoint the book's subtitle, suggested by the bookseller Urbain Canel, is revealing: *A Few Scenes from a Parisian Drawing Room in 1827*. Although Stendhal was unacquainted with the *Faubourg Saint-Germain* he was curious about the morés of his time and he placed his heroes in official positions, not without leaving himself open to certain criticisms. This picture of the aristocracy, in which his imagination utilized known information, objectively reconstructed an atmosphere which should be fairly accurate. But the drama of Octave and Armance is too primordial to concern itself for long with satirical aspects.

The character of Armance de Zohiloff, who embodies Métilde's gentleness, was "copied" in its externals "from the companion of M. de Strogonoff's mistress, who always used to be at the *Bouffes* a year ago," the author tells us. According to a letter of his to Mérimée, Mme. d'Aumale is the Duchess de Castries "made wise." Mme. de Bonnivet, who is not absolutely necessary to the plot, seems to be a composite image of the Duchess de Broglie, Mme. Swetchine, and Mme. de Krudener; she was brought upon the scene in order to give some idea of the sanctimonious tone which the aristocracy of that era owed to the Jesuits. Stendhal always proceeded this way when he created his characters.

The literary scandal aroused by Latouche had assured his *Olivier* a success which was due to curiosity; but Stendhal's anonymous novel had no readers. The author consoled himself in a note of June 9, 1828. Not that he complained: "The vulgar do not appreciate my novel and, actually, do not feel it, because it is not the fashion. So much the worse for the vulgar. . . ." Even his friends, though, were reticent. Di Fiore told him on several occasions that "there is nothing in it, absolutely nothing good in this novel." André Gide was to recognize that for the common reader, and even for Stendhalians, *Armance* has not yet been raised to a level much above Sainte-Beuve's original estimation of it. Gide himself regarded the work as the most delicate and finely written of all Stendhal's books—the purity of its feelings, the Racinian rhythm of its phrases, drawing us gradually into a realm of verbal music. The book's protagonists, whom Maurice Bardèche regarded as possessing something of the "Proustian," seem dedicated "to eternal stainless avowals."

Stendhal himself judged the work, on his Civitavecchia copy, to be as "delicate as *The Princess of Clèves*." Although it cannot be regarded as a masterpiece—it is actually an unsuccessful book with a cumbersome Introduction—it is nevertheless useful as a basis for comparison, for one can discern within its course the first, still very muted, accents of that "music of happiness" which the last novels were to express with such abundance. In it the writer's contempt for Restoration society takes shape; but his hero is by no means the rebel that Julien Sorel is to be. He belongs to another world, and he lacks that leaven of ambition which constitutes the Napoleonic adventure.

The *Promenades in Rome,* occurring at a pivotal point in the life and work of the author, draws a portrait of ancient and modern Rome under the threefold aspect of its political, social, and artistic monuments. Composed in Paris because Stendhal needed money, with the help of Romain Colomb, this book crowned the series of Stendhal's writings on Italy. It followed on the heels of his first novel and preceded the masterpiece of his maturity, *The Red and the Black.* Appearing two days before the July Revolution, it seemed almost a prelude to his consular life. He had written more outstanding books, certainly, but none that were more eclectic. The memory of Métilde can still be discerned in it, although the *Promenades* belongs much more to "Mme. Azur."

Did Stendhal possess in 1829 the ability required to compose an erudite itinerary? He had been assembling material since 1817, all of which could hardly be incorporated into his second

edition of *Rome, Naples and Florence*, for which it had been
intended. Other of this material, abandoned in Milan in 1821,
was not pertinent enough to be utilized. There was, in addition,
a considerable amount of actual, direct documentation on the
work, which in no way resembles any of the classic itineraries.
It has a seeming disorder, but only on the surface. The author
adopted, as opposed to *Corinne*, the informal style of a travel
diary and of notes from a not yet drafted notebook. He loved
the lively tone of P.-L. Courier and the President de Brosses.
Between these positive and negative poles was struck the spark
of the *Promenades*. Although he himself stated that there was
absolutely no use in praising the book since three-quarters of
it consisted of extracts from better works, it was an extremely
personal work, communicating both a real and an ideal impression of Italy.

Nibby, Lalande, Nardini, and their peers documented the
sections dealing with monuments of antiquity, churches, and
museums and furnished several odds and ends concerning ancient history; but he turned the pages of remote centuries with
emotion. Indifferent to the catacombs, about which Stendhal
breathed not a word, he reserved his keenest interest for the
Middle Ages, the Renaissance, and his own age. Avowing that
civilization wilts the soul, he had persuaded himself that energy
blossoms in anarchy or under tyranny. Hypocrisy, he claimed,
is an element of that unbridled *virtù* by which the "human
plant" affirms itself. These theories, of course, owed a great
deal to Sismondi and to Potter. Once again he ran the entire
gamut of plagiarism. He would copy the first phrase of a paragraph, faithfully summarizing its major points and rectifying
its style; then, the need for literary freedom ripening in him
during the course of this fastidious toil, he would depart further
and further from his model as his paragraph came to a close.
Above all else he strove for conciseness, neatness, and vigor,
stripping from the hand of the master all colorless prose and
keeping only the best. Upon a simple suggestion he grafted a
development of his own thought, or invented arguments. Re-
jecting Sismondi's slow narrative form, he substituted action
for the narration of action, by always using the most direct word,
dramatizing the statement, excising extraneous adjective, and

generally compressing the style. With the surety of a surgeon's hand, he removed everything that was adipose tissue and exposed the nerve of the sentence. This residue was often composed simply of words effectively used by Sismondi or Potter, but Stendhal gave life to them; the personalities presented became efficacious actors whose responsibility was found to be linked with circumstance. Thus he attained psychological truth and thus he found the use of those dramatic elements that he had despaired throughout his life of bringing to the stage. His references were secondhand, and if the author here and there interpolated a short paragraph, one could be sure that it had no historical precision but rather some psychological insight or allusion which was probably a hazy reminiscence. Stendhal wanted to point out to his reader the simultaneity of events and, above all, to combine an artistic period he knew well with an historic period for which his references furnished him material. Forced to choose between the picturesque and the psychological, he would always unhesitatingly sacrifice the picturesque. Was he ignoring the originals? To say this would be incorrect, although appearances condemn him. Only secondhand syntheses were usable, if the book were to be completed quickly; they did away with all the effort of research and made possible an artistic effort.

It happened, on occasion, that he had the chance to recover a bit of his own—such was his article on the Conclave of 1823, which appeared in the first issue of the *Revue britannique* of 1828, and which was simply a translation of one of his articles from the *London Magazine*. Contemporary newspapers and periodicals gave a little spice to his documentation and he proceeded from this to a more savory amalgamation. The mocking remarks of Misson's *Voyage to Italy* were a windfall for his anticlericalism. Stendhal's political ideas and his reflections on morals reiterated his previous statements, but they were strangely in accord with Simonde de Sismondi's *Voyage to Italy*. He applied, in the *Promenades*, esthetic ideas that had already appeared in a simpler form in his *History of Painting*, in other cases directly utilized. Fifteen pages dedicated to Michelangelo were extracted, line for line, from the enormous work of 1817. Such selectivity is displayed in its research, such

art in its narrative, that it is a model of this type of résumé.
Moreover, although the material is the same, the vision is new.
In regard to Michelangelo, Stendhal, who had been very much
the art critic in his *History of Painting*, proved himself in the
Promenades to be a passionate worshipper of great souls, above
all. Quotations and anecdotes abound, borrowed from every
hand—his own work *On Love*, the *Edinburgh Review*, the
Gazette des Tribunaux, *Laoreins*, *Duclos*, the *Journal des
Débats*, the *Globe*, and the *Revue britannique*. The martyrdom
of Saint Perpetua, for which he referred to Delamotte's translation of Tertullian, came originally from his cutting of an
article unearthed in the *Globe*. The narratives relating beautiful crimes committed out of honest conviction foreshadowed
his *Italian Chronicles*. The dramatic story of the suppression of
the Bajano convent was taken from an anonymous work, published shortly before the *Promenades*, with which Stendhal
must have been acquainted. He had no hesitation in moving
from the sixteenth to the nineteenth century an anecdote into
which carbonarism bizarrely intruded, as in *Vanina Vanini*
(1829). This process of the contamination of two epochs was
to be, ten years later, the origin of *The Charterhouse of Parma*.
In relating the tragic amours of Fabio Cercara and Francesca
Polo, he had modified, by changing its one and simplifying its
plot, a novel of Bandello's which had originally treated the
theme of amorous substitution in the most comic vein.

His evocation of Roman social life owed more than one fea-
ture to the *Revue britannique*, although it is difficult to know
what part memory may have played in it. His evocation of the
Roman countryside was a reaction against the "hypocritical
farrago" of Chateaubriand; and yet, this Frenchman who had
best known Italy was the being least capable of depicting the
Italian temperament. He suffered inhibitions when it came to
conveying his impressions, and although he occasionally had
the patience to describe accurately, he had not the patience
to describe at length. His words did not convey his initial magical feeling and his landscape remained an interior one. How
many times had he remarked, in trying to evoke his memories,
that they had "lost style by waiting." Only his emotion, expressed in a few words, prompts the reader to pursue the work

of the artist because—due to his modesty, his timidity, his self-criticism, his scorn for others, his egotistical dilettantism, his egotism—Stendhal was often negligent in his work. But perhaps we who are weary of *style noble* owe him thanks for the restraint that gives his *Promenades* its everlasting freshness. And it is possibly this book, a turning point in his intellectual preoccupations, which presents the best opportunity to accurately judge what Stendhal owed, in the acquisition of his mastery, to the lengthy labor of rewriting which most of his works had imposed upon him until that time.

Once again his learning is only adulterated, and the manner in which he employs it is often rather unscrupulous. Keeping references that could lead one to believe it an erudite documentation, he silently ignores certain authors, whom he scorns at the very moment he is plundering their works. And in 1829 these authors often possessed the added fault of still being very much alive. From this arose his systematic method of rewriting, designed to mask his most deliberate larcenies. Stendhal's originality therefore often stems from the fact that he was forced, in order to hide his thefts, either to contradict a source or to change its details. And what is true of his style is no less true of his composition; the rambling quality of the *Promenades*, which has only the surface appearance of a journal, is also the skillful negation of the forms of its predecessors. For the reader who is not forewarned the illusion is otherwise perfect.

The *Promenades in Rome*, however, is much more than either a reaction or a negation. To explain the conditions of the work and to suggest its limitations is neither to destroy its charm nor to misconstrue its perceptiveness. This would be a pity, for no book yet written about Rome can match it. A sculptor of the style and ideas of others, with what spirit Stendhal transfigured his borrowed thoughts, with the energy of his quips, the brilliance of his wit, and the vigor of his phrasing! What richness this masterful and learned literary collection thus acquired! What cleverness of style! He cuts, pares, interpolates, inverts, deletes, comments, approves, contradicts, enters the scene, disappears, and reappears again; it is perpetual motion; it is Figaro in all his irreverence. In a rapid

succession of ideas, emotions, rancors, sympathies, predilections—of aversions, even—he fashions with light jests or bitter
barbs an animated frieze, in which it must be clearly recognized, without concern for its larcenies or similarities, that this
Beylist Italy is most accurate when all is said and done. What
does it matter if systematic synthesis was the basis of its creative force? Completely immersed in his subject, the author
dominates it and abandons himself to it; laboriously fashioned
material thus gives birth to the most delicate of discoveries.
The *Promenades* exceeds the boundaries of the Eternal City.
It had been over a century since that very fascinating Rome
which had for its background an Italy awakened by "the sound
of a cannon on the Lodi bridge." Even the Europe Stendhal
knew, and the America and Turkey his imagination conceived,
served as bases for comparison in an itinerary that condensed
all the human experience of an author who was everlastingly
curious about comparative psychology. And although *Promenades in Rome* is, on the surface, a systematic guide, it is still
more a breviary of Beylism and one of the most total expressions of Stendhalian egotism, if not the most novel. It reveals
both the heart and mind of its author, with all their deficiencies
and all their inexpressible fascination.

Although he was moved by poetry on the death of Tasso,
Stendhal did not have the gravity necessary to probe into any
spiritual problems which the Eternal City might have posed
for meditation. He did not view every aspect of Rome, both
pagan and Christian, with equal profundity; and although he
reconstructed its atmosphere with talent, to our satisfaction at
least, he was not particularly apt at regarding his own image
in Rome's mirror. For the Rome he so painstakingly described
was a constant pretext for escape. Italy was always the "promised land" of his pursuit of happiness—as in his youth. It was
the spiritual homeland of an imaginative epicurean, the ideal
climate for retrospective amoralism, à la Benvenuto Cellini—
and particularly when he was in France and in financial
straits. Occasionally, looking backward past the Italy of the
Renaissance and the Middle Ages, an oversimplified vision of
pagan Italy, voluptuous and uncomplicated in its psychology,
presented itself to Stendhal like the longed-for and refreshing

image of some lost paradise. With all the bitterness and poignancy of memory, Stendhal poured into this book, in minute careful phrases, his great, unquenchable desire for a life without shackles.

The most surprising thing about this itinerary, which reinvigorates traditional themes by making light of them, is that even the most obvious documentary hoax attains, with ease, an infinitely engaging artistic sincerity; more profoundly still, it attains through brief and abstruse allusions a human sincerity of lyric fullness.

Within the course of this sinuous and varied text are light touches, opening into marvelous abysses of silence, from the heart of which suddenly arises a wave of sound, with the purest tone, touching a secret chord within us: love, beauty, music, passion, death—every dream and every despair.

But the capricious Stendhal is already carrying us along. He has recovered himself and is on his way again. He is no poet and does not wish to be one. He goes back to his historians and archeologists—to Lalande, the most "glacial" of them all. Nevertheless, for one brief moment and with a singular mastery over himself, he has captured the accent and emotion of the *Reisebilder*.[3]

3 Tr. note: Six volumes of travel sketches by Heinrich Heine (1826–31).

7 · The Red and the Black (1830)

ONE NIGHT in Marseilles, on his way back from Catalonia, between the 25th and 26th of October, 1829, Stendhal had an "idea for *Julien*," just as he was putting the finishing touches on the *Promenades* in the wee hours of the morning. In one fell swoop he committed the novel to paper, and in May he chose this enigmatic title: *The Red and the Black*. The writer found himself, at that time, at a sentimental crossroads. During the writing of his itinerary he had fallen in love, "with a fury" but for only a short time, with Alberte de Rubempré. Then Giulia Rinieri de' Rocchi had flatteringly declared her love to him and had kept her word. He therefore regarded himself as "very passably happy in 1830." Although his first draft was a bit meager, Stendhal had a habit of always completely reworking his first version during the course of its final composition. Ordinarily, an anecdote picked up in his reading, a diverting fact, served as a stepping stone; before long, these had become only a subsidiary structure, so many details had he accumulated for the purposes of truth, so many elements had he crystallized around the characters he was justifying, tirelessly researching the birth and evolution of their thoughts and feelings.

Three months later, as he was expanding the theme, Stendhal began to see his hero as "the young provincial, a student of Plutarch and Napoleon." He left for Trieste, leaving the manuscript behind, like a bottle in the sea, never suspecting that he had just written the most important novel of the century and ranked himself the foremost psychologist of his age. He had reread each morning, enthusiastically resuming work, the last pages of the previous night, without troubling to follow a rigid plan. The "July Days" (during which the armed Parisians finally defeated the king's men) found him absorbed in Las Cases' *Memorial of Saint Helena*. His own book, a veritable pamphlet against the society created by the Jesuits and émigrés, had the ill luck to appear after the revolution that it had foreshadowed and even hoped for. But the book had been conceived long before that and carried the hopes of all the obscure Julien Sorels who were hoping to find their fortune again. Napoleon's example had nourished the energy of a generation that was rebelling against its lot. Gustave Lanson claims that *The Red and the Black*, in five hundred pages, "teaches us as much about the secret motives of actions and the internal quality of souls in the society created by the Revolution as does the entire *Human Comedy*, in forty volumes." The particular case of Julien Sorel is, in itself, fascinating enough.

The background and plot of the novel were furnished by two contemporary trials in the Court of Assizes. One of them concerned the condemned Laffargue, who displayed "more soul in himself alone than had all the poets taken together." The other and more important trial was that of Berthet, which took place in Brangues and Grenoble. These two events had fascinated Stendhal from the outset, as he was always intrigued by fine crimes of passion. Had he not, only recently, inserted in his *Promenades* a long excerpt from the *Gazette des Tribunaux* (1829), which recounted the trial of Laffargue, a cabinet maker? Delighted at discovering the French equivalent of that "human plant" which Alfieri had revealed to him, Stendhal, more than a year before *The Red and the Black*, had borne this significant judgment concerning Laffargue, who had shot his mistress with a pistol:

While the upper classes of Parisian society seem to be losing the ability to feel with force and constancy, in the petite bourgeoisie the passions seem to exert a frightening energy among these young people who, like M. Laffargue, have received a good education, but whose lack of wealth compels them to work and exposes them to real needs. Removed, by the need to work, from a thousand little duties imposed by good society and from a way of seeing and feeling which etiolates life, they keep their strength of will because they possess strength of feeling. Doubtless every great man will henceforth emerge from the class to which Monsieur Laffargue belongs. Napoleon once combined these very circumstances: a good education, an ardent imagination, and extreme poverty.

The atmosphere of *The Red and the Black* is already present here, and again in the following remark:

Because an artillery lieutenant became emperor and raised to social heights two or three hundred Frenchmen born to live on one thousand *ecus'* income, a mad and necessarily ill-starred ambition seized all Frenchmen. It is not so with the young people, who are simply relinquishing every pleasure of their age in the mad hope of becoming deputies and eclipsing the glory of Mirabeau (but they say Mirabeau had a few passions, and our young people seem to have been born at the age of fifty . . .)

Thus we find linked with the notion of social class the name of the emperor, whose example was becoming contagious. He was viewed as the prototype of the ambitious man, a "burner of bridges," a speculator in the malady of social climbing, a "disciple," and even an "expatriot." This, then, provided the background of the book. As for its concrete circumstances, these were provided by a celebrated Grenoble trial related in the *Gazette des Tribunaux* of December 28–31, 1827—the Berthet trial—from which the author drew, changing none of the essential elements of this peculiar affair.

In 1827 Antoine Berthet, a former Dauphinois seminarist of peasant origin, shot a woman during the middle of a service in the Brangues church. The woman was Mme. Michoud de la Tour, aged thirty-six years, the wife of one of Beyle's friends and a cousin of one of Grenoble's judges. The young man, a former tutor of her child, had seduced this woman, whose reputation had been spotless until that time. As she knelt during the elevation of the host by the side of her friend, Mme. Marigny, Berthet grievously wounded her and then tried to kill himself. He was condemned to death and guillotined in the Grenoble drill ground on February 23, 1828, at the age of twenty-five. Another circumstance in this story furnished Stendhal the basis for the novel's second part. Long before the bloody drama provoked by love and jealousy, Berthet, driven from the seminary, from his paternal household, and finally from the Michoud household, had entered the service of one M. de Cordon on the recommendation of the same Mme. Michoud. There Mlle. de Cordon became infatuated with him; once again he was driven out. Cast adrift, he wrote despairing letters to Mme. Michoud, whom he blamed for his misfortunes: "My position is such that a catastrophe will occur if it does not change." And so it did, not without Berthet's having expressed this regret: "It is a great pity that I should have missed the career for which I was destined; I would have made a good priest; I feel particularly that I might have skillfully stirred the power of human passions." Berthet and Laffargue, avenging themselves identically on the women they loved, were already Stendhalian heroes. What transformation would the novelist's soul impose on them?

They were the occasion of a "chronicle"—"the chronicle of 1830"—in which they personified and indicted a precise stage in French society. The author's first step was the choice of a title. At that time the use of colors was very much in vogue. Stendhal had once toyed with the idea of entitling *Lucien Leuwen* as *The Amaranth and the Black*, then *The Red and the White*, and had considered writing a book entitled *The Red and the Green*. As for *The Red and the Black*, there have been numerous speculations concerning the title's meaning. Could he, perhaps, have been alluding to the hazards of destiny, as opposed to the game of chance? If so, it would seem that he should have used the feminine form: *la rouge et la noire*, as it would be in French; whereas, he used the masculine form: *le rouge et le noir*. Could these colors have symbolized the priest and the executioner, or perhaps the blood that was to stain the seminarist's soutane? Or might they be, instead, considering the importance of the novel's political elements, symbolic of the struggle between the liberals and the Congrégation? By the author's own admission, according to Emile Forgues, the meaning is this: had he lived under the Empire, Sorel would have been a soldier; whereas, the only outlet for his ambition under the Restoration was in the priesthood. The novel would thus express Julien's yearning for heroic times, rather than the republicanism of this disciple of Plutarch.

The *Red* symbolized, first of all, the age of the Revolution

and the Empire, with everything these words implied to an ambitious youth certain of his value, his audacity, fearing neither
bullets nor death. This was the glorious career of arms, in
which merit astonished the eyes of all, in which courage boldly
asserted itself, in which foresight and *sang-froid* won their
place in the sun. This was the age of action, superior to the
word, an enemy of the word, which had for its yardstick only
itself and for its judges only its peers. This was the age of immediate and irremediable decisions, of clear visions, followed
by immediate consequences, of wagers in which everything was
risked, both for oneself and for others. Real obstacles must be
overcome. Daydreams must be mastered and victories won. It
was a time of responsibility and power for the man who commanded, for the leader of men, sure of himself and sure of his
soldiers—a time when feelings were high, when man was testing himself and judging himself, when one was involved in
events that had repercussions in the farthest reaches of Europe,
instead of squeezing by under the wire with the dust of circumstances on one's breast in an anemic, factitious, passionless
world. This was a time of great horizons and unleashed ambitions, when "one is either killed, or a general, by the time
he is thirty-six."

The *Black* represents the Restoration, with all that word implied, lacking prestige, connoting renunciations and early dis-
avowals to the ambitious youth, who saw the career of arms
closed to him and who found in its place the all powerful
Congrégation. "Black" symbolized the ecclesiastical career, the
only one henceforth open to an ambitious youthful appetite;
the eager young man who had dreamed of nothing but wounds
and blows, glory and violent action, was forced to sheathe his
useless courage. He had to renounce the blisses of action and
resign himself to the insipid satisfactions of shabby thoughts,
small advantages slowly gained, and long meditations silently
savored. The art of directing or restraining the word succeeded
that of maneuvering armies. That store of audacity within him
would aid him to no end but prudence; that need to spend
himself physically and morally would aid him only to prove
himself impassive; that heroic burst of his entire being would
have to be restrained; his shining uniform would become a

soutane, his military gait would become ecclesiastical unction, his tone of command a tone of prayer, and his martial bearing a false face of piety. The ambitious youth who wanted to become general or die would become a bishop with an income of 100,000 francs, and the arm created to brandish a bold sword would scatter benedictions for hypocrites.

Such was the contrast that Stendhal wanted to emphasize by his creation of Julien Sorel. The contemporary critic has long delighted in regarding him as a specimen of the ambitious man and the déclassé. But the writer's worth is not so much in having contrasted the spirit of two epochs as in having recreated the drama from beginning to end through the continuous insights of his own personality. *The Red and the Black* is much more than a novel about morals or politics, although both are of a high standard in this book, in which the author again takes up *Armance's* satirical theme, extending his indictment of the hated régime to include the provinces; it is the psychological aspect of this novel of ambition and love that is particularly fascinating. Freely reconstructing the story, Stendhal carefully contrived every detail of it, stripping bare the motives of great passions and always respecting the logic of his characters.

His depiction of various social milieus and of minor characters was neither less precise nor less evocative. He always drew as much from his observations and memories as he did from his fancies and dreams. We often witness composite images. The surface untruthfulness of certain situations and characters—of Mathilde de la Mole, for instance—disappears in that truth of detail and gift for life which sustains the total structure. In vain might one search, by analyzing, for a chink in the armor. Can one possibly forget the fantastic humor of Mme. Azur, so probing of mind, so purposefully energetic, so scornful of appearances? Can one forget the noble character that masked Giulia's frail silhouette, her audacious frankness, her reckless gift of herself to Stendhal at the time the book was written—perhaps because she had just read *Vanina Vanini*, in which the heroine pursues a carbonarist? Lastly, can one forget the scandal that then touched French aristocracy—the abduction, by Edward Grasset, of the niece of a minister of

Charles X; the escapade of the girl, Méry de Neuville, and her
lover in London; and then the return to her family of the
heroine of this adventure, who refused to marry her seducer!
Stendhal was interested in the affair, as his letter to Mareste of
January 17, 1831, testifies:

This ending seemed right to me when I wrote it; I had in mind
the image of Méry, a lovely girl whom I adore. Ask Clara if Méry
might not have done such a thing. The young Montmorencys and
their family have so little strength of will that it is impossible to
fashion a denouement that isn't flat, with these elegant and unob-
trusive beings. . . . This view of the upper classes' lack of character made me take one exception; it is wrong; is it ridiculous?
Quite possibly. The why of it—it *is because I was thinking of
Méry.* I would not know what to do in a novel about a young
Rohan-Chabot of really high quality.

The case of Méry de Neuville, then, was a revealing and decisive illustration.

The Red and the Black must be read a little at a time to
be fully appreciated. Every new reader reaps a harvest of new
discoveries. The ensemble is beautiful and powerful; its shad-
owed maze of psychological undulations is more fascinating
still. Sacrificing nothing to description or fine style, Stendhal
wrote a novel that is all nerves by sole means of analysis and
internal monologue; and through the power of this taut analysis, he brought to life new, robust, dramatic characters—not
so much through external events as through their own substance—characters made for the passions and their upheaval.
There is no doubt that this taut book was a difficult one to
approach. The author confessed as much in 1804, on his Civitavecchia copy:

[For me] [1]—to condense it, to add a line here and there in order to
make it easier to understand. . . . It lacks physical descriptions
of the characters. . . . For want of three or four descriptive words
per page and two or three additional words per page to keep its
style from resembling Tacitus, several of the preceding pages seem
like a moral treatise. The reader is always faced with something
too profound.

[1] Words enclosed by brackets written in Beyle's English.

We must point out that *The Red and the Black* was contemporary with *The Hunchback of Notre Dame*, and the average reader of 1831 would have preferred Quasimodo, Claude Frollo, Captain Phébus, Esmeralda, or even Esmeralda's goat, to Julien Sorel.

One of the chapters of *The Red and the Black* bears an epigraph in these words of Saint-Réal: "A novel is a mirror which is borne along a great highway." The critic, taking Stendhal at his word, has seen him as a painter of social types. Julien Sorel appears to be an ambitious man tortuously pursuing his designs of conquest and pleasure—proud, vindictive, clear-sighted, and insensitive. If one grants him a romantic *noblesse* unknown to his heirs, he is regarded, above all, as a déclassé, an envious man, a frenzied pleasure seeker, the "principal danger of our society"—which is another story entirely! As René Doumic has said, "sad are the heroes of Stendhal, that goes without saying"; and he is echoed in our own time by Paul Claudel, after Victor Giraud. To reproach Stendhal for his lack of moral feeling is to confuse art with morals, to misunderstand the scope of his clearsighted analysis, to forget that the real moralist mocks the moral. From the standpoint of ambition alone, Julien Sorel presents quite another image than does Rastignac, for example. Balzac's method, on the other hand, was to illustrate through patiently accumulated facts. Stendhal sounds out the secret of the soul and then builds again from the source. His continuous analysis is never tedious to the person with a taste for living psychology and not for systems. Whatever may be the importance of the social problem incarnated in this déclassé, paying no attention to anyone but himself and hastening brutally to win his place in society, it is his psychological problem that is most fascinating.

This "chronicle of 1830" is less an example of "realist" than of "true" art; there is a shade of difference that becomes clearer if one reads this statement from the margins of the Civitavecchia copy, dated 1834:

I wrote in my youth several *Biographies*, which are a kind of history. I regret it. The truth of the greatest, as of the smallest, events seems to me almost impossible to attain, at least any minutely detailed truth. Mme. de Tracy told me: "There is no longer any truth except in the Novel." I see more and more every day, as everywhere else, this is a pretension. . . .

In *The Red and the Black* Stendhal pursued this "minutely detailed truth" by dint of self-examination. His realism is therefore completely subjective; it is Stendhal's ego that is reflected by his characters and milieus.

Julien Sorel has done the writer a great deal of harm, for he has permitted the following syllogism to grow: Julien typifies the antipathetic careerist; Julien is a personification of Stendhal; therefore, Stendhal was an antipathetic careerist. One is struck, certainly, by the purely autobiographical circumstances in the narrative. There are allusions to the Sixth Dragoons; the receipt from Prince Korasoff can be found in his *Correspondence;* M. de la Mole's secretary writes *cela* with two "l's," just as Pierre Daru's secretary had. And although Beyle never scaled to any window that we know of, Menta certainly hid him well enough in her chateau at Monchy, just as Mme de Rênal hides Julien after an unexpected visit. Julien seems to be the one, among all of Stendhal's heroes, in whom the author himself is most completely incarnated. If the narrative which smoothly introduces Mme. de Rênal into the story often evokes *La Nouvelle Héloïse,* and even the *Confessions,* the novel's setting is very plainly inspired by Dauphinois country from the outset, and not by Franche-Comté country. The good priest, Abbé Chélan, frequently visited with Dr. Gagnon. And many another Grenoble inhabitant appeared under Stendhal's patronym: Gros, the geometrician; his classmate, Chazel; Ducros, the librarian. Mme. de Rênal's confidante, Mme. Derville, took her name from one of Pauline's friends. One episodic character is called Rubempré. The Count Altamira is none other than Stendhal's Neapolitan friend, Di Fiore. M. Valenod was modeled after a director of the Saint-Robert poorhouse, Victor Casimir Michel. The Abbé Frilair seems to have had for his model one of Grenoble's vicar-generals; Father Pirard was inspired by the terrible Abbé Raillane; Fouqué resembled Bigillion, a friend of Stendhal's early adolescence. With an eye toward certain Grenoble inhabitants, he created Barnave and Genoude, two brilliant parodies on social climbing. M. de

Rênal's aristocratic ambitions are reminiscent of Stendhal's father's. And is not Julien's own father, Sorel, with his revolting peasant greediness, the same Chérubin Beyle, exaggerated in the extreme? Who was Mme. de Rênal? Was she Métilde? Menti? Alexandrine Daru? Or still another? Or is she a mixture of memory and dream? By his own admission to Balzac, the novelist Stendhal always chose from reality among models he knew well, leaving them their moral habits, and then giving them "more wit."

Julien Sorel, filled with aversion for his father, anxious to escape from his environment—with his mania for reducing every action to military tactics, foreseeing life's smallest event as if it were a battle, and planning for love as if it were war—represents rather well, in the first part of the book, the kind of youth Henri Beyle had been. Actually, however, the writer's idolatry of Napoleon had come later than that of his hero. However, this "realistic" work, except for its modified method of exposition, is elevated, little by little, to a lyric transformation. With the experience of his mature years, Stendhal caught himself playing the game of his own life in his imagination. This confused life, with a few mistresses in the game, which had ended by winning an obscure counsulship, at last understood its own age and deposed on Julien Sorel its unrealized dream of energetic ambition. This analyst, who owed some of his rarest joys to his life of action and who worshipped too late at Napoleon's shrine, represents himself as acting, with his hero as spokesman, long after the hour of inaction had struck. For Stendhal's energy was not intended for practical realization. It was an energy of the imagination, which dictated his attitudes and furnished him a moral of life—a completely internal energy, which made it possible for him to persevere in the enervating and deceptive cult of the self. He did not have the stuff of an arriviste or a careerist, for he placed other less common pleasures too high. It is hardly a paradox to say that Julien was an antithetical transposition of Stendhal, for he seems, in fact, to have bestowed on his hero all the qualities that he himself most lacked.

Is Julien, however, actually such a perfect model of ambition? The early part of the novel presents him as "a poor young man who is ambitious only because the delicacy of his heart makes him need a few of the pleasures that money can give." There is nothing vulgar about him. His ambition is, above all, a love of sport, a taste for risk, and a need for struggle and for struggle against himself, alone able to give zest to life, to happiness. "He preferred less certainty and more vast opportunities," inscribed the author in the margin of his Civitavecchia copy; he "saw nothing between himself and the most heroic actions but the lack of opportunity." He triumphs ultimately through an internal victory, rather than through concrete success. Julien is a sentimentalist, filled with all the charm that Stendhal had lacked, making a show of being a roué and wanting to free himself from every social and financial restriction. He maintains his lucidity in action and his mastery in passion, in revolt against society and against morality. Stendhal, who was to rejuvenate himself through Fabrizio, gave Julien the soul he possessed in 1830: " 'There is everything in this young man,' said the old officers mockingly, 'except youth.' " To equal Napoleon by competing with Sixtus Quintus—"the Hercules of modern times" who deceived "forty cardinals for fifteen successive years by his modesty"—this is an extremely austere goal for a twenty-year-old seminarist as passionate as he is greedy. Julien has a need for mad feelings of heroism, and he is at the mercy of his feelings, despite his heroism. There is a constant dichotomy between his sensibility and his intelligence. He is a taut chord in perpetual vibration. Undeniably, he struggles to the top through the sheer force of his own perseverance, through his ability, his intellect, his flexibility, and through a voluntary hypocrisy which is actually contempt for society. From the outset, he places himself beyond good and evil. And he persists in a single path, no more than Stendhal, courting a single disaster. Although his cleverness easily wins him partial battles, the return of a certain flame unexpectedly occurs within him—and it is this most unreasonable, most spontaneous sensibility, insanely disinterested, that checks this ambitious creature in his ambition. "Within this peculiar being there was a tempest almost every day," which might be a matter either of deeply personal problems or of dangerously explosive political and social problems.

In his prison, his love for Mme. de Rênal, elevating him to a paroxysm of the spirit and senses, drives this cry of deliverance from him—the ultimate expression of Beylist philosophy and happiness—"Leave me my ideal life!" Julien is less an ambitious man than an egotist for whom ambition is only a means to an end; although he believes himself ambitious, his supreme goal has actually been to ingest everything in order to reflect on everything. He is more avid than he is hedonistic; his imagination projects him into the future and prevents him from enjoying the present. He obstinately tests the power of his energy and his calculating intelligence until the day, shortly before his death, when he finally realizes the value of surrender and simplicity of heart. This heroic seducer, scornful and chivalrous, cannot consent to scorn himself; that instinct for nobility which he calls his "honor" is his morality; he deeply feels a certain pride at the idea of this "duty" upon which he was bent, to which he had clung, rather than be swept away by chance. The hypocrisy with which he arms himself has made almost no dent on his integrity. His death is a defiance thrown in the face of those who exclude him, the last protest of the vanquished, rebelling against the social order. His ambition is forgotten: "He was still very young," comments the author,

but in my opinion this was a beautiful plant. Instead of moving from the tender to the crafty, like the majority of men, age might have given him the goodness to be easily moved, he might have been cured of his mad mistrust . . . but what good are these vain speculations?

We have come a long way from the seminarist Berthet! This "mad mistrust," this "goodness to be easily moved," was this not Stendhal himself, as he really was, with his prideful soul, his tender heart? Julien Sorel, with the limitations already mentioned, casts light on Beyle's nature; less, however, than do Mme. de Rênal and Mlle. de la Mole, who permitted the writer to imagine himself in that role of seducer which he played so badly in life.

Mme. de Rênal, with her modest tenderness, embodies the passion he never knew, born without any previous inkling and recognizing itself too late; a passion that age renders slightly maternal, slightly reminiscent of Mme. de Warens: "There were certain days when she had the illusion that she loved him like her child." She loves her children more because they love Julien. She endures all the extremities of love, remorse, and pleasure. She views the illness of her son, Stanislas, as a punishment of God; but this remorse, which is the other side of her love, sometimes gives "their happiness the appearance of a crime"—the most typical of Stendhalian sensations. Her passion is subject to contradictions:

She would gladly have sacrificed her life in order to save that of her husband had she seen him in peril. . . . Nevertheless, there were certain fatal days on which she could not dispel the image of the excess of happiness she would taste if, suddenly become a widow, she might marry Julien.

But although she sees these contradictions, she does not, in her naïveté, need to explain them to herself. It is Julien, a completely tamed Julien, who savors them, senses them, and dominates them. He absorbs Mme. Rênal's personality, which is unclear to herself: "I knew her thoughts before she did; I saw them born; I had as an antagonist in her heart only her fear of the death of her children." But the imminence of material danger is enough to make her forget her remorse, and this simple provincial then finds in his innocently cynical ladylove coolheadedness, courage, and feminine wiles which must have delighted Stendhal. During her separation from Julien, what she calls her "remorse" is only Julien's absence. To die at his hand, after his wound, would be for her "the acme of blisses." And when she proclaims to her lover that she feels for him what she should feel only for God—a mixture of respect, love, and obedience—she is echoing the words of Métilde, related in the *Promenades in Rome*. In this respect, Mme. de Rênal symbolizes Métilde, as Stendhal's worshipful mind re-created her. But the tender Métilde was also the haughly Métilde—and the first name of the woman who inspired *On Love* was reserved for the prideful Mlle. de la Mole.

These two heroines, who love him no less when they resist than when they abandon themselves, are among the most complete character studies in the French novel. Mathilde, in her pridefulness, seeks vainly to conquer her passion for this plebeian, and there enters into her love for him as much class hatred as physical and emotional attraction. Mlle. de la Mole represents cerebral love, with all its complicated psychology, as opposed to spontaneous love, which asks itself no questions: "Cerebral love undoubtedly contains more intelligence than real love, but it has only a few moments of enthusiasm; it is created solely by the power of thought." We know where the preferences of the author lie, because of the prison scenes— after Julien, void of all feeling and pursuing one fixed idea, has accomplished the homicidal act that he believes, through a kind of lucid hypnosis, has avenged him, but that ironically gives him back the love of Mme. de Rênal, tenderer than ever. However, although Stendhal relished the total devotion of Mme. de Rênal for Julien, he also savored in his imagination the voluptuousness of bending Mathilde's frenetic pride, which he had been able neither to move nor to conquer in real life. Thus, with Julien as his instrument, he carried off a double victory and created two immortal heroines, giving the occasional impression, in a book as taut as a bow string, that he was writing a novel about happiness. If Stendhal was ambitious, he was so only for love.

One could enlarge endlessly upon this incomparable book, and from other points of view—particularly that of its eminent worth as a social and historical document. Let us note, only, that this "chronicle of 1830" is swept along by the spirit of the "red," although the spirit of the "black" ought to prevail. Julien is much more than a déclassé. He is a man out of his time who longs for the Napoleonic epic. Because he had felt the black mane of the Davout Dragoons streaming to his shoulders during his late adolescence, Stendhal saw etched on his brain, as the years passed, the great vista of the Empire, stretching out before his imagination and assuming an almost mythological aspect. The power of his imagination coupled itself with a deceptive regret! Henceforth, the Napoleonic stamp was to mark his work indelibly, and it was under the sign of the "Red" that the great prelude of *The Charterhouse of Parma* would open in 1839. In *The Red and the Black*, however, Julien Sorel is much more the seeker after tenderness, at heart less parched for happiness than for the pangs and sufferings of love, like Stendhal, who crowned with a dream, at the will of his pen, the intoxicating resurrection of his memories.

8 · Novels and Short Stories (1820-39) * Souvenirs of Egotism (1832) * Lucien Leuwen (1834-35) * The Life of Henri Brulard (1835-36) * Memoires of a Tourist (1838) * A Voyage in the South of France (1838)

THE STENDHAL who authored the *Short Stories* was far from insignificant, but he had not the same scope as Stendhal the novelist. The author cheated a bit with the former genre; his short stories are not so much brief narratives as they are chapters from a novel. If the summary of the action is striking in "The Coffer and the Ghost" and "The Philter," the narrator intended, above all, to make several disconcerting characters psychologically plausible and to attain emotion by the most direct methods. He succeeded in this, thanks to that "spirit of analysis in action" which Paul Bourget has recognized in him. We cannot go into detail here concerning the *Novels and Short Stories*; we will deal with Stendhal the storyteller, in connection with his *Italian Chronicles*. In addition to the two stories referred to above, however, must be mentioned "The Rose and the Green," "Mina de Vangel," "Souvenirs of an Italian Gentleman," "The Jew," "The Knight of Saint-Ismier," "Philibert Lescale," and "Feder, or the Wealthy Husband."

The boredom that suddenly overcame the newly appointed Consul of Civitavecchia brought him back in spirit to the literary salons, to the Parisian friends whom he would see again only two or three times before his death—and he was desolated. Thus, in 1832, the *Souvenirs of Egotism* resurrected, for his private delectation, the last years of the Restoration. And was it his fault if, among these friends, there had been a few joyous rakes—whence the bracing liberty of certain anecdotes?

The book took an unexpected turn; it was rather like what the *Regrets* were to Du Bellay, or the *Sorrows* to Ovid. Neglected by his Parisian companions, Beyle became a prey to the demon of memory, abandoning himself in Civitavecchia to the delusion that he was hauting the Palais-Royal. But after two weeks of this his enthusiasm waned. He did not recoil at the most intimate confidences. The frankness of the book corroborated what the *Journal* and the *Correspondence* had already indicated and what *The Life of Henri Brulard* was to confirm: the prideful complexity of Stendhal's soul, ever anxious to conceal the timid core of his nature. His need to confide in order to find peace and to understand himself without any self-delusion drove him to an egotism quite different from that of Chateaubriand, whose "I" and "ego" exasperated him. This examination of his conscience revealed "the frailty of the animal" as well as his relentless idealism. How can one forget these pages, which resurrect the "tender, profoundly sad, phantom" of Métilde, whose image disposed him "to good, just, indulgent thoughts!"

Shortly after this, the consul Stendhal began drafting a new novel, *Lucien Leuwen*, whose subject brought him back again to France. The third part of this novel, none of which was actually written, was to have had Rome as its setting. Our own era has tended to place this novel on a level with *The Red and the Black* and *The Charterhouse*. It contains some of Stendhal's most exhaustive character analysis; Lucien Leuwen and Mme. de Chasteller are characters as intricate as those of his major novels. Nevertheless, there is a breach of importance between this work and the others. It might be somewhat redeemed by the fact that we have, in this case, a manuscript that permits a complete study of his novelistic technique; but the value of this cannot be reckoned.

Stendhal hesitated for some time over his choice of a title: *The Orange of Malta*, *The Telegraph*, *Leuwen*, *The Amaranth and the Black*, *The Woods of Prémol*, *The Green Huntsman* (in memory of Brunswick), *The Red and the White* ("red" for the young republican, Lucien, and "white" for the young royalist, de Chasteller). He finally chose *Lucien Leuwen*. Here again, the protagonist is no more than the author's double; but the genesis of this book is not as well known as that of his other novels, and its hazardous composition was subject to more fluctuations.

We are acquainted with Beyle's loving friendship for the "amiable Jules"—Mme. Jules Gaulthier, born Rougier de la Bergerie; she was a brilliant woman, witty, kind, and compassionate. In 1833 she had sent him the manuscript, soliciting his opinion, of a novel entitled *The Lieutenant*, whose protagonist was called Leuwen. Faithful to his principles, Stendhal replied with "absolutely no consideration for self-pride," and his criticisms shed some light on the rules he was accustomed to imposing upon himself:

At least fifty minor characters must be removed from each chapter. Never say: "Olivier's burning passion for Hélène." The poor novelist must try to create belief in this "burning passion," but must never name it. That is against discretion. . . . Read Marivaux's *Marianne* and Mérimée's 1572, as one might take a magic potion, in order to rid yourself of this provincial phoebus. When describing a man, a woman, or a place, always think about someone or something real.

Did he ever do anything else?

So it was that, intrigued by the idea, he took up the mishandled plot, which was about to occupy him for eighteen months. A new novel was on its way. From the manuscript which had been entrusted to him he retained the initial episode concerning a lieutenant in the Nancy garrison. Still, he had actually foreshadowed this character in his *Racine and Shakespeare:*

So it is that a young man to whom heaven has given a certain delicacy of soul, if fate makes him a second lieutenant and flings him into a barracks, into the society of certain women, believes in good faith, upon seeing the success of his companions and the manner of their pleasures, that he is insensitive to love. One day fate at last presents him with a simple, natural, honest woman, worthy of being loved, and he feels that he has a heart.

But Stendhal did not stop at describing the provincial life of an officer. His hero becomes secretary to a minister in Paris, and he had intended making him an embassy secretary in Rome before marrying him off to a woman who "revealed the pangs and delights of crystallization" to him.

This is, once again, an attempt to picture the birth of love—but with what happiness! Following the style he had set himself in *Armance* and *The Red and the Black*, he evoked, at the same time, the extremist circles of a provincial city and the intrigues that are woven about power. He had undoubtedly intended to use for the novel's third part his outline of 1832, *A Social Position*, which dealt with diplomatic circles in Rome. Such was the general theme to which all of his outlines led him; its variants bear upon the details. How many times did he change his mind along the way! It is regrettable that the author had not planned some ending that might have done justice to that of the *Charterhouse*. Five heavy manuscripts, drafted in two-hundred days, deluded him that the essentials were in place; and he did not wait until he had finished the whole thing to begin correcting it. This was a mistake. This constantly going back over the work caused him to revise whole chapters for phrasing and style and depleted his energy. On his return to Paris in October, 1836, he was absorbed by other interests; and undoubtedly, he could not very well write about Roman diplomatic circles while he was still a consul of Civitavecchia. *Lucien Leuwen* was therefore doomed to incompletion.

According to the manuscript, the plots often resemble simple retrospective résumés: "Having done a history, I do the plot as my heart dictates, otherwise the call of memory kills imagination (at least with me)." Whence the accumulation of a thousand notes in the margins of the earliest version of the text, all of them destined to be inserted in good time. In the introduction of his characters, he wanted to avoid any resemblance of his book to the *Memoires,* and he envied Fielding's ability in *Tom Jones* to describe the feelings and actions of several characters at the same time, while he had to content himself with only one at a time. He transformed the narrative into dialogue to enliven it. Once again, Métilde served as a model, this time for Mme. de Chasteller—so gentle, so muted—and he based Lucien's nature on his own. As for his cast of minor characters, they were the usual mixture of reality and imagination, adroitly handled. Mme. Grandet embodies several traits of Mme. de Saint-Aulaire; Lucien Leuwen's father is reminiscent of Di Fiore. Stendhal's scrupulous phrasing was intended to express "even the most intense flights of passion with reason"—"I copied the characters and events from nature, and I constantly *weakened* them," he admitted. He concerned himself with style only after he had made a thorough attempt to express the thought, whipping himself to action during a month's stay in Paris for final polishing of the work and last observations from the social standpoint.

The reading of *Lucien Leuwen* is like the ascension of a very gentle slope; it bears the dual stamp of youth and melancholy. Its protagonist, despite his dashing horse, has something of the feminine about him—recalling Clélia Conti's brother, or Octave de Malivert. The simple narrative unfolds like a tapestry. By means of delicate touches, the author steals in upon our sensibilities. And he can be recognized in so many characteristics! This transposition offers us the very image of the father of his dreams: an opulent father, a banker by profession, indulgent and good natured, whose most earnest desire is to put an agreeable and flattering mistress into the arms of his timid and sentimental son! What amiable dialogue there is between this aging and fascinating man who knows how to live and the son who loves him, possibly envies him, but cannot imitate him, for he has discovered a mysterious domain which the author of his days does not suspect! As for Mme. de Chasteller, shy and exquisite, given to intermittent audacities but completely hemmed in by scruples and timidities, she reminds one of the Métilde whom Stendhal once likened to "an orange tree." In this book, more than in *The Red and the Black*, which is so tightly constructed, Beyle gently draws us away from the world of reality, like a poet, before that final and total uprooting which was *The Charterhouse of Parma*.

The Life of Henri Brulard, which deals with the author's life from his childhood through his adolescence, is his most outstanding biographical narrative. This is the point at which Stendhal readers divide themselves into three major categories: the devotees of *The Red and the Black* (the "*Rougistes*"), those of *The Charterhouse* (the *"Chartreusistes"*), and those who would trade his entire work for these pages which plunge so boldly and directly into the "remembrance of things past." Must these memoires, destined for a problematical posterity, have been written, as Paul Hazard suggests, to convey "the dazzling image of his ego?" His aim would seem to us to have been more modest: "This is new to me, to discuss people about whose turn of mind, type of education, prejudices, and religion one is totally ignorant! What an incentive to be truthful and simply truthful, that is the only thing one can cling to." It was his concern to know the truth about himself, once and for all, which prompted him to take up his pen. It was a matter of recalling a period much more remote for him than that of the *Souvenirs of Egotism;* the effort was more arduous. The writer's visual memory being exceptional, it was often through the accuracy of a sketch that a recalcitrant image would be wrested from his memory. We are faced with the *Memoires of Dominique,* whose tone is the exact antithesis of Rousseau's *Confessions.* Stendhal had had the idea for it in 1832; he made his decision to go ahead with it on November 23, 1835, at San-Pietro in Montorio, as he faced the sun-drenched panorama of Rome against the ashen background of the Alban Mountains. He pursued its composition until March 17, 1836, going as far as his first Milanese sojourn. But then the news of his leave reached him and his thoughts flew to France. Therefore he did not complete *Henri Brulard,* any more than he had *Lucien Leuwen.* Those French years, however, yielded us in compensation *The Charterhouse of Parma.*

Why this pseudonym "Brulard"? Stendhal must have taken the name from an antecedent of his on the Gagnon side, a notary of Bédarrides—a very strong-willed man, critical and rude—who was a first cousin of Dr. Gagnon. Preventing himself from excising any part of the first draft, so that he would not "lie out of vanity," Stendhal left behind a rough copy almost totally without corrections. There is a seething passion in this retrospective quest. Never before had the author attained such a degree of honesty with himself or with the reader of a doubtful posterity. He re-created a very vital and indelible image of the child and the adolescent he had been. Is it the best commentary on his work? One can see his awakening sensibility, the formation of his thought; and he does not flatter himself—quite the reverse, he makes himself appear worse than he was.

Neither Grenoble and its inhabitants nor his paternal family are spared—and not without an occasional injustice. Stendhal was slow to forgive Grenoble. At last we can understand this proud soul, disappointed in his thirst for affection and protecting himself against being hurt. He would bequeath this to his heroes, in love with glory, in love with love, just as he had been at sixteen. He was romantic, certainly, but without rebelliousness, without any vanity in the face of distressing confessions which might have been costly to someone else. There is no altering of events to put himself in a better light. He does not plead *pro domo*. These pages, of very mild historic interest, offer a great deal of human interest. Everything converges on a being destined to become the surest psychologist of his age. Absorbed in the task of resurrecting a personal past, he sometimes had the feeling that he was "making discoveries about someone else." But can he be taken unreservedly as a guide? Paul Arbelet has had to rectify more than one of his assertions. This is because it happened that Stendhal had no head for facts and dates; his emotional memory, however, preserved forever the imprint of anything he had experienced. The adult's rancors sometimes take the place of the vision of the child and the portrait suffers from this. It must again be emphasized that Chérubin Beyle and the Abbé Raillane were not, historically, the sinister characters Stendhal depicted. But does historical truth really matter in such a subjective case? Isn't it, rather, the psychological reaction of the child to these people that really matters? And the truth of this reaction was precisely as *The Life of Henri Brulard* expressed it. His analysis of the child Henri Beyle's delight over the young women of Les Echelles in the splendor of their attire further confirms the author's instinctive reticence in the face of all description:

Here, already, I lacked the phrases. Where to find words to express that perfect happiness, relished with delight, without satiation, by a soul sensitive to the point of prostration and madness? I don't know if I shall not renounce this effort. It seems to me that I could not depict this ravishing happiness—pure, fresh, sublime—except by enumerating the evils and boredom which were suddenly completely absent. Now this is certainly a sad way to depict happiness.

It is regrettable that Stendhal did not go further with these confessions, as they constitute a priceless document and they have served many a time as a countercheck on his work. Jean Prévost made an interesting observation concerning the internal rhythm of this book: "In it the present alternates with the past, impression with fact, mistrustful effort with abandonment to dreams." Beyle, a true precursor of the moderns, has given more importance to memory than to chronology in his analyses. His attempt at explication, on the other hand, never fails to encroach upon the logical order of events, so that the mature man appears in these pages to be dedicated to the child and the adolescent. As one recaptured detail leads to another, little by little a blurred scrap of existence is revived. Chance definitely plays its part, but Stendhal knew how to choose and communicate a true and living impression, working back from the qualitative memory of a feeling to the concrete scene which gave birth to it; but without always being able to reconstruct it, despite the precision of his notes. "I have no great confidence, at heart," he wrote, "in the opinions with which I have filled the last 536 pages. Only the feelings are really true; except, in order to arrive at the truth, one must put four sharps to my expressions. I render them with the coldness and the jaded emotions of a forty-year-old man." He had already referred, in his treatise *On Love*, to this same inhibition.

Stendhal led this inquest into his past scrupulously, and although it happened that the author's excessive mental effort modified his original feeling, this was over his dead body. "What a marvelous document this book is," wrote Emile Henriot,

In which so many riches abound, in all their glory! It is completely Stendhal, in sum and in promise, with his sharp particuarity, because, although it was written thirty years after the period he is relating, it is the impression and sensation of the moment which he depicts. Moment and memory! The keenness of the latter has made the former live again and has captured it forever.

Certainly Stendhal, who had roamed so much throughout
Italy and Europe and who was enraptured by every new journey,
owed it to himself to discover France. And in 1838 his opportunity arrived. Traveling was fashionable then, and the French
romantics were exploring their own country. Having decided
to give *Promenades in Rome* a French counterpart, he started
on his way. He intended to present himself to the reader of this
book not as a man of letters but as a traveling iron salesman, a
cousin of that salesman of cotton bonnets who had once made
such a droll entry into Mme. Ancelot's salon.[1] His dilettantism
had the most noble requirements in his *Advice to Gay Gad-
abouts Going to Italy*.[2] The *Memoires of a Tourist* would permit
him to verify the accuracy of the picture drawn in *Lucien
Leuwen* of Louis Phillipe's France; and he hoped, in this way,
to fill his purse.

He began to collect material, never hesitating to press his
friends—occasionally the authors of learned works—into his
service: Dr. Edwards instructed him on ethnography; Mérimée,
who accompanied him on several journeys, on religious architecture. Just as in his early books, however, he knew how to
mix original observations with borrowed material. Arcisse de
Caumont's *History of Gothic Art* (used to Italian churches,
Stendhal found the French ones gloomy), Millin's[3] *Voyage
in the South of France*—these were among his major sources.
Crozet furnished him the episode concerning Napoleon at
Laffrey. But in certain other areas, how completely he drew
from his own imagination!

Basically never particularly concerned with historical truth,
Stendhal wrote the book in a simple and personal style. It is
mordant and concise, if not inspiring, and makes enjoyable
reading, although one wearies, at length, of this fictitious traveling salesman. Despite certain preconceptions and the knowledge
of a neophyte given to certain prejudices, the author presents a
fairly accurate picture of the provinces through which he is
passing. He piques the curiosity, enters wittily upon the scene,

[1] Tr. note: The author refers to an incident in Stendhal's Parisian
life. He arrived at Mme. Ancelot's disguised as a cotton merchant and
engaged in a wild improvisation, until finally he was recognized.

[2] Tr. note: This was a humorous letter written to his sister Pauline,
who was about to go to Italy with a friend.

[3] Aubin Louis Millin de Grandmaison (1759–1818).

and—recalling certain truths which he had once unleashed against the French in English periodicals—he pushes frankness to limits against which his contemporaries protested. "To please simpletons by proving to them for seven hundred pages that they are simpletons is impossible," he said to Di Fiore, concerning the book. It is stimulating to see such an alert mind judging men and events, even admitting that it might be mistaken. As he had already done with Italy, he turned his attention most particularly to social habits, although with less inward pleasure. The tiniest, unexpected nuance in this realm fascinated him.

What were his predilections? From the very beginning he had praised the charm of "the ascent behind Poligny," and we are already acquainted with his wholehearted admiration for the Alps. But Stendhal had come to speak with a certain disdain of the whole of that country "which the idiots call 'la belle France.'" Italy had left too great a mark on him; he could not appreciate the subtle grace of a Touraine landscape in the Loire Valley. His bitter criticisms of Lyon and the Lyonnaise temperament left him as he admired the view from the height of the Fourvière cathedral; but he felt himself really alive only when he left Valence. Twenty years later Mistral was to place the doorway to "the land of love" at the *Pont Saint-Esprit*. Stendhal sensibly placed this boundary further north.

His outmoded anticlericalism provokes a smile. One might well take exception to it, inoffensive though it may be, for is this a traveling salesman who is speaking? The critic of that time might reproach him for his political ideas and for his Anglomania, which changed the cannotation of the word "tourist" in France; but he was grateful to him for having written "sometimes like Stern and at other times like Montesquieu" and could even divine the author's delicate sensibility through the paradoxes in which the book abounds (and which are occasionally reminiscent of Diderot). Many of the journals, however, did not even deign to mention this topical work, which ranks with *Rome, Naples and Florence* and *Promenades in Rome*.

The *Voyage in the South of France*, a posthumous work edited from Stendhal's notes, revives the title of Millin's book, with which Stendhal was thoroughly acquainted. It constitutes a complement to his *Memoires of a Tourist* and employs much the same approach. The writer was undoubtedly diverted from the work's completion by his sudden compelling urge to write *The Charterhouse of Parma*. (For so many pages devoted to France had given him a thirst for the Italy from which he was separated and plunged him anew into imagining and remembering it.) His trip through the south of France took him 135 days, and it took him to Bordeaux, Toulouse, Marseilles, Pau, Toulon, Grasse, Cannes, Valence; and he returned by way of Switzerland, Germany, and the Low Countries. He might have envisioned noting his impressions from the banks of the Rhine, even though he did not care as much for the northern countries.

This companion to the *Journal*, filled with freshness and artless joy, does not disdain information about the material aspects of the journey. The author's *Promenades* had already dealt with these concerns. After two years in Paris the mournful melancholy of his Civitavecchia days seemed dissipated; never had he felt younger in spirit, more spontaneous, more ready to enjoy everything, finding in these happy emotions something of that eternal quest he was pursuing; but suddenly a tender reverie crept into his confidences, betraying a vulnerable Stendhal:

In earlier days when I was alone I used to dream of love affairs which were tender and romantic, rather than flattering to my self esteem. Since then I have become less foolish . . . This fine knowledge has perhaps made me less gauche, although I shall probably always be very much so, but it has robbed me of my charming flights of fancy. . . . I find myself fallen into an epoch of transition, that is to say, of mediocrity . . . I would almost like to become a dupe and a simpleton again in the facts of life, and to take up those charming and terribly absurd fancies which made me do so many foolish things. . . . Since I have learned a little about what to do in this war, I often disdain entering the field of battle . . . As long as one is able to love a perfectly stupid or supremely comic woman for her delightful wit, for her perfect naïveté, as long as one is able to have a completely ridiculous illusion, one is able to love. And happiness is loving much more than being loved.

Thus did the aging Stendhal, in a simple travelogue, subtly recapture the tone of his treatise *On Love*.

9 · The Charterhouse of Parma (1839)

THIS MAGICAL BOOK, in which the complexities of life itself are expressed by highly individual characters couched in a brilliant narrative and bathed in unparalleled poetry, introduces us more than any other of his works into the world of Stendhalian lyricism. Although Stendhal made only a few fleeting trips to Parma, in 1811, 1814, and 1824, the unforgettable sight of the Correggios at that time inspired in him the desire to create "Correggian" characters. Although he had had an idea for the novel since 1832, he accomplished its actual writing in only 52 days, toward the end of his Parisian stay. And no book better reveals the psychological arsenal he had accumulated during the forty years he had spent in the pursuit of happiness! Turning once again to his spiritual homeland, Stendhal transferred to it one last time the imaginary novel of his life, by presenting a vast chronicle of the Italy of the Holy Alliance. But it is the internal quality of the book which is especially moving, because of its freshness and spontaneity.

The apparent suddenness of his inspiration had been made possible by a slow maturation:

Charming women . . . how superior you are to the de Staëls of Paris and England, who always recite a single lesson and consider themselves brilliant! If I could bring back from my Italian journey nothing but the acquaintance of these two friends, I should be well paid. I am at last assured, then, that such souls exist in the world!

Such was the intoxicating discovery Stendhal made one evening in 1818 in a Milanese salon, in the presence of Métilde Dembowski and Maddalena Bignami. Knowing this passage and the lines that preceded it—unpublished until recently—is it mere coincidence that the image of Maddalena Bignami and the story of her unhappy loves should spontaneously evoke in us the fleeting silhouette, the tortured soul, of Clélia Conti? It extends even to the maternal sorrow of the one they used to call Lenina, inconsolable over the death of her child—long before Clémentine Curial wept for her Bathilde. This incident furnished the writer a touch of sentiment that perfected his heroine's poignant sweetness and grace, and that makes the following admission, on May 24, 1840, not so surprising:

I make no outline at all. The page I am writing gives me an idea for the following one; this is the way the *Charterhouse* was created. I used to think about the death of Sandrino, and that alone caused me to undertake the novel. I saw much later the terrible difficulty of overcoming: 1) a hero who is in love only in the second volume; 2) two heroines. . . .

With Stendhal the plot is secondary; it is in the book's masterly network of details that its vehement passions reveal themselves. It fairly teems with facts, sensations, emotions, intrigues, biting observations on war and politics, a flowing and impassioned imagination—with flights of tenderness here and there, like those subtle vistas of Lake Como and the Po Valley. The factual mind can perceive that the author takes up too much time with minor characters and divergent circumstances, recalling the "cloak-and-sword" novel or re-creating the mood of the *roman noir*, or even the great *opéra-bouffe* scenarios. But the mind that possesses even a touch of fancy permits itself to revel in his intoxicating poetry, which never strains the style, and in that gift of life which gives his characters a reality their real-life counterparts might well have envied them.

After a painting of Napoleonic Italy, to the delight of some and the furtive resistance of others, Stendhal chose for his hero a young and handsome Italian, specimen from a race born for conquest and politics—Fabrizio del Dongo. Fabrizio is really the natural son of the Marquisa del Dongo and Lieutenant Robert, a young French officer who was with Bonaparte's army in Milan, but this rather ironic innuendo is so subtle that it is often missed. Fabrizio runs away at seventeen to fight with Napoleon's army. He witnesses the battle of Waterloo, hardly noticing that it is a surrender. Returning home, he becomes a protegé of his young aunt, la Sanseverina, a woman of charm, wit, and energy, who urges him to join the priesthood to make his fortune. He consents and proceeds to lead a thinly disguised life of pleasure while he continues to seek ecclesiastical honors. Involved in intrigues of politics and love, he is arrested and confined in the citadel of Parma, where his exalted soul becomes infatuated with Clélia Conti, the daughter of his captor. From this point on, the novel centers about the prodigious passion of the two young lovers; but without neglecting the passion, of another variety but just as rich, of la Sanseverina for her handsome nephew and of Count Mosca for la Sanseverina. It is Fabrizio, however, who is at the center of this ardent life. With the combined efforts of the two women who love him, Clélia and la Sanseverina, Fabrizio manages to escape. After many a hardship, he attains the highest ecclesiastical offices and returns to the court of Parma, where he finds himself still in love with Clélia, who has married against her will. He sires a son by her, but the son dies. Shortly after this Clélia dies and Fabrizio retires to a charterhouse in which he himself finally expires. This last, simple circumstance furnished Stendhal with the book's title. This work is, at the same time, an adventure novel, a romantic novel, and a historical novel (for even a character as apparently caricatural as the poet Ferrante Palla had his place in the Italy of 1820); but it is, above all, a psychological novel and a muted lyric novel in which the most antithetical and most transparent transposed autobiography is offered to the "fancier of souls."

Again taking up the theme of *The Red and the Black*, the book brings us back into Italy after Napoleon's fall. The same drama begins again—that of a youth thirsting for military glory, forced to accommodate himself to the Italy of the Holy Alliance. Stendhal was not the only one to speak out on this subject. In Alfred de Musset's *Confession of a Child of the Century* the same desolate note resounds: "When the children used to speak of glory, one said to them: 'Become priests!'—when they spoke of ambition: 'Become priests!'—of hope, of

love, of power, of life: 'Become priests!' " Such is the counsel
that follows Fabrizio after his escapade at Waterloo. His innate
amoralism accommodates itself to his religious faith, and he is
forced to become a hypocrite in order to gain his material ends.
And yet, what indifference Fabrizio displays toward his own
ambition!—and not only because others are so preoccupied by it.
It is simply that his real life unfolds outside of the world of
reality. So it is that prison serves once again as an occasion for
ideal deliverance.

This novel is less the work of an observer than the spontaneous creation of a poet; its sources are nevertheless obvious.
Its prison scenes were inspired by the atmosphere of the Spielberg, widely diffused by Silvio Pellico and Alexandre Andryane.
However, strange as it may seem, it was the sixteenth-century
Italian, above all, who constituted the essential basis of the
narrative. Since 1834, Stendhal had been living in the atmosphere of "Roman short stories" and "Neapolitan anecdotes,"
from which he would later draw his *Italian Chronicles*. Moreover, he believed in the veracity of these written accounts, which
revealed matters about which official historians did not breathe
a word. Their tone of scandalous gossip and antipapal propaganda appealed to him. He was particularly fascinated by a
text entitled *Origine dellè grandezze della famiglia Farnese*,[1]
upon which he had considered basing a short novel, in 1838.
The characters that appeared in it had been familiar to him
since his *Promenades in Rome*. In this narrative the beautiful
Vannozza Farnese, aided by her love, Roderigo Borgia, creates
the fortune of her handsome nephew, Alessandro. Alessandro
is imprisoned in the Castel Sant' Angelo for abducting a young
Roman girl. He escapes, is appointed Cardinal despite his im-
moderate life, and eventually becomes Pope Paul II, after the
death of the mistress who has borne his children, a young
noblewoman named Cleria. Cleria would be called Clélia;
Alessandro would become Fabrizio; Vannozza, la Sanseverina;
and Roderigo, Count Mosca. The young woman whom Alessandro kidnapped would become a little actress; and the Castel
Sant' Angelo, moved to Parma, would be embodied in the
illusory Farnese Tower. *The Charterhouse of Parma* might there-

1 Origin of the Greatness of the Farnese Family.

fore be considered the first and longest of Stendhal's *Italian Chronicles*.

Stendhal was not afraid to transfer to the early nineteenth century "several habits and customs by which one sought happiness in Italy, around 1515." A breath of liberty moves through the book's second part, giving it a contemporary quality. Stendhal thought he detected in this new spirit the energy which had given such tone to the republics of the Middle Ages; beyond the petty, suspicious, inquisitorial life, with its complicated etiquette of reactionary principalities, he divined that desire for unity which was inspiring the carbonarists. Fabrizio's adventures, his murder of Giletti, his imprisonment, and his escape, reproduce the very circumstances of Cardinal Farnese's life. A great reader of Benvenuto Cellini, Stendhal was particularly fond of the story of Cellini's escape from the Castel Sant' Angelo, and his account of Fabrizio's second imprisonment retains many of its details. The Roman manuscripts on which he was nourishing himself at that time had further revealed to him the vital statistics of one Duchess Barba San Severino, who, after conspiring against Ranuccio the First, Prince of Parma and a Farnese, was beheaded with an axe in 1618. He gave her name to the beautiful Vannozze. Count Mosca had for his model—without forgetting what Stendhal contributed of his own personality—Metternich, Sarau, and most particularly the French minister, Du Tillot, servant of the Bourbons of Parma and friend to Marquisa Malaspina, the great mistress of the palace.

Autobiographical memories abound. The Milan of 1796, suggested with winning lightness, is the one Henri Beyle had known in 1800. So delicately does he evoke the shores of Lake Como or Lake Maggiore, so well do they answer the feelings of his characters, the daily tragedy which rouses them against each other—the party of Napoleon against the party of Austria —that we sometimes discover here in advance the atmosphere of Antonio Fogazzaro's *Little World of the Past*, transposed with a modestly epicurean tone. Like Julien, like Beyle himself, Fabrizio instinctively despises his father—not knowing that this is not his real father. On the other hand, the writer conveys, through Abbé Blanès, the beloved qualities of the good

Dr. Gagnon, who likewise used to operate his telescope on the terrace—where "Stendhal's climbing vine" can still be seen. He was doubtless thinking of Angela Pietragrua when he created la Sanseverina, who is first named Angela Pietranera: Angelina, Gina. Clélia Conti recalls Métilde, and also, if a fascinating theory of Paul Arbelet's is to be believed, the young Eugénie de Montijo, at least in her first appearance in the novel—a discrete homage to her youthful loveliness! The Fiscal Rassi contains more than one of the heinous Lysimaque Tavernier's qualities. As for la Raversi, she appears to be a woman named Traversi, born Francesca Milesi, Métilde's first cousin and confidant, whom Stendhal considered to be his sworn enemy. One recognizes everywhere the writer's faithfulness to his own method of always basing his imaginary characters on reality.

Stendhal himself appears first of all within the flattering image of Fabrizio; he even divided himself, appearing also under the guise of the humane but disenchanted Count Mosca. If *The Red and the Black* is, in its primary conception, the French novel about ambition and energy, *The Charterhouse of Parma* is most of all a novel about the pursuit of love on Italian soil. Julien is an intellectual, first of all, depending upon himself alone for his luck. Fabrizio, a southern type, is especially endowed with a sensual imagination; although struggle is also a condition of felicity with him, he is lucky enough to be able to disassociate himself from his career. Temporal success crowns this novel of pleasure and satisfied ambition. What bewitching charm there is in this Fabrizio, trailing feminine hearts behind him, from the little Flemish innkeepers who coddle him after Waterloo to the beautiful Annetta Marini, the captivating Gina, his docile mistresses in Naples and Bologna—barely glimpsed—la Fausta, his young chambermaid Marietta, the beautiful penitents of Parma, and finally Clélia Conti—his one great love!

Fabrizio del Dongo enters into life through an act of enthusiasm and courage. He is seventeen when he overtakes Napoleon, just as Henri Beyle was at the fort of Bard. And although Stendhal was not at Waterloo, he transmitted to his hero his own impressions of that baptism by fire when he crossed the Alps—

his lack of experience, his naïveté, his brutal initial contact with the army, with danger, and with death; and with the help of his later experience—the Austrian campaign, the retreat from Russia and from Bautzen—he wrote about the war in these pages, to the admiring despair of Balzac and the delight of Tolstoi, in order to entertain his young friends from Spain, Paca and Eugénie de Montijo. This hors d'oeuvre chapter could serve as a standard for descriptions of war, as false as the pictures of history with which many a closet writer has burdened us. For Stendhal presents 'Waterloo as seen by a raw recruit, a patch of ground filled with truth, accuracy, incoherence, nameless horror, in a total event of whose import the young man has no idea, but which dominates the narrative without his realizing it, as tiny realistic details gradually clarify the situation. The continuous boom of the cannon; the barrages of grapeshot; the "brute" that pushes ahead, making the soil and branches fly; the noise, which upsets him; the fear—and the fear of being afraid; the joy at being under fire, soon followed by the suspicion that this may not be the real battle; there are so many detailed impressions captured from life that they must have been deeply felt—with as much involvement as Marie Louise—to have been noted with so much precision and so little exaggeration. Like Stendhal, Fabrizio "was one of those hearts of too delicate a fabric, which requires the kindness of those around it." The sympathy of an unforgettable canteen keeper, the joy over having seen Marshall Ney, at having killed one of the enemy during the retreat—is all quite exciting to him.

The defeat at Waterloo having put an end to his adventure, Fabrizio goes back to Lombardy. His beautiful and ardent aunt is so taken with his youthful *gloire* that if Fabrizio were to speak of love she would fall in love with him. His feeling for her, however, is merely that of affectionate gratitude, and "she would have been horrified at herself had she sought from this almost filial affection any other emotion." She urges Fabrizio to take up an ecclesiastical career, for military life after 1815 would be for him "the life of a squirrel in a revolving cage." She does not realize that this is also a way of keeping him for herself, or at least of preventing him from belonging to anyone else. After her husband's death in the war she marries, for a second time, a senile duke who assures her social position without imposing his presence on her, and she becomes the unimpassioned mistress of Count Mosca, First Minister to the Prince of Parma, to whom she is faithful. But although she displays the utmost frankness with him about everything, she never discusses Fabrizio without carefully choosing her words. Meanwhile, although Fabrizio continues his pursuit of love in numerous affairs, he finds only pleasure. He returns to Parma, where his fortune awaits him, after four years at the seminary in Naples. Fabrizio differs from Julien in that his sensual appetites and his intelligence have in no way corrupted his faith. This novel, in which several men of the church appear, is judged by Pierre Martino to be "hopelessly secular and pagan." Nevertheless, the author's agnosticism does not prevent him from disposing on his hero—whose sensibility is never at odds with reality—a character that is both egotistical and believing. Certainly no metaphysical abyss yawns before the future Archbishop of Parma! And yet Beyle's profligacy was not profound impiety, and the novelist proved himself esthetically susceptible to Catholicism. He sensed the psychological enrichment which his characters might, by chance, draw from the religion. And although Stendhal never prayed, it happens that his heroes do. He sensitively rendered the profound piety, tinged with a certain Italian superstition, of Clélia Conti, whose love and tortured modesty would possess the religious and mystic taste to a fault. Fabrizio could not have loved an emancipated woman so much.

From this day forward Fabrizio is another man in the eyes of la Sanseverina. Count Mosca, whose jealousy is quickly aroused, comes within a hair of avenging himself. But he perceives that Gina has not yet given a name to the emotion she feels. Fabrizio, more lucid, is extremely uneasy in the horrible role of "the man who does not want to guess." Should he pretend a grand passion? a base love? Why taint so sweet a friendship with the one person in the world for whom he has the greatest affection: "She will think I lack love for her, whereas it is love that is lacking in me." Fabrizio's heart is empty. Stendhal has admirably depicted the ardent and painful melancholy of expectant youth. He is in love with love, and it is in prison that he will see his dream fulfilled.

It would have been worthwhile to study the slow, insinuating commanding "crystallization" of the tender and noble Clélia Conti, passionate in its very purity; her pity for Fabrizio, which is metamorphosed into a limitless love; her compassion for la Sanseverina, which is soon tinged with jealousy and transformed into hatred. It suited the author, instead, to follow the same "crystallization" in the more clearsighted Fabrizio, who sometimes recalls Julien Sorel; but whose sincerity and intensity prompt him to cry out for his ideal life from the heights of his tower, like Julien, while efforts are being made on every side to free him: "I do not want to save myself. I want to die here!" But one would have to stop la Sanseverina, who, in her passion, sacrifices everything for him: Count Mosca, whom she is beginning to scorn and from whom she is separated; and her position at the court of Parma. She reveals that she loves Fabrizio instinctively for the simple courage which he is totally unaware of, for his nobility of soul, and for his exquisite grace. "Finally, if he is happy I can be happy," she declares to the count. Henceforth, any talk of love wearies her: "Remember, I am sixty years old, the young woman within me is dead . . . I am no longer able to love." Fearing that Fabrizio may be poisoned, she can think of nothing but effectuating his escape. And when, upon Clélia's entreaties, Fabrizio consents to attempt the feat— having thought about la Sanseverina in his cell as little as had Julien Sorel about Mathilde under analogous circumstances— the headstrong, spiteful, witty, amorous Gina painfully discovers that she has saved an ingrate. In place of the frivolous and dissolute Fabrizio, who, although he did not love her as she might have wished, might possibly have loved her some day, she finds a heart forever fixed. He proves himself to be kind, concerned, and grateful; but this is obviously due to his goodness, his eagerness to show his gratitude! She has no more than second place in his affections. Never does he speak of Clélia, and yet she suspects that he is always thinking of her. Worse than this, her rival, not content with stealing Fabrizio's love, has also stolen from her the joy of having set him free, as she would certainly never have succeeded in this had it not been for the help of Clélia Conti.

This is the core of the novel—the rivalry between la Sanseverina and Clélia Conti over Fabrizio, the central figure of the book, who lives like Julien Sorel, caught between the love of two women. Stendhal has tastefully depicted the love of la Sanseverina, who dares not awaken herself to its realization, who pours out in mad devotion a sensuality that is never dissipated by embraces, discouraged as soon as she becomes aware of it—discouraged and disappointed—and also a trifle humiliated. Hers is a slightly maternal love, unlike the tenderly feminine love of Mme. de Rênal; rather if one likes, similar to the love of an older Mathilde de la Mole, under the same circumstances, with as much wit and energy, more amiability, and less prejudice and aristocratic coldness.

Fabrizio himself is a young Stendhal with an Italian soul, with his feelings of honor, his freshness of heart, his lusts, his parched young egotism, and his tendency to change his mind over the merest trifle, to gamble his life in an immense need for action, absorbing everything completely into his personality: characters, milieus, and setting. Count Mosca, on the other hand, infinitely more attractive than M. de la Mole—so human, so tenderly in love with la Sanseverina, who is moreover indebted to him, so alone despite everything—is a still older and disappointed Stendhal. He escapes the ridicule that might so easily have been attached to his person because of his gallant kindness and his cleverness as a diplomat. Within him, as has been said, "Beyle deposited, with his artist's curiosity, the residue of his knowledge and his disappointments—the supreme irony of a too ambitious ego which 'set its nets too high.'" Last of all, the book contains an attitude, with Fabrizio as its instrument, which permitted Stendhal to imagine himself again in the role of preacher, and this is no recantation. He had not had occasion to use it in *The Red and the Black*, or rather, Julien's argument took its place. But the Berthet case had afforded a pathetic element that he could not ignore: "I would have made a good priest," wrote the accused; "I feel particularly that I might skillfully have stirred the power of human passions."

Fabrizio returns voluntarily to prison to await the review of his case. Clélia, who has succumbed to him at a moment when she feared he had been poisoned, is forced by her father to marry the Marquis Crescenzi. La Sanseverina is overjoyed at this, although she believes she no longer wants Fabrizio's love. After his release from prison, Fabrizio becomes coadjutor of the Archbishop of Parma, whom he is to succeed, but he remains indifferent to such honors. He imposes long retreats upon himself; his face, which once breathed voluptuousness and gaiety, becomes the face of an anchorite. The court of Parma brings him back into the presence of the married Clélia and—with the help of music—all of his fine resolutions vanish. He can no longer think of anything but winning her back. It is then that he begins to preach, in the hope that Clélia will one day come to hear him; and he proves to be a great mover of human souls. After some time, at the beginning of a sermon, Fabrizio suddenly notices Clélia in the front row of his congregation and he is unable to go on preaching. He reads instead a short written prayer—meant for her—which does the job of Galahad and re-unites the lovers, by virtue of the Stendhalian principle that a woman really belongs to the man who loves her most. Clélia, who has promised in her prayers to the Virgin that she will never see him again, consents to receive him, but only at night in darkness. It is Psyche, this time, who refuses to look at love! The lovers produce a child, Sandrino, for whom Fabrizio feels the same love as had Julien for his future son; he wants to tear the child away from the Marquis Crescenzi. But the infant dies; Clélia, feeling that she has been dealt a just punishment, survives her son by only a few months. Fabrizio retires to the charterhouse of Parma, in which he dies. La Sanseverina, now the Countess Mosca, having indulged the fancies of the new Prince to save Fabrizio, despite her revulsion—the final sacrifice and last proof of her love—barely survives Fabrizio.

Considered in relation to Stendhal, *The Red and the Black* seems to be a kind of imaginary revenge on life. This appraisal is even more true, if possible, of *The Charterhouse of Parma*. Stendhal had always dreamed of a love capable of equal mutual devotion and of a life filled with strong and delicate emotions.

Despite their marked personalities, his heroines are all sisters under the skin by virtue of that power of absolute devotion, ignoring all the rules of society, which he would have given anything to find in even one woman. They are the creation of his immovable desire. Unmindful of the inroads of age and the disgraces nature had inflicted upon him, Stendhal presented himself—after an interval of forty years—in the guise of a young and vigorous hunter in the teeth of the wolves, proud of his strength and his young hunger—this was Julien and, even more so, Fabrizio. It was a dream of energy, a dream of pleasure, of happiness, of egotism, but one that leaves an impalpable melancholy in the heart.

Besides being a psychological novel and a lyric novel which particularly strikes one's attention, *The Charterhouse* is also a historical and social novel. Ever since the time of carbonarism, Stendhal had recognized the Italians as having virtues worthy of the Renaissance; and, in order to depict Italy after 1815, he had moved from Modena to Parma the finicky and reactionary politics of Duke Ferdinand IV which the *Promenades in Rome* had already denounced.

Faithful to his own method, Stendhal constructed a universe around the impulse he received from his heart, his experience, and his imagination. Bloody episodes follow Correggian pages. Originally part of a brief account dedicated to the youth of Alessandro Farnese, the idea of making this work into a novel began to take shape when, on April 3, 1838, he considered transferring events which were over three hundred years old to the nineteenth century. Occupied at around this time with his *Life of Napoleon*, he took it into his head to recount the Battle of Waterloo for his young Spanish friends. In a flash of inspiration, the possibility of tying these three disparate events to a single narrative occurred to him. Two months later, he began the task, writing it in one burst—writing the Waterloo episode a second time when the first version of it was mislaid by his publisher. This brilliant improvisation was his revenge on the effort and frustration of his early books. Into this imaginative work he put the most delicate and tender memories, the most poignant regrets, the hopes that had so often been disappointed in life— satisfied, this time, in an unreal life! Truth and poetry! What book, as much as this one, deserves to be considered under this double transfigured aspect? How else could Stendhal have achieved such a rapture of total passion, such an absolute worship, surpassing morality and law, as Fabrizio found in these two women—so unlike each other, and yet so similar in their fervor and devotion? What better idea could he have left to posterity of his thirst—less a carnal thirst than a thirst of the soul—which could have been quenched, as if by magic, by one simple gesture, or the heartfelt word of one being: "Enter here, friend of my heart." [2]

The chance buffeting of his heroes by the most unforeseen circumstances, the continual ricocheting of the plot, is far from weakening the book's characters. On the contrary, they are always faithful to their own law, assuring the unity of this disparate, and yet marvelously unified novel. Julien Sorel is almost always, with the exception of rare blessed moments, on the alert with men and events. Fabrizio, on the other hand, is abandoned to his urges and passions, as well as to his caprices. His Italian fire is coupled with an adventurous spirit inherited from a soldier of the Empire. While *The Red and the Black* is a novel of revolt, *The Charterhouse of Parma* is a peaceful book. A melodic resonance emanates from it, reflecting the tranquillity of the scenery, heralded by an epigraph from Ariosto: "There was a time when beautiful landscapes, through their sweetness, spurred me to write." And if the author placed his charterhouse in Parma, this was in homage to the painting of Correggio; to the perfect grace of the *"amorini"* of Casin San-Paolo; [3] to the frescoes of the cupulas; to the Assumption of the Virgin, turning gold in the warm colors of the sunset; and, above all, to those paintings of unforgettable delicacy, so thrilling in form, so naunced in color, so vibrant, which are always a wonder in their Farnesian setting. The whole of Stendhal's emotional life had led him to his two heroines—la Sanseverina and Clélia Conti, voluptuous and idealized figures—while he imagined, through Fabrizio, the life he would love to have led, and while he poured

2 Tr. note: Clélia's words to Fabrizio.
3 Tr. note: A *palazzo* in Milan, where Beyle had attended a ball, during which he first observed the amorous intrigues of the Milanese, which completely delighted him.

into Count Mosca the disillusionments of his experience, even
to the solitudes of his own decline.

At the insistence of his bookseller, Stendhal had to shorten
the book's conclusion, which seems a little abrupt. In this last
episode, however, in which everything rushes forward headlong,
in which all of the characters die within a few pages—with the
exception of Count Mosca—he attains an intensity of expression
which is the mark of great art. During the closing moments of
his book he seems to have had in mind a rhythm identical to
that in the closing of Montesquieu's *Greatness and Decadence
of the Romans.* Nothing could more aptly follow the death of
the passions he had just created than the death of an Empire:

I haven't the heart to speak of the miseries which were to follow.
I will simply say that under the last Emperors the Empire, reduced
to the outskirts of Constantinople, ended like the Rhine, which is
no more than a trickle when it loses itself in the sea.

This sadness—with the taste of ashes, somnolence, and nothingness—is identical to that in the last lines of the *Charterhouse,*
enveloping like a shroud the beautiful skeleton of an Italy fallen
anew into the hands of reactionaries: "The prisons of Parma
were empty, the Count immensely rich, Ernesto V adored by
his subjects, who were comparing his government to that of the
Grand Dukes of Tuscany." "[To the happy few!]" [4]

4 Words in brackets written in Beyle's English.

10 · *Italian Chronicles* (1839) * *Lamiel*

(1839-42) * *Italian Ideas on Certain*

Celebrated Paintings (1840) * *Intimate*

Miscellanies and Marginalia (1804-42)

THE BOOKS that Stendhal had thus far dedicated to Italy had already included several narratives which were actually chronicles. Searching through the *novellieri* for illustrations of primitive energy, the author discovered, around 1834, in either a secondhand bookstore or a family archives a few "ancient manuscripts in yellowed ink" dating from the sixteenth or seventeenth century, which he carefully copied down. Most of these were "little histories, each of them about eighty pages, and almost all of them tragedies." They contained "nothing risqué," as did those of Tallement des Réaux, but love played a major role in most of them. Stendhal saw them as a useful complement to his history of Italy: "These are the customs which gave birth to the Michelangelos and Rafaels, which it is so foolishly supposed have been revived with academies and schools of the arts." He flattered himself that he understood these texts "in the *demipatois* of the time" rather well. They had neither the uniqueness nor the veracity which the author attributed to them, but their dramatic interest was intense. He translated them "with absolutely no pretentiousness," devoted himself to his customary habit of polishing, and emerged with several candid and moving accounts depicting an Italy fierce in its instincts. A beautiful crime was not in the least offensive to him, and he related it with cold objectivity and a secret and lucid delight.

His first idea was to entitle these pages "*Roman Short Stories,* faithfully translated from accounts written by contemporaries (1400–1640)." Or should one say, "short story from a tragic account?" He discarded this as being inappropriate and published only "The Abbess of Castro," "Vittoria Accoramboni," and "The Cenci," toward the end of 1830. The collection bore the title of the first of these stories, which had previously appeared in the *Revue des Deux Mondes*. In 1855 Colomb chose, for the Lévy collection of complete works, the title *Italian Chronicles*. Stendhal, who had collected "seven volumes full of Roman facts" and "two volumes of Neapolitan anecdotes" and had them bound, heralded twelve of them to Di Fiore in 1835. At the time of his death he had fourteen of them. The interest of this material, which he never completely utilized, can well be imagined. His original text takes strange liberties with history and chronology. It is actually a collection of more or less romantic *causes célèbres*, rather than a precise account of the facts. Stendhal introduced into his reworking of the facts an excitability and a psychological precision that subjugates the reader. With his force of analysis, Stendhal ransacks souls and probes hearts, re-creating circumstances that illuminate these narratives with moving vigor. He hastens toward his denouement with mastery and simplicity. The experience he had acquired from so much study, so much observation of human nature, caused him to discover nuances in these chronicles —which he subjectively reappraised—nuances which their primitive authors had never dreamed of—an incomparable feast! He re-created the setting and prevented himself from interfering with the narrative (which he loved to do in his own novels), carefully keeping the souls of his characters in a state of tension. Scorning every romantic device, he strictly applied the technique of the short story. Note that "The Abbess of Castro," dramatic and closely knit, is contemporary with *The Charterhouse of Parma*, so filled with oases of freshness and reverie.

As for the question of the esthetic value of crime, always so fascinating to Stendhal, which people insist upon posing from the standpoint of morality, let us ask its solution from a writer who certainly cannot be suspected of having exalted violence —Renan—who states in his *Essays on Morals and Criticism* (1855):

What a strange peculiarity! Man is more willing to accord fame to a grandiose crime than to shabby usefulness; that is because crime itself, when accompanied by a certain glamour, presents a powerful idea of human capacity and implies a dimension of perversion which only the vigorous races are capable of; it is no small matter today to be called a Borgia. But that which is merely useful will never ennoble.

As restrained as imagination's part may be in the *Italian Chronicles,* to which André Suarès pays fervent homage in his *Voyage of a Condottiere,* they remain among the most striking of Stendhal's works, among the most widely read and revealing in regard to the worship of *virtù* which was such an integral part of Beylism.

From amid the plots for novels, outlines for short stories, and pages of autobiographical data which date from Henri Beyle's last stay in Civitavecchia, we retain *Lamiel,* an extremely incomplete sketch which is a feminine transposition of the writer; here is a female Julien Sorel, just as independent, just as unprejudiced, in revolt against an environment that forces her to be a hypocrite. Jean Prévost has described Lamiel as the most advanced specimen of Stendhal's "amazons." This heroine, more cerebral than emotion, more liable to be "a loved enemy, rather than a true lover," embodied several of Mina de Vanghel's traits. Only the first part of the book has come down to us.

Certainly everything that came from Stendhal's pen deserves attention, and this effort is not without its value. It was conceived in the setting of French society at the beginning of the July Monarchy, and it is significant that he chose for its heroine an awakened young peasant girl, rather reminiscent of Marivaux's *Marianne,* raised in a provincial chateau, seeking love but always unsatisfied, destined to end in the barrenness of a criminal underworld, and preferring the uncertainties of a life of chance to the security of a settled existence. The famous assassin, Lacenaire, whose trial made a great stir in 1835, furnished Stendhal more than one element for the depiction of this unsavory environment. Frankly speaking, the interest that *Lamiel* has aroused seems surprising; although it seems to have its admirers, for not only does incompleteness become a major vice in it but also those parts of it which are complete are boring—perhaps the only boring pages Stendhal ever wrote. The novel does not go anywhere, and its characters do not engage the reader. The fetishism of Stendhalians has, in this case, done a disservice to a writer who always dedicated his genius to nothing but the most poetic transpositions. He did his best to substitute the "narration of action" for "the moral summation of action," to tell the story "narratively" and not "philosophically," and managed to avoid the trap of introducing his characters one by one. Unfortunately, though, he became entangled in the composition of it, and its impetus was lost; and although he saw his characters clearly, he did not conceive his plot carefuly enough.

A prolonged friendship united Stendhal with Abraham Constantin, the miniature painter. Both of these men possessed an open and independent spirit; they shared the same artistic tastes —the one for reproducing masterpieces with probity and talent, the other for discoursing on them. They spent several years side by side in Rome, in "absolute independence" and friendly camaraderie, leading similar social lives, delighting themselves with similar works of art, and sharing their memories of Paris. They became friends again in Paris in 1837, and then again in Rome in 1839. Their extremely frank relationship gave rise to a collaboration. This work, *Italian Ideas on Certain Celebrated Paintings*, was published in 1840 under the sole authorship of Abraham Constantin and was intended as a kind of guide for dilettantes, but it was not authored by the Genoese artist alone. Its technical observations are his, but its general remarks concerning human nature and the arts are those of Stendhal, drawing again from his own fund of familiar opinions. Romain Colomb found among Stendhal's papers an outline of one chapter, and Paul Arbelet has proved that three-fourths of the book is his. Friendship thus prompted him to relinquish his own rights without reservations. These pages add nothing to our knowledge of Stendhal, but it is gratifying to close our study of a writer who entered the field with such casualness toward his predecessors with a compensatory gesture of generosity on his part.

There remains to be mentioned the exceptional importance of the two volumes published by Divan: *Intimate Miscellanies* and *Marginalia*. In addition to his actual autobiographical work, Beyle was constantly making comments in the margins or on the blank pages of his interfoliated books. With commendable shrewdness the Beylists were able to find there, with meticulous research, solutions to many a problem and counterchecks on whatever remained to be guessed about the man through his work. Dominique—the pseudonym was probably a subtle homage to Cimarosa—was perpetually analyzing himself, commenting on himself, and educating himself. Fearful of the police, he often employed ingenious and complex devices to lead the prying eye astray, although the mystery was usually transparent. There exists a veritable epigraphic science of his scribbling, written in an increasingly shaky hand. This labor of deciphering, which already had facilitated the publication of his entire posthumous work, has been applied to the smallest trifles, furnishing many a physical detail and many a psychological notation; this work, all told, has made Stendhal one of the most thoroughly understood writers in French literature. There exist testaments, medical opinions, veiled confidences, noteworthy dates noted, all of them contributing additional biographical data. There are plans for his amorous battles (*Advice for Banti*), truncated accounts of his love affairs (*Earline*), dedications, prefaces, and so on; all this material, although not particularly novel in style, remains on a par with the *Journal*, the *Correspondence*, and *The Life of Henri Brulard*, although in a more fragmentary and perhaps still more immediate fashion. All these minute trifles have permitted an almost total renewal, over several decades, of our acquaintance with both the man and the author.

Conclusion

> I imagine that some critic of the twentieth century will discover Beyle's books in the hodge-podge of nineteenth century literature and render them the justice they have not found among his contemporaries.
>
> (Mérimée) H. B.*

* Excerpt from an article written by Mérimée after Stendhal's death.

WE HAVE WITNESSED the tentative experiments by which Stendhal became a novelist. His ideas are remarkably consistent. From the political standpoint, however, he found it suitable to conform. This outspoken liberal rallied by degrees to the social ideal that was flourishing around 1780. The boundaries of the principles of 1789 could become very vague, on his own authority: "I submit to my aristocratic penchant, after having declaimed in good faith for ten years against the entire aristocracy."—"I passionately adore a great gentleman, gay and well brought-up. . . . A society deprived of these light-hearted, charming, amiable beings who take nothing too seriously seems to me almost like the year stripped of its spring." Should we wonder, then, that his heroes have such glamour?

Stendhal, whose quality of thought possessed a penetrating singularity, but who was less gifted for synthesis, made his reputation with two terms: "Beylism" and "egotism." These do not define a doctrine; they merely express an epicureanism that was always prepared to resume the game of life, no matter what its disappointments. Is it enough to regard him as "a superior and *manqué* genius," like Paul Arbelet, or to echo Paul Hazard's statement: "To create pleasure was his supreme law, and, having created it, to defend it against others, against itself, against himself—is that egotism?" This is only a *first step*. As one recreates, in the writer's wake, his theory of pleasure and happiness, one gradually begins to realize the misery that lay behind it and that slowly accumulated his bitterness. This epicureanism was too loudly proclaimed to be solidly founded. Stendhal possessed a wealth of stoicism, which sometimes almost approached a taste for asceticism. There is a surprising reflection from his youth in his *Filosofia Nova:*

When I read Pascal it seems to me that I am rereading myself, and since I know what a reputation this great man has, I take great pleasure in this. I think he is the one, among all writers, whom I most resemble in my soul.

Since 1806 he had foreseen the danger to happy living of a too intensive introspection. The secret melancholy of certain of his pages was the unforeseen reward of a spirit that belatedly attained the modulation of its *Song of Songs.* But this is only a *second step,* and the reverse side of his egotism.

The writer was no less faithful to his syle. They denied that he had one because they were unable to penetrate the mystery of a form that purified what had already been purified by emotion. A Racinian modesty linked his subtle musicality to a precision of touch; and the resulting style, a marvel of intelligence, is alternately active, relaxed, virulent, and volatile, rushing ahead with the dialogue and then suddenly abandoning it for a passionate internal monologue, leaving everything to the imagination and yet casting no doubt in the heart. If the author strained at morality, it is because living psychology, which was his domain, admits of more things than orthodoxies can imagine. The veracity of his analysis and "the forward step taken by the spirit," as he called it, carrying their own justification in themselves, are thus the surest antidote.

Stendhal occupies a unique place in French literature. He ranks with the followers of Montaigne and the moralists. He was steeped in the classics, particularly Racine, of whom he had a substantial knowledge. Their heroines, consumed by feeling and submitting to the all-powerful yoke of the flesh, are lovers every minute of their lives. That early predilection that dedicated him to the psychological novel made him instinctively fond of *The Princess of Clèves.* An enthusiast of the *Memoires,* he studied men through them, while at the same time pursuing his study of them in life and in the theater. Shakespeare, Alfieri,

Goldoni, as well as Molière, contributed to forming his tastes. Subject to the opposing forces of the eighteenth century, whose double influence he experienced, an admirer of the President de Brosses, Choderlos de Laclos, and Paul-Louis Courier, Stendhal came to the age of romanticism armed against the *mal du siècle*. As has been witnessed, he was a romantic, but in his own specific sense. Parallel to a romanticism in which he distinguished himself and which he surpassed—only to see himself occasionally referred to as old-fashioned because of his fidelity to Helvétius—he leaped beyond realism and naturalism to overtake an epoch more prepared to understand him. How could the Stendhal who subtly juggled the fall of Clélia Conti have taken pleasure in the *fiacre* scene from *Madame Bovary*, or even the description of a Normandy wedding? Can one imagine him chaining himself to the inventory of a caretaker in the Vauquer lodging house?

The contrast of a Flaubert, issuing from everything that writer created around a character through little light touches, was not at all suited to Beyle, who understood everything from within. Nor was the realism of a Balzac, who proclaimed the necessity for laborious didactic preparations, at all his style. In *The Charterhouse of Parma* the city of Parma is never described; its atmosphere is merely suggested in a stylized geographical framework. People matter too much, in his opinion, to concern oneself too much with things. This novel, constructed totally through nuances, truly proves that Stendhal's first condition of art was to be "stronger than Nature is"—a requirement against which Balzac revolted. Maurice Bardèche has put the accent on that "pleasure of the demiurge," which prompted Beyle to create like a sculptor heroes who did not conform to type, while Balzac created like an architect, by constructing through mass. A novelist of action, Blazac used his initial gift for the dramatic, sometimes to excess. Stendhal, a novelist of reflection, improvised on his accumulated memories and never injected into his work anything but his own love. Untiring in his pursuit of revelatory character detail, he balked at emotion and required from the reader an active participation that binds him so much more deeply to the writer.

Stendhal was misunderstood by his contemporaries, although

one could not include the entire elite of his time in this reproach. For he was, after all, in close touch with almost everything that mattered in Paris from the intellectual standpoint
and was regarded as the head of a literary school. Mérimée,
Sainte-Beuve, Duvergier de Hauranne did not fully realize the
true scope of his originality, but Balzac proclaimed in 1840 in
the *Revue Parisienne*: "In my opinion *The Charterhouse of
Parma* is, up to and including our time, the masterpiece of
French literature."

Stendhal's fortune was slow to rise. The press was not always
eulogistic. We must point out one important article in *Débats*,
however, dedicated by Jules Janin to *The Red and the Black* on
its publication. After Balzac's dithyramb, however, the writer
became the subject of a serious study by Bussières in the *Revue
des Deux Mondes* in 1843. Before long Colomb began to re-
consider reissuing the writer's works; already fetishistic, he
wanted to reprint everything, including the unpublished works.
Balzac, whose *Psychology of Marriage* was inspired by *On Love*,
advised a choice, as did Mérimée. Crozet wanted to keep only
On Love, the *Promenades*, the *Charterhouse*, and "perhaps"
The Red and the Black! In 1846 the editor Hetzel launched a
series with *The Charterhouse of Parma*. This whole fiasco seems
to confirm Bussières' statement that Stendhal was "among those
whom posterity alone will elevate above the judgment of his
contemporaries." Michel Lévy reappeared with greater success
in 1843, publishing the *Promenades* as the first work in a series
of eighteen volumes. Sainte-Beuve dedicated two articles to this
event in the *Constitutionnel* of January, 1854, which evaluated
the dilettante, if not the novelist. The friends of Stendhal
themselves came to the rescue. Colomb dedicated a voluble
Notice to him; and Mérimée wrote a few reminiscences about
him, which he signed with the initials "H.B.," and although
they were actually rather discreet they were considered quite
shocking.

Stendhal's fortune, luck aiding, began to rise during the
middle of the nineteenth century. Jaquinet, a lecturer at the
École Normale, introduced his writing to Hippolyte Taine,
who was quite interested at that time in the psychology of love,
according to Francisque Sarcey. His masterful works appeared

in *French Philosophers* and *Essays on Criticism and History*, rendering a conclusive homage to Stendhal, whom he considered the greatest psychologist of his time, and perhaps of all time. A. Colignon, in a book whose first part alone was published, offered the first sufficient information about the author. Paul Bourget, in his *Essays on Contemporary Psychology*, was to write some very perceptive pages which, through a kind of critical mimicry, captured the author perfectly, and which dealt with the quality of "believability" that Beyle gave to his situations, as well as his characters. At about that time the first Beylist clique was formed. It became fashionable to be *rougiste*, as it was called. The initiated used to assemble to recite pages from the novel; the most infinitesimal details were tracked down. Paul Bourget and Jean Richepin particularly excelled in this sport.

Curiosity was aroused, but critical bases were still shaky; nevertheless, a mass of ideas and facts was circulated by Emile Faguet, Edouard Rod, Arthur Chuquet, and still others, in studies that were of varying quality, but that testified to the novelist's growing reputation. Scrupulous researchers could understand fully the interest of the unpublished works. One can read further penetrating studies on Stendhal, such as those of Léon Blum, who regarded the novels as "fanciful biography"; the *Stendhaliana* of Emile Henriot; the *Reflections* of René Boylesve; the judgments of Pierre Lasserre, and of so many others. Who has not had his word on Stendhal? The observations of Alain and of Henri Delacroix on Stendhal's art and psychology are of the highest quality. These works, however, might mave multiplied without really revitalizing the material had not exegesis—the sole means of preparing foundations for future syntheses—replaced critiques concerning his personality and general ideas, for a time, through the force of circumstances. Stendhal has been literally scrutinized with a magnifying glass. Not that the first generation of scholars was always so precise; we are well aware of the carelessness of such men as Casimir Stryenski, Rémy de Gourmont, Jean de Mitty, L. Belugou, and Adolphe Paupe. Nevertheless, they were very valuable in that they opened a new path, and their task was arduous. Then came the time of the real scholarship—Pierre Martino,

Paul Arbelet, Henri Martineau, Louis Royer, Henri Debraye. Armed with the most scrupulous techniques, sparing neither time nor energy, even in the face of the most minute problem, persuaded that art and erudition are compatible—and they proved the truth of this—they established a precedent of textual accuracy for their successors, leaving nothing of a biographical or critical nature in the shadows. So it was that after so many inaccuracies arose certain works, a good many of which are practically exhaustive.

In 1915, Édouard Champion and Paul Arbelet undertook the presentation of a critical edition of Stendhal's complete works, as sound as it was sumptuous. Two successive wars and the upheavals that followed interrupted a publication that involved the reputation of French scholarship. This temporary halt heightened the value of Henri Martineau, who succeeded in editing for *Divan* the complete works, published and unpublished, due entirely to his own efforts. Each separate volume contained an up-to-date study of the most recent, and sometimes entirely new, works. The text was scrupulously collated.

A few recent works like those of Jean Prévost, *Stendhal's Creation*, and Maurice Bardèche, *Stendhal, the Novelist*, have given contemporary Stendhalian criticism an echoing force and a note of truth which had possibly never before been attained. Critical, or simply correct, editions are currently multiplying. Although a journal of Stendhalian studies is lacking, Beylism has had for its platform the *Editions of the Stendhal Club*, *The Critical Review of Ideas and Books*, and, since 1912, the irreplaceable *Little Stendhalian Notes*, and many an article or criticism in *Divan*—not to mention the literary rubrics of the larger papers, weeklies, and periodicals. It is obvious, then, that posterity has appealed against the disdain of Stendhal's contemporaries. There is even a mythical *Stendhal Club*, which is significant! And, however mythical it may be, three volumes of *Evenings at the Stendhal Club*, the last of which recently appeared through the efforts of Martineau and François Michel, are definitely a reality.

One finds Stendhal at the end of almost every avenue of contemporary literature; at least he seems to be claimed on every side. Although he may have inherited his worship of the ego and his glorification of passion from romanticism, he broke with that school in order to give free rein to the development of his "self" in the world of reality, rather than that of poetry and morality. Whence it is only one step to the literature for which he has been blamed—of egotism and introspection, passion and conquest, positivistic and realistic, lacking faith and poetry— which dominated the latter nineteenth century and made him the scapegoat of succeeding generations. His supposed "disciples" have not always understood the truth about his humanity. The ballast of action has generally been missing in his successors, who seem occasionally to have been victims of their own leisures, certain ones of whom recall that student of Jules Lemaitre's tale who experienced everything "although he had never gone anywhere except from his room to his studies at the University."

Through the lucid notation of ideas, through the agreement between fact and the psychology of a character, with passion being always the motive of action, Stendhal made his characters revolve around a protagonist who was the projection of his "self." Doing this, as Socrates had once done with philosophy, he brought the ego from heaven to earth, without any moral concerns, and again took up the old adage: "Know thyself." His entire rationalist, sensualist, and ideological education should have led him into a sense of realism, or indeed of "scientific" naturalism. The champions of these schools could point to him, without realizing that he never took details and facts for ends in themselves, but for what they might reveal about the mind and the passions. Stendhal was a born psychologist; he was not trying to prove anything; he needed neither thesis nor anti- thesis. Through the intensified truth of a transposition, he ob- served and tried to account for what took place in the "magic lantern." He relived every emotion a thousand times in his mem- ory and mediation and transformed it. Disdainful of "slices of life" before their time, everything in him was opposed to ex- haustive realism and a naturalism with "scientific" pretensions, whose eventual outcome was to be an extreme populism of which he was the living negation. He wrote for himself and for the "happy few," with absolutely no *a priori* ostracism; and we have watched for several decades as the Beylist chapel became a

great cathedral. It could never be transformed into a fair
ground.

Stendhal's influence is felt not only among the novelists.
Hippolyte Taine and Joseph-Arthur Gobineau utilized his observations on the psychology of races; Edgar Quinet submitted to
the attraction of his Italy; Baudelaire affirmed, in his wake, that
he existed as much for the *beauties* as for the *means* of pursuing happiness.

Paul Bourget plundered *The Red and the Black* for his *Disciple*; and his *Physiology of Modern Love* is indebted to *On
Love*. The Barrès of the "cult of the self" is influenced by him,
particularly. Of course, Barrès the enchanter is equally sensitive
to the spells of Chateaubriand, but what ardent ideological
meditations does he not owe to Stendhal! The same can be said
of the egotism and amorality of an André Gide or a Marcel
Proust. On a closer scrutiny, though, this "cult of the self" to
which our contemporaries have addicted themselves with such
relish has nothing in common with Stendhal but its name.

For Henri Beyle never fell into the narcissism in which those
who call themselves his disciples take such pleasure. It was
not within him to experience that infinitely jaded attitude toward life, that sick longing for desire, which takes the place of
real desire. Stendhal had too sound a head for such vertigoes.
If he analyzed himself tirelessly, it was certainly not through
any concern to discover within himself "oh, the most irreplaceable of beings!" He had no Nathaniel in whom to mirror himself; he wanted only to understand himself. Contemporary literature, often involved with presenting the abnormal, unusual,
and decadent aspects of life, is fascinating; but these delicate
and jaded writers are artists in quite a different way from Stendhal, for in order to attain their exquisite art they have had to
renounce all energy. Furthermore, any writing that gives prec-
edence to style, or that gives such an impression, is opposed to
the Beylist spirit.

Stendhal knew how to escape from his "self." Even his most
personal books, which completely reveal him, give an impression
of objectivity. He discusses himself not without pleasure, but
without complacency, as he would discuss a stranger, always
introducing objectivity into his speculations in some way. His

egotistical cosmopolitanism could still be objective: "For a long time I have been indebted to him alone," Sainte-Beuve recognized, "for the lively and gay Italian spirit, without leaving my room." What does the cosmopolitanism of Maurice Barrès, on the other hand, teach us, "draining every kind of emotion in Europe"; what do we learn except Barrès, and a jaded Barrès at that? Where is the healthy and fresh ardor that animated Julien and Fabrizio? Where are those enigmas, nourished by realist wit, that Henri Beyle cause to surge forth? Will we discover them in the rather vulgarly partisan remarks of Barrès' *Déracinés*, or in the biting theses of the *L'Etape* and *Disciple* of Paul Bourget, incensed against the Faubourg? Stendhal was neither a closet writer nor a commercial writer. He demanded that a person stop and think for himself. His characters have nothing to prove but themselves. They "are." Although he was an egotist, he was not intentionally an immoralist. He was a prose master of the poetry of veiled nuance, of suggested sensuality, a peerless revelator of the authentic and shifting life of the emotions.

He had not expected to be translated as far away as Japan or to influence so many foreign writers. Charles Simon has followed his wake into Germany—from Goethe, who had great admiration for his wit, to Nietzsche, who idolized him and viewed him as a predecessor, "a man of question marks,"—"the last of the French psychologists." The Tolstoy of *War and Peace* was indebted to him for his understanding of war. And is not the Raskolnikoff of *Crime and Punishment*, haunted by the image of Napoleon, a peculiarly Russian Julien Sorel? The influence of Stendhal on the contemporary novel, then, has been considerable.

The importance of foreign critical works to Stendhal studies must not be overlooked. The Italian contribution, by far the most important, has recently been enriched even further by several notable works.

Was he merely talented? Or was he a genius? This seems to be an interminable debate, as if it were simply a matter of solving a riddle. It is generally agreed that one can define him as a "superior intellect," rare rather than great, which seems equitable enough. But he had certain superiorities of intellect which might be considered preferable to the outbursts of genius. Some people consider his influence to have surpassed his merit.

Actually, Stendhal had "nuances too fine" for the civilization that was springing up, and he had a premonition that literature —and the novel alone seemed to him capable of truth from that time on—would go into analytical complications sometimes surpassing the means of art. With an intelligence so subtle, constantly dulling its point against itself, how could he have entered into trances and predicted? He preferred to do and to say. But in this failure of genius which he implicitly proclaims, neither depth nor human truth had anything to lose.

Certain anxious minds have ranked him among the "evil prophets" and chased him from the temple. As Paul Arbelet said: "It is not Stendhal they are judging, it is themselves. Why be offended? Certain types of minds are incompatible, and Stendhal would be the first to have his intimate enemies, from the literary standpoint. Let them at least thank him for his gratuity, even though his ideas may shock! Is he so immoral? His gods are courage, honor, love, and friendship. He despises hypocrites. And, undoubtedly, he laughs at the powerful and important. He is a great awakener who has questioned everything once again, who thinks irreverently and speaks irreverently; his virtues mock virtue and he is not mounting a soap box. Isn't this the attitude that Socrates assumed, long before him? And wasn't Socrates, like himself, accused of corrupting youth? Listen to Henri Beyle's answer, trumpet-toned in its brevity: "I do not corrupt, I deliver!" Still, one must have felt slavery in order to have a taste for deliverance.

He is the only one, among the romantics, who plainly stated what he was. Ought he to be censured for his honesty? Life was hard for him, on the whole. Basically, he was only seeking the success of the psychologist and the dilettante. More often than not he was poor. And yet the frustrations of his writing never forced him to pander to the public—although his work brought him only 9,900 francs in twenty-eight years. He was an honor to his profession, even in this respect. Protecting himself from the excesses of his passions through self-discipline, he proved himself worthy even in misfortune. And although he boasted of an ethics of self-interest inherited from Helvétius, and pretended to seek happiness through *"lo-gique,"* he was constantly building new castles in Spain only to see them tumbling down again. It was always the same. Persuaded in theory that the world is divided between the cheaters and the cheated and that heroism is often motivated by base emotions, he luxuriated in his *espagnolisme*. And though he tilted at windmills, he tirelessly examined their turning vanes.

A fanciful and lucid soul bound to reality, he preferred to simple pleasures the pursuit of strong emotions and the vain and constant pursuit of happiness which was his cloth of Penelope. Aristocratic in his tastes, occasionally demagogic, using Julien as his spokesman, Stendhal came within a hair of ending his hero as a self-satisfied aristocrat named "de la Vernaye"—for he did not believe in revolutions and even less in revolutionaries. Stendhal's suffering sometimes inclined him toward neurasthenia and pessimism, which was only the reverse side of his tender, idealistic nature, constantly strained by life, which had even in the end imposed upon him the martyrdom of obesity! He presents an efficacious lesson in psychological sincerity and in the free examination of dogmas and political theories. His intellect had its blind spots, certainly, but he was a writer whose style will never grow old, who knew how to be—in every sense of the word and every day of his life—a free man.

Bibliographical Note

BIBLIOGRAPHICAL NOTE

I. THE MANUSCRIPTS

Bibliothèque Nationale: Copy in fourteen volumes of novelettes which are the source of the *Italian Chronicles.*

Bibliothèque Municipale de Grenoble: A considerable store of Stendhal's manuscripts.

Fonds Donato Bucci: Was at Civitavecchia, but is no longer there; numbered around 200 volumes, a great many of which were annotated, and among these were several of Stendhal's interfoliated volumes.

II. BIBLIOGRAPHY

Henri Cordier, *Bibliographie Stendhalienne* (Stendhalian Bibliography), Champion, 1914.

Adolphe Paupe, *La vie littéraire de Stendhal* (The Literary Life of Stendhal), Champion, 1914.

Pierre Martino, *Stendhal,* Boivin, 1914, revised in 1934.

Louis Royer, *Bibliographie stendhalienne* (Stendhalian Bibliography), (1928–37), Champion, 1930–32, 1934, Editions du Stendhal-Club, nos. 30, 33, and 34.

V. Del Litto, *Bibliographie stendhalienne* (Stendhalian Bibliography), 1938–46, Arthaud.

Henri Martineau, *L'oeuvre de Stendhal* (Stendhal's Work), Divan, 1945. *Collection Champion:* Refers to bibliographical prefaces.

Pierre Jourda, *Etat présent des Etudes stendhaliennes* (The Present State of Stendhalian Studies), Belles Lettres, 1930.

L. F. Benedetto, *Arrigo Beyle Milanese,* Bilancio dello stendhal-
ismo italiano a cento anni della morte dello Stendhal (An
Account of Stendhalism in Italy One Hundred Years after
the Death of Stendhal), Firenze, Sansoni, 1943.

Carlo Cordié, *Interpretazioni di Stendhal dal Bourget ai nostri
giorni* (An Interpretation of Stendhal from Bourget to Our
Day), Milano, Montuoro, 1947.

III. MODERN EDITIONS

Edition Champion, published under the direction of Paul Arbelet and Edouard Champion, then of Paul Arbelet. Fourteen works appeared between 1913 and 1940.

Edition du Divan, furnished by Henri Martineau in seventy-
nine volumes, four of which are dedicated to an index of
names.

Note: The documented editions or criticisms of Stendhal's
isolated works has multiplied in the last thirty years.

Note: The reproduction in facsimile of the Chaper copy of
La Chartreuse de Parme, with a Preface by Paul Arbelet and
transcriptions of Stendhal's corrections by Henri Debraye
(Champion, 1921); the editions of *La Chartreuse de Parme*
by Pierre Martino (Bossard, 1929), Pierre Jourda (Belles-Lettres, 1933), Henri Martineau (Garnier, 1942; Hazan, 1946); the
editions of *Le Rouge et Le Noir* by Pierre Jourda (Belles-Lettres,
1929), Henri Martineau (Garnier, 1939); *Armance,* by Henri
Martineau (Garnier, 1950); *Lucien Leuwen,* by Henri Rambaud
(Bossard, 1929); *De l'Amour,* by Henri Martineau (Cluny,
1947).

Because of their immense richness of documentation we
should like to call particular attention to the critical editions
published by Henri Martineau in Divan, together with the collection of complete works: *Souvenirs d'égotisme* (1 vol., 1941
and 1950); *Vie de Henri Brulard* (2 vols., 1949).

IV. BIOGRAPHICAL and CRITICAL WORKS

Pierre Martino, *Stendhal,* Boivin, 1914; revised in 1934.

Paul Arbelet, *La jeunesse de Stendhal* (Stendhal's Youth), 2
vols., Champion, 1919.

Paul Hazard, *La vie de Stendhal* (Stendhal's Life), Gallimard, 1927.

Pierre Jourda, *Stendhal, l'homme et l'oeuvre* (Stendhal, The Man and His Work), Desclée de Brower and Cie.

Pierre Jourda, *Stendhal raconté par ceux qui l'ont vu* (Stendhal Discussed by Those Who Observed Him), Stock, 1931.

Jules Marsan, *Stendhal*, Editions des Cahiers libres, 1931.

Albert Thibaudet, *Stendhal*, Hachette, 1931.

Paul Arbelet, *Trois solitaires, Courier, Stendhal, Mérimée* (Three Solitary Men, Courier, Stendhal and Mérimée), Gallimard, 1934.

Jean Prévost, *La création chez Stendhal* (Stendhal's Creation), ed. by Sagittaire, 1942. New edition by Mercure de France, 1951.

Maurice Bardèche, *Stendhal romancier* (Stendhal the Novelist), ed. by la Table Ronde, 1947.

Note: Two recent volumes by Henri Martineau are a mine of information, while we await his promised *History of Stendhal's Heart*. These volumes are: *Petit Dictionnaire Stendhalien*, Divan, 1948; *Le calendrier de Stendhal*, Divan, 1940.

V. THE STENDHAL LIBRARY

Inaugurated in 1934, this library is situated on the rue Hauquelin in Grenoble and offers the keenest documentary interest. Louis Royer was its founder.

BIBLIOGRAPHICAL SUPPLEMENT

V. Del Litto, *Bibliographie stendhalienne* (1947–55) (Stendhalian Bibliography: 1947–55), Arthaud, 1955; V. Del Litto, *Bibliographie stendhalienne* (1953–56) (Stendhalian Bibliography: 1953–56), Éditions du Grand Chêne, Lausanne, 1959.

Note: Stendhalian bibliography is henceforth assured by the pains of V. Del Litto in the magazine *Stendhal-Club*, whose founding editor he has been since 1959 (Éditions du Grand Chêne, Lausanne).

Since the death of Henri Martineau, *le Divan* has ceased to appear; Henri Martineau, *Le coeur de Stendhal* (The Heart of Stendhal), Albin Michel, 1952–53, 2 vols.; L. Aragon, *La lum-*

ière de Stendhal (The Light of Stendhal), Denoël, 1954; V. Brombert, *Stendhal et la voie oblique* (Stendhal and the Oblique Path), Presses Universitaires, 1954; V. Del Litto, *Compléments et fragments inédits* (Unpublished Additions and Fragments), Presses Universitaires, 1954; *Journees stendhaliennes internationales de Grenoble, Discours et Communications* (International Stendhalian Days of Grenoble, Speeches and Papers), sold by Divan, 1956; F. Marill-Albérès, *Le Naturel chez Stendhal* (Naturalness with Stendhal), Nizet, 1956; F. Marill-Albérès, *Stendhal et le sentiment religieux* (Stendhal and the Religious Sentiment), Nizet, 1956; G. Blin, *Stendhal et les problèmes de la personnalite* (Stendhal and Problems of the Personality), Corti, 1958; G. Blin, *Stendhal et les problèmes du roman* (Stendhal and Problems of the Novel), Corti, 1958; V. Del Litto, *La vie intellectuelle de Stendhal, 1802–1821* (Stendhal's Intellectual Life), Presses Universitaires, 1959.

Index